Jewels of the Rainforest –
Poison Frogs
of the Family Dendrobatidae

Jerry G. Walls
Art by John R. Quinn

Photos by A. v.d. Nieuwenhuizen,
R. Bechter, R.D. Bartlett,
and others

Contents

Acknowledgments 3
Dedication 3
The Rainforests 5
Some Taxonomic Background 11
Checklist of the Poison Frogs 19
As a General Rule 29
The View from the Terrarium 45
Dendrobates auratus, the Green and Black Poison Frog 61
Dendrobates azureus, the Blue Poison Frog 74
Dendrobates granuliferus, the Granular Poison Frog 84
Dendrobates histrionicus, the Harlequin Poison Frog 89
Dendrobates leucomelas, the Yellow-banded Poison Frog 111
Dendrobates pumilio, the Strawberry Poison Frog 117
Dendrobates tinctorius, the Dyeing Poison Frog 139
Dendrobates ventrimaculatus, the Amazonian Poison Frog 157
Other *Dendrobates* 166
Epipedobates tricolor, the Phantasmal Poison Frog 207
Epipedobates trivittatus, the Three-striped Poison Frog 212
Other *Epipedobates* 219
The Genus *Minyobates* 247
Phyllobates terribilis, the Golden Poison Frog 253
Phyllobates vittatus, the Golfodulcean Poison Frog 259
Other *Phyllobates* 267
Of Rockets and Skunks 272
The Social Poison Frog 277
Appendix: A Different Poison Frog Classification 283
Bibliography 284
Index 286

Cover: *Dendrobates speciosus*, the Splendid Poison Frog. Photo: A. v. d. Nieuwenhuizen.
Endpaper: *Dendrobates tinctorius*, the Dyeing Poison Frog. Photo: R. D. Bartlett.

© Copyright 1994 by T.F.H. Publications, Inc.

Distributed in the UNITED STATES to the Pet Trade by T.F.H. Publications, Inc., One T.F.H. Plaza, Neptune City, NJ 07753; distributed in the UNITED STATES to the Bookstore and Library Trade by National Book Network, Inc. 4720 Boston Way, Lanham MD 20706; in CANADA to the Pet Trade by H & L Pet Supplies Inc., 27 Kingston Crescent, Kitchener, Ontario N2B 2T6; Rolf C. Hagen Ltd., 3225 Sartelon Street, Montreal 382 Quebec; in CANADA to the Book Trade by Macmillan of Canada (A Division of Canada Publishing Corporation), 164 Commander Boulevard, Agincourt, Ontario M1S 3C7; in the United Kingdom by T.F.H. Publications, PO Box 15, Waterlooville PO7 6BQ; in AUSTRALIA AND THE SOUTH PACIFIC by T.F.H. (Australia), Pty. Ltd., Box 149, Brookvale 2100 N.S.W., Australia; in NEW ZEALAND by Brooklands Aquarium Ltd. 5 McGiven Drive, New Plymouth, RD1 New Zealand; in Japan by T.F.H. Publications, Japan—Jiro Tsuda, 10-12-3 Ohjidai, Sakura, Chiba 285, Japan; in SOUTH AFRICA by Multipet Pty. Ltd., P.O. Box 35347, Northway, 4065, South Africa. Published by T.F.H. Publications, Inc.

Manufactured in the United States of America by T.F.H. Publications, Inc.

ACKNOWLEDGMENTS

Acknowledgments

My thanks to Joe Collins, Alex Kerstitch, and especially Eric Rundquist for making available some of the literature I needed for the project and for various other assistance. Drs. J. S. Simmons, L. Trueb, and W. E. Duellman allowed indirect access to facilities at the Division of Herpetology, Mus. Nat. Hist., Univ. Kansas, and Drs. Duellman and Trueb allowed access to their personal libraries. Drs. C. W. Myers and Darrel Frost of the American Museum of Natural History also helped in various ways, though of course any misstatements and misinterpretations here are strictly my own. The indirect help of the Zimmermanns and other Continental researchers and hobbyists through their many publications cannot be forgotten. A book like this is dependent on its photography, and the marvelous photos by A. van den Nieuwenhuizen of Holland and Rolf Bechter in Switzerland that form the core of the book speak for themselves, but the work of Dick Bartlett and the other photographers should not be slighted. Dr. Herbert R. Axelrod is directly responsible for this project and pushed it through as part of his continuing effort to focus hobbyist interest on the importance of the American rainforests to their hobby.

The artwork by accomplished natural history artist John R. Quinn has for the first time made it possible to illustrate every described poison frog in color. The paintings are based on published photos and written descriptions, most in original descriptions, and a bit of artistic license. The paintings are meant to convey the appearance of the frogs so they can (we hope) be recognized in life, but no attempt has been made for structural or proportional accuracy—in other words, don't bother checking toe lengths or relative sizes. Enjoy the paintings for what they are, small works of art.

Warren Burgess, Ray Hunziker, and Wil Mara served as sounding boards for the organization of the book, and I thank them for their patience. Finally, Maleta as usual understood that sometimes it is necessary to spend nights and weekends at the computer to birth a living thing like a book manuscript, and I love her for it. Much of this book was written during the throes of a series of New Jersey ice storms and sub-zero weather, and every word served as a reminder of how much I would have loved to be in Costa Rica at the time, which didn't make me any easier to live with.

Poison frogs are delicate little frogs that require much attention from the hobbyist to maintain them successfully, and many or most of the species are beyond the capabilities of beginning and intermediate hobbyists. I would hate to think that this book will make hobbyists run out and without proper preparation purchase poison frogs, even captive-bred specimens, only to have them die within weeks or months. Please do your homework before you obtain a poison frog and be prepared to spend hours maintaining fruitfly cultures and keeping terraria spotless...these gorgeous little animals are not easy to keep successfully but certainly are worth a determined attempt if you start with a large captive-bred species such as *Dendrobates auratus* or *D. tinctorius*. Good luck!

Dedication

To the memory of Chester F. Carlson (1906—1968), the developer of xerography. Without his invention this book would have been almost impossible to research and would have taken years to write.

THE RAINFORESTS

Tropic splendor. Central American forests often serve as home to thriving populations of poison frogs. Photo: D. Conkel.

SOME TAXONOMIC BACKGROUND

Mantellas, though few in species, show quite a bit of variation from species to species. Contrast the *Mantella viridis* above and at center left with the adult *Mantella aurantiaca* at center right and bottom left. It still is uncertain whether mantellas are related to typical frogs (ranids) or not. Recently the relationships of the small, colorful, diurnal frogs (mantellas and dendrobatids) have been questioned, and some scientists would say that mantellas and dendrobatids are rather closely related.

In the pair of Golden Mantellas at center right, by the way, the female is the stout-bodied specimen, the male more slender. Full color patterns develop rather slowly in mantellas as in poison frogs. The *Mantella aurantiaca* froglet at the bottom right looks nothing like the adult female at the bottom left. All photos by A. v. d. Nieuwenhuizen.

SOME TAXONOMIC BACKGROUND

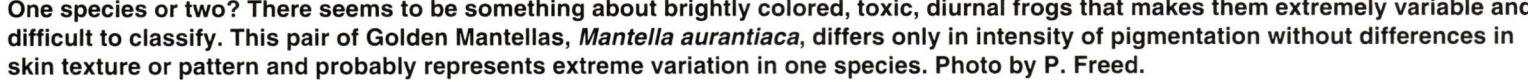

were put in *Dendrobates* and *Phyllobates*. In *Dendrobates* the first finger was shorter than the second, the discs on the fingers tended to be obviously wider than the fingers (especially in males), and teeth usually were absent from the jaws. In *Phyllobates* the first and second fingers were about equal in length or the first was longer than the second, the fingers discs were not much wider than the fingers, and usually there were teeth in the jaws.

In the late 1970's and early 1980's, research by Myers and Daly into the chemistry of skin secretions of the dendrobatids led to the creation of a rather different system of genera based on the admittedly "difficult" character of the presence or absence of various toxins. These toxins are complex organic chemicals, technically called lipophilic alkaloids, usually based on a six-membered ring of five carbon and one nitrogen atoms (a piperidine ring). Most of these alkaloids (there are over 100 types identified in the dendrobatids) belong to a class called "pumiliotoxin-C," a relatively inefficient and primitive toxin. Of the dendrobatids so far tested, the species formerly contained in *Dendrobates* and *Phyllobates* all contain pumiliotoxin-C, while those assigned to *Colostethus* lack the toxin (and, in fact, all toxic alkaloids). The assumption is made that alkaloids, even if not dangerous to predators, are at least distasteful because they affect the mucous membranes of the mouth and nostrils and appear to be very bitter or numbing to most animals. The frogs that possess the alkaloids also tend to have bright colors and are active during the daytime when they are relatively conspicuous. The bright colors would be associated by predators with a bad-tasting frog. Such bright warning colors are termed "aposematic" by scientists and are common in many different groups of animals where bright colors are associated with various chemicals causing bad tastes in predators—Monarch Butterflies come instantly to mind. Assumedly the ancestor of the poison frog genera developed pumiliotoxin-C, while the ancestor of *Colostethus* never did.

Other types of alkaloids are present or absent in the four genera of poison frogs as restricted by Myers in his 1987 paper. Thus, histrionicotoxins are absent in *Minyobates*, while the powerful batrachotoxins are present only in *Phyllobates*. *Epipedobates* lacks a group of toxins called the 3,5-disubstituted indolizidines as well as histrionicotoxins, both of which are present in *Dendrobates*. This system of genera is tentative and probably will change again in the near future as other research continues, but because it seems closest to expressing what probably are real relationships it is followed here.

Briefly, the four genera of poison frogs we'll use in this book, based mostly on the descriptions presented by Myers in 1987, are as follows:

DENDROBATES: Small to relatively large (20 to 50

One species or two? There seems to be something about brightly colored, toxic, diurnal frogs that makes them extremely variable and difficult to classify. This pair of Golden Mantellas, *Mantella aurantiaca*, differs only in intensity of pigmentation without differences in skin texture or pattern and probably represents extreme variation in one species. Photo by P. Freed.

SOME TAXONOMIC BACKGROUND

Compared to any true poison frogs, the harlequin toads tend to look like emaciated froglets with long snouts and stubby, webbed hind feet. The lack of broadened pads on the hands should be sufficient to distinguish them from dendrobatids at a glance. Shown here are a nice female Costa Rican *Atelopus varius* (upper left); an unidentified *Atelopus* from Panama that probably is a form of *A. varius*, as you might expect; and two views of *Atelopus flavescens* from Surinam, one of the few harlequin toads that can be kept and even bred on occasion by fairly advanced hobbyists. Photos by A. v. d. Nieuwenhuizen.

Some Taxonomic Background

Oh no...Latin names again!! Relax, it's not as bad as you think. Taxonomy is necessary if you are to identify poison frogs correctly (a difficult task even for specialists), and you have to identify them if you want to successfully keep them. Different poison frogs have different ecologies and breeding behaviors. I've tried to make things as simple as possible by using common names for each species (many are from Silverstone's 1975 and 1976 reviews), but in many cases a little Latin is necessary. Also, taxonomy is more than names, it is relationships.

First, the Dendrobatidae is a family that in all features is very closely similar to the Leptodactylidae, a gigantic and variable American family that includes several hundred species of rainfrogs (*Eleutherodactylus*), the edible mountain chickens (*Leptodactylus*), the bizarre but popular horned frogs (*Ceratophrys*), and dozens of other varied genera. The families differ in small characters of muscle attachments and development in the thigh and the jaws, plus the presence of scutes on usually expanded and disc-like fingers and toes of the dendrobatids. (See Ford, 1993, and Ford and Cannatella, 1993, for a discussion of phyletic relationships. New interpretations may suggest dendrobatids are closely related to ranids, but the evidence seems equivocal.) In the past the dendrobatids were divided into three genera on the basis of characters that today are considered to be almost meaningless. In the system proposed by Silverstone and based largely on structure and admitted convenience, *Colostethus* comprised frogs with "plain" colors, usually brown and white, that tended to be relatively aquatic or at least were associated with streams. The frogs with more "brilliant" colors, usually with red, green, blue, or yellow on at least the belly, and also usually relatively terrestrial (not associated with streams)

Again, this is not a poison frog, though it does have somewhat toxic skin. This is a Golden Mantella, *Mantella aurantiaca*, from Madagascar, a very common frog often imported for the terrarium hobby. Photo by R. D. Bartlett.

THE RAINFORESTS

A stunning specimen of the most brilliant Splendid Harlequin Toad (*A. varius*) color pattern. The only color missing from this toad is bright blue, which is found in the patterns of some specimens. Photo by A. v. d. Nieuwenhuizen.

THE RAINFORESTS

This little male Strawberry Poison Frog shows the color pattern typical of Costa Rican *D. pumilio*: tiny dark speckling on the back and deep blue-black hands and feet. In male poison frogs the vocal pouch or sac often appears to be located far back on the throat, almost between the front legs at first glance. Photo by R. Bechter.

vent. A dozen or so species of true poison frogs are kept by terrarium hobbyists on a regular basis, many of these being bred with some regularity.

There are many other colorful little frogs from rainforests around the world, and hobbyists often have trouble telling them from the poison frogs. The mantellas of Madagascar, for instance, may be just as colorful as any poison frog, are of similar size and shape, and also are active during the day. How do you tell a dendrobatid from a mantella or some of the little rainfrogs (Leptodactylidae) likely to be abundant in American rainforests? The answer is that there is no sure way to make the determination. The characters of the Dendrobatidae are largely internal features of the skeleton and muscular system, fine details that even a specialist has trouble distinguishing with certainty. All the dendrobatids have toe discs, and the last bone of each finger and toe is T-shaped. The only obvious (sometimes!) external character for the family is the presence of a pair of raised lumps (scutes) on top of each finger and toe, the scutes separated by a valley. In species with greatly widened discs (those of *Dendrobates* and *Minyobates*) the scutes can be quite conspicuous, but in those genera with narrower toe discs the scutes may be hard to see. Other than that, you have to match up the species and work backward through genus to the proper family.

I have to give a few lines to the harlequin toads, *Atelopus* and allies, strange little toads found in and near Neotropical streams. Though often called poison frogs by hobbyists and dealers, they are not dendrobatids by any stretch of the imagination and cannot be kept like dendrobatids. They usually are adapted to running streams, their tadpoles often having a sucking disc behind the mouth to help prevent them from being swept away by the current. Though their skin secretions may be distasteful like those of any toad, they are completely different from the toxins of poison frogs. Harlequin toads may have colorful patterns on the back (though many are plain brownish), but none resembles the pattern of any poison frog. The hind feet usually are large and heavily webbed, the webs thickened; many species have a distinct projecting snout. As a rule, harlequin toads fare poorly in captivity and have short lives; they are considered to be virtually impossible to breed successfully. These are animals for the real frog specialist, and they are not—repeat, not—poison frogs.

Before we start talking about individual species of poison frogs and their relatives, you will need a bit of background about both their taxonomy (how to tell them apart) and their batrachiculture (how to keep them alive and breed them). We'll discuss these topics next.

Another selection of harlequin toads. These all represent various color forms (often individual variations) of the common Central American *Atelopus varius*. Both the specimens in the center and the pair at the upper right are from the San Jose area of Costa Rica. Splendid Harlequin Toads, *A. varius*, are as variable as some of the species of true poison frogs, almost matching the possibilities found in *Dendrobates histrionicus*.

The black and yellow *A. varius* at the bottom probably are from Panama, as is the individual shown at the upper left, but similarly colored specimens also are found in Costa Rica. Unfortunately, structural characters are almost as variable as color patterns in these toads. All photos by A. v. d. Nieuwenhuizen.

No, these are NOT poison frogs; they are harlequin toads of the genus *Atelopus*, close relatives of the common garden toads. Shown at the top is the Golden Harlequin Toad (*A. zeteki* or *A. varius zeteki*). All photos by A. v. d. Nieuwenhuizen.

In the center is an unidentified but quite colorful species of *Atelopus* perhaps related to *A. varius* (as is almost anything you are likely to find on the terrarium market). At the bottom left is an *Atelopus varius*, the poorly distinguished subspecies or color variety often called *ambulatorius*. At the bottom right is that troublesome unidentified *Atelopus* species again.

THE RAINFORESTS

Of the three common Central American poison frogs, *D. speciosus*, the Splendid Poison Frog (bottom), is most poorly known. Its extremely smooth skin contrasts greatly with the coarsely granular skin of *D. granuliferus* (top). Photos by R. Bechter.

frogs. (From now on, when I use "poison frog" I will mean only the colorful, toxic species; "dendrobatid" will be applied to members of the family as a whole.) Rocket frogs belong to the genus *Colostethus* (currently under review and being broken into smaller genera) and comprise about 100 species of small (under 40 mm) day-active brownish frogs that often are near or in shallow rocky streams, tend to have webbed hind feet, and lack the skin toxins found in the true poison frogs. Their taxonomy is very confused, but a few species have worked their way into the terrarium hobby, so we'll talk about them a bit toward the end of the book. The skunk frogs so far consist of a single species in the genus *Aromobates*, an odd animal discovered only in 1981 and described in 1991 from specimens collected near shallow streams in the northern Andean cloud forests of Venezuela. We'll talk more about them when we take on the rocket frogs.

POISON FROGS IN GENERAL

Poison frogs proper are unusual in being mostly ground-dwellers that are active (often in the open) during daylight hours and have bright colors. As far as known, none frequents streams or hides under rocks during the day and they don't emerge at night to call and mate like typical frogs. Their activities take place in the ground litter or low shrubs (with some exceptions), where they actively pursue ants, their major prey. Eggs are laid in small batches during the rainy season or throughout the year on damp protected spots on land and the tadpoles are transported to usually individual water spots by the parents for separate rearing (many are notorious cannibals as tadpoles). Amplexus or clasping, the usual frog behavior of the male holding the female in position for mating, appears to be absent or reduced to grasping the head, the frogs often mating vent-to-

Rarely seen in captivity, the Splendid Poison Frog is closely related to the Strawberry Poison Frog, and the two could be confused. Notice the absence of dark hands and feet in the Splendid, however. Photo by R. Bechter.

act and decided it would be more accurate to call them either "dart-poison" or "arrow-poison" frogs, making four common names circulate for the group. Recently specialists in the group have simplified and—in my opinion—solved the problem by referring to the toxic dendrobatids simply as "poison frogs," an approach followed here. It might be noted that only a few (apparently three) species of the 65 discussed here actually have been used to treat darts, but all as far as known have potentially dangerous though not especially toxic skin secretions.

The family Dendrobatidae can be broken into two groups: poison frogs proper and rocket and skunk

The Rainforests

This is the decade of "biological diversity." It is hard to pick up a magazine, read the morning newspaper, or listen to radio or television news without running into the expression. Everyone knows that the rainforests are being destroyed at a rapid rate, taking with them the literally hundreds of thousands of plant and animal species that make rainforests unique. This isn't the first time a major ecological realm has been devastated (think of the eastern forests and the Great Plains in the United States), but it is the first time that television cameras have been there to instantly apprise everyone of the situation.

The American tropics from Nicaragua in Central America south to the limits of evergreen rainforest vegetation in South America (about 20° latitude, a line running from Peru through the Bolivia-Paraguay border area and cutting off the southern "finger" of Brazil) are home to a unique family of tiny frogs that have capture the imagination of naturalists, photographers, and terrarium hobbyists the world over. The dendrobatids, family Dendrobatidae, comprise about 170 species of brownish to highly colored frogs, but hobbyists are interested mostly in the (currently) 65 colorful little jewels here dubbed the "poison frogs" and often called poison-arrow or poison-dart frogs in terrarium literature. These species presently are placed in four major groups or genera (*Dendrobates*, *Epipedobates*, *Minyobates*, and *Phyllobates*), the subjects of this book. They have a long history in scientific literature, the first species being described by European scientists at the end of the 18th century, but only in the last 20 years have modern scientists realized just how odd these frogs really are.

Today you can book a tour to visit the homes of some of the most colorful species of poison frogs. Parks in Costa Rica and Panama boast large populations of *Dendrobates granuliferus*, *D. auratus*, and *D. pumilio*, three of the species that are collected in relatively large numbers for the terrarium hobby and, in the case of *D. auratus*, sometimes bred in captivity. In the humid lowland forests of islands lying off Panama some localities literally "hop" with tiny Strawberry Poison Frogs (*D. pumilio*) in a bewildering variety of patterns, while more somberly colored *Phyllobates* and *Minyobates* species, as well as rocket frogs, are just tantalizingly beyond the next ridge of litter or beyond the next tiny stream. Western South America is less accessible to ecotourists, but the expanding array of parks in Venezuela, Colombia, Ecuador, and Peru has produced a large number of the new species described in the last decade. As unprotected rainforest is timbered or cultivated, the parks become the only concentrations of habitat for many species with already restricted ranges. Though poison frogs occur in the Amazon basin, they are not particularly abundant or diverse in the inundated Amazon River forests. The Guianas of northeastern South America host a much more interesting diversity of species, but only recently have the forests of these countries been opened to tourists.

Two of the most commonly seen poison frogs, both usually imported from Costa Rica. At the top is one of the more typical Costa Rican color forms of *Dendrobates pumilio*, the Strawberry Poison Frog, while at the bottom is its Pacific Coast relative the Granular Poison Frog, *D. granuliferus*. Photos by R. Bechter.

WHAT'S IN A NAME?

Dendrobatids are called poison frogs for a simple reason—the skin of many species secretes toxins that are potent poisons to predators, including man. Secretions of the species belonging to the genus *Phyllobates* are used by various Amerindians to treat blowgun darts for use in hunting and warfare. Over the years they acquired the common name "poison-arrow" frogs, but eventually it was pointed out that Amerindians used blowguns rather than bows and arrows, so they then began to be called "poison-dart" frogs. Next various grammatical purists got into the

SOME TAXONOMIC BACKGROUND

Mantella crocea, one of the several species of mantellas that reaches the market on a sporadic basis. I don't think that anyone with any experience with poison frogs could confuse this species with any dendrobatid, but.... Photo by R. D. Bartlett.

mm adult length); first finger shorter than second; finger discs usually conspicuously wider than fingers; teeth absent; bright oblique lateral stripe absent; histrionicotoxins and 3,5-disubstituted indolizidine alkaloids present; amplexus normally absent; tadpole with oral disc unindented laterally and anus median.

MINYOBATES: Tiny, under 20 mm adult length; first finger shorter than second; finger discs usually conspicuously wider than fingers; teeth absent; back usually unicolored; a bright oblique lateral stripe often present but incomplete, as are bright dorsolateral stripes; histrionicotoxins and 3,5-disubstituted indolizidine alkaloids absent; cephalic amplexus may be exhibited; tadpole with oral disc laterally indented and anus dextral.

EPIPEDOBATES: First finger equal to or longer than second; finger discs usually not conspicuously wider than fingers; teeth often present; a bright oblique

Leptodactylid frogs such as *Lithodytes lineatus* seem to be close relatives of dendrobatids, or at least several herpetologists believe this to be the case. Notice the shortness of the upper front leg, leading to a horizontal resting pose, and compare the proportions to most dendrobatids. *Lithodytes*, by the way, often is found in ant and termite nests, where dendrobatids are never found. Photo by J. P. Bogart.

The tiny *Eleutherodactylus limbatus* of Cuba has a pattern similar to some of the *Colostethus* but has much shorter limbs and differently shaped toes. Photo by J. P. Bogart.

SOME TAXONOMIC BACKGROUND

Recent collecting in Madagascar has produced many interesting new mantellas, most of which are available to hobbyists. This beautiful little frog seems to represent an undescribed species (probably being described by a German or French scientist) closely related to the Golden Mantella but with a more granular skin and differences in color pattern (notice the dark eardrum). Photo by R. D. Bartlett.

lateral stripe usually present, bright dorsolateral stripe often absent; 3,5-disubstituted indolizidine alkaloids absent; cephalic amplexus may be exhibited; tadpole with oral disc laterally indented and anus dextral.

PHYLLOBATES: First finger equal to or longer than second; finger discs usually not conspicuously wider than fingers; teeth usually present; a bright oblique lateral stripe absent but a bright dorsolateral stripe present at least in juveniles; histrionicotoxins absent or poorly represented, 3,5-disubstituted indolizidine alkaloids and batrachotoxins present; tadpole with oral disc laterally indented and anus dextral.

Again, this classification is tentative, and *Epipedobates* especially is likely to be broken into more genera.

Not everyone has accepted this generic classification (we'll call it the Myers system here). Because the four genera are almost impossible to distinguish without chemical tests and there are indications that the classes of alkaloids can change over the life of an individual (*Phyllobates terribilis*, for instance, gradually loses batrachotoxins in captivity and in later captive-bred generations), they are not very practical for identification, a feature that many herpetologists feel is important. In 1988, Zimmermann and Zimmermann, two researchers known for their success in breeding dendrobatids and other frogs, erected two new genera: *Allobates* for *femoralis*, and *Phobobates* for *bassleri, silverstonei,* and *trivittatus*, species included by Myers in *Epipedobates*. *E. bassleri, silverstonei,* and *trivittatus* form the *Trivittatus*-Group in the Myers system, but *femoralis* is only one of seven species in the *Femoralis*-Group of Myers. Myers, et al. (1991) provided good reasons for not recognizing *Allobates* and *Phobobates* at this time, including the opinion that they obscure already uncertain relationships even more.

Still another classification was proposed by Bauer in a series of short papers, summarized in 1989. His classification recognizing three subfamilies and a

SOME TAXONOMIC BACKGROUND

Many mantellas, such as this *Mantella viridis*, have fairly distinct glandular skin folds (dorsolateral ridges) on the sides of the back that are absent in poison frogs. Mantellas have somewhat toxic skin and lay eggs on land like dendrobatids, but otherwise their behavior is not much like the poison frogs. They often are found near roads and fields and often do well in densely inhabited regions. Photo by P. Freed.

total of nine genera has not been accepted, but two of his new generic names may be validly proposed and in one case (*Ameerega*, 1986) may predate *Epipedobates*. Further inquiry by nomenclatural specialists seems to be necessary before the Bauer classification might be more widely used. See the appendix for more details.

One rather paradoxical aspect of dendrobatid taxonomy that has not been explored is that of chromosomal variation. Limited research has displayed the presence of three different chromosome numbers in the family. Typical *Dendrobates* (*pumilio*, *histrionicus*, *granuliferus*) have ten pairs of chromosomes (2N = 20), while *Epipedobates trivittatus* and *Phyllobates lugubris* have 12 pairs (2N = 24). (*Colostethus inguinalis* and *C. trinitatis* also have 2N = 24.) Curiously, *Dendrobates auratus* has only nine pairs (2N = 18). Structurally *Phyllobates* and *Epipedobates* are similar, so a similarity in chromosome number is not unexpected. *Dendrobates auratus*, however, is not an atypical member of its genus structurally, so the difference in chromosome number is hard to explain. It may be that *Dendrobates* comprises several distinctive lineages that might be worthy of generic rank; *D. auratus* belongs to the *Tinctorius*-Group, while the other species belong to the *Histrionicus*-Group, recognized for unusual tadpole morphology.

Behavior has been used to a minor degree in attempting to unravel the relationships of dendrobatids, but it apparently is much too early to even attempt to summarize the literature. Much of the controversy surrounds the presence or absence of true amplexus in dendrobatids. At least some *Epipedobates* have cephalic amplexus, where the male clasps the female during mating by placing his arms under her head, his hands under her chin. However, an action very like cephalic amplexus occurs during fighting (aggressive behavior) in many poison frogs, and different researchers have different interpretations of what this means—if anything. The various calls of poison frogs also have been studied and may eventually prove to be of some use in taxonomy, but so far it is hard to determine any constant patterns. One of the problems is that the calls of most poison frogs in nature are low, soft trillings (*Phyllobates*) or buzzes. *D. auratus*, for instance, produces a slurred "cheez-cheez-cheez," while *D. pumilio* and *D. granuliferus* produce low insect-like buzzes. The sounds seldom carry far and often are heard only an hour or two after sunrise and an hour or two before sunset. These usually are "advertisement calls" produced by males to attract females. Different calls may be produced by both sexes later in courtship. The Zimmermanns have tried to use the presence or absence of certain components of the call for taxonomy, but they have not been followed by most workers. Though behavior may prove useful as a taxonomic adjunct, it still is too early to guess exactly what behavioral aspects will prove valuable with further research. Detailed observations on captive animals (especially mating behavior and recorded calls suitable for spectrographic analysis) may provide a valuable contribution to the understanding of the group.

Numerous undescribed species of poison frogs are

SOME TAXONOMIC BACKGROUND

known to specialists and slowly are being described in scientific journals. Many of the wider-ranging "species" are known to consist of two or more species that are difficult to identify and might even exist together in the same localities (examples are *ventrimaculatus* and *pictus*). The wheels of science grind slowly and the major workers in the field cannot devote their entire lives to describing little red, yellow, and black frogs, so it may be decades before the group finally is figured out—and by that time most of the rainforests probably will be gone.

I would be the first to admit that to a non-specialist the poison frogs are difficult or perhaps even impossible to identify with certainty. Some of the species (*pumilio*, *histrionicus*, and *tinctorius*, for instance) exhibit incredible variations in colors and patterns, while others currently recognized as valid (*reticulatus*, *fantasticus*, and *imitator* come to mind) seem to a disinterested observer to be just extreme patterns of one variable species. Silverstone, for instance, in his 1975 revision of *Dendrobates* provided drawings to display the extreme pattern variation in *D. quinquevittatus*, including in his opinion the patterns called *reticulatus* and *fantasticus*. There is no doubt that color pattern alone cannot be used to reliably identify poison frogs; size, locality, and knowledge of skin toxins also must be known before a firm identification can be made and certainly before anyone should even think of describing a new species. Breeders now are successfully hybridizing some related species of poison frogs in the terrarium, making identification of hobby specimens even more confusing.

When trying to identify an unknown poison frog, first try to make sure it is not a variation of one of the dozen relatively common terrarium species. Make a note of the body length (tip of snout to vent) of adult specimens and notice if the finger discs of a male are especially wider than the fingers or just a bit wider. Is the skin of the back smooth or granular? Is there a bright (usually yellow or blue) oblique line on the side of the body? Are there bright (yellow, usually) "flash" spots in the armpit and groin? Next look at the overall pattern of both the back and the belly, which are most likely to vary from population to population or even from individual to individual. *Never assume that just because two frogs look different they really are different.* We've tried to present a large number of pattern variations for the common species, but *histrionicus*, *pumilio*, and *tinctorius* seem to be almost infinitely variable. When preserved, most poison frogs lose their bright colors in a matter of days, turning into solid black or black and white specimens that may be virtually impossible to identify (even for a specialist) without detailed notes on collecting locality and detailed color photos. This is a difficult group of animals, and the few scientists who have dedicated years to their study deserve the thanks of the entire terrarium hobby for their perseverance.

A fairly typical little rocket frog, *Colostethus olfersoides*, in this case a female from Brazil. I've not attempted to cover the rocket frogs in great detail in this book because: 1) they are not especially toxic; 2) their taxonomy is totally confused; 3) they all look much alike to the average hobbyist; and 4) they are unavailable to the average hobbyist. A couple of the more common species are covered in a later chapter of this book, however, enough to give the interested hobbyist a sampling of rocket frog care and behavior. Photo by J. P. Bogart.

New poison frogs are described almost every year, and so are new mantellas. This interesting little species, *Mantella expectata*, is one of the most recently described species. Considering the mantellas are restricted to Madagascar, a very large island with diverse though threatened habitats that have been poorly studied in the past, more new species should be expected. Photo by P. Freed.

CHECKLIST OF POISON FROGS

Checklist of the Poison Frogs

As mentioned, for our purposes the poison frogs consist of just those species in the four genera that produce certain skin toxins and usually have bright (aposematic) warning colors. These are the species currently of most interest to hobbyists and naturalists. The remaining genera and species of the family Dendrobatidae, the rocket and skunk frogs, will be considered briefly in a later chapter.

The classification used here follows as closely as possible that presented by Myers in 1987, recognizing four genera based on chemical and minor structural characters. Attempts to correlate this classification with the earlier revisions by Silverstone in 1975 and 1976 are confusing to many hobbyists, so Silverstone's classification is summarized briefly here. Silverstone's works appeared before the descriptions of several species, and his concepts of some species (such as *quinquevittatus*) differ from those currently accepted:

[*Dendrobates*: First finger shorter than second, finger discs conspicuously wider than fingers, teeth usually absent.

Histrionicus-Group: *histrionicus, leucomelas*
Minutus-Group: *altobueyensis, fulguritus, minutus, opisthomelas, quinquevitttus, steyermarki*
Pumilio-Group: *granuliferus, pumilio, speciosus*
Tinctorius-Group: *auratus, azureus, galactonotus, tinctorius, truncatus*]

[*Phyllobates*: First finger equal to or longer than second, finger discs not much wider than fingers, teeth usually present.

Bicolor-Group: *aurotaenia, bicolor, lugubris, vittatus*
Femoralis-Group: *anthonyi, boulengeri, espinosai, femoralis, tricolor, zaparo*
Pictus-Group: *bolivianus, ingeri, parvulus, petersi, pictus, pulchripectus, smaragdinus*
Trivittatus-Group: *bassleri, trivittatus*]

An additional name, *Dendrobates labialis* Cope, 1874 (*Proc. Acad. Nat. Sci. Philadelphia*, 26: 130-137), was inadequately described from an uncertain locality and the holotype has been lost; the name has never been placed with certainty and usually is ignored.

Currently there are about 65 described species of poison frogs that are considered to be valid by the leading workers in the group, but there are many synonyms and described subspecies that are not presently accepted. The taxonomy of poison frogs still is poorly understood and the last word certainly has not been written. Phantasmal Poison Frogs, *Epipedobates tricolor*, for instance (shown here is a typical multi-generation captive-bred specimen), are highly variable and actually may be comprised of several good species or subspecies. Photo by R. D. Bartlett.

CHECKLIST OF POISON FROGS

Another problem with dendrobatid taxonomy is that captive-bred animals often differ greatly from their wild-caught ancestors. This captive-bred *Epipedobates tricolor* is one of the most brilliantly colored poison frogs I've ever seen, but it really is not too similar in color to typical wild-caught specimens. There are strong indications that skin toxins also change (both in quantity and quality) in captive-bred poison frogs. Photo by R. D. Bartlett.

The following checklist presents the described species in alphabetical order in the genus to which they were assigned by Myers, 1987, and later papers. Also given are a citation of the original description, an English-language common name, the type-locality (often reworded for brevity and to place country first—please check original citations for exact type-locality) or restricted locality, general statement of range, and comments on synonymy and (in *Dendrobates* and *Epipedobates*) species-group. The list has been compiled from Frost (1985) and Duellman (1993) and checked where possible against original descriptions. Be aware that several undescribed species are known and are in the process of description by several specialists.

DENDROBATES Wagler, 1830 (type-species: *tinctorius*)

D. *arboreus* Myers, Daly & Martinez, 1984. *Amer. Mus. Novitates*, No. 2783: 5.
POLKA-DOT POISON FROG
Panama, border between Chiriqui and Bocas del Toro Provinces,' cloud forest above upper Quebrada de Arena.
Range: Vicinity of the type-locality.
Histrionicus-Group.

D. *auratus* (Girard, 1855). *Proc. Acad. Nat. Sci. Philadelphia*, 7: 226.
GREEN AND BLACK POISON FROG
Panama, Taboga Island.
Range: Central America from southern Nicaragua south on the Atlantic versant and from Costa Rica south on the Pacific; also northwestern Colombia. Introduced to Oahu, Hawaii, in 1932 from Taboga Island, Panama.
Tinctorius-Group.

D. *azureus* Hoogmoed, 1969. *Zool. Meded., Leiden*, 44: 134.
BLUE POISON FROG
Surinam, Nickerie, Sipaliwini Savannah, western slope of Vier Gebroedersberg near Brazilian border.
Range: Mountains of western Surinam.
Tinctorius-Group.

D. *biolat* Morales, 1992. *Caribbean J. Sci.*, 28: 195.
BIOLAT POISON FROG
Peru, Dept. Madre de Dios, Prov. Tahuamanu, Reserva de la Biosfera del Manu.
Range: Upper Amazon drainage of southern Peru.
Quinquevittatus-Group.

D. *captivus* Myers, 1982. *Amer. Mus. Novitates*, No. 2721: 14.

OK, give up? No, these frogs do not represent three or even two species. They all are variations of *Dendrobates histrionicus* from Colombia. The frogs above are plays on the "bull's-eye" pattern, where there is a large, bright spot in the center of the back (absent in the frog at top right). Color means little in this pattern.

Often the yellow spotting on the back is of medium to small size, and either regular or very irregular in shape and placement. The bright orange head of the frog to the lower right never fails to draw the attention of observers. Any of these patterns could be found in adjacent valleys over a short distance. All photos by A. v. d. Nieuwenhuizen.

CHECKLIST OF POISON FROGS

Though poorly known in nature (where it appears to be restricted to the vicinity of one valley), hobbyists have succeeded in breeding *Epipedobates silverstonei* in captivity with some regularity. A good Silverstone's Poison Frog is one of the most desirable and beautiful, as well as largest, of the rainforest frogs kept in the terrarium. Photo by A. v. d. Nieuwenhuizen.

RIO SANTIAGO POISON FROG
Peru, Dept. Amazonas, mouth of Rio Santiago.
Range: Rios Xingu and Tapajos, Para, Brazil.
Captivus-Group.

D. castaneoticus Caldwell & Myers, 1990. *Amer. Mus. Novitates*, No. 2988: 3.
BRAZIL-NUT POISON FROG
Brazil, Para, near Cachoeira Jurua, Rio Xingu.
Range: Rios Xingu and Tapajos, Para, Brazil.
Quinquevittatus-Group.

D. fantasticus Boulenger, 1884. *Proc. Zool. Soc., London*, 1883 [1884]: 636.
RED-HEADED POISON FROG
Peru, Yurimaguas, Huallaga River.
Range: Upper Amazon basin of Loreto and San Martin Dept., Peru.
Quinquevittatus-Group.

D. galactonotus Steindachner, 1864. *Verh. Zool. Bot. Ges. Wien.*, 14: 260.
SPLASH-BACKED POISON FROG
Brazil, Para, Rio do Muria, Pedro Gurcao's farm, north of Virgia to Frequenza.
Range: Central Brazil south of the Amazon.
Tinctorius-Group.

D. granuliferus Taylor, 1958. *Univ. Kansas Sci. Bull.*, 39: 10.
GRANULAR POISON FROG
Costa Rica, Puntarenas Prov., about 3 miles north of Palmar, north of the Rio Diquis.
Range: Golfo Dulce area, Pacific Costa Rica.
Histrionicus-Group.

D. histrionicus Berthold, 1846. *Nachr. Ges. Wiss. Gottingen*, 1845 [1846]: 43.
HARLEQUIN POISON FROG
Colombia, Popayan Prov.
Range: Choco area of western Colombia and Ecuador.
Histrionicus-Group.

D. imitator Schulte, 1986. *Sauria*, 8: 11.
MIMIC POISON FROG
Peru, Dept. San Martin, Tarapoto-Yurimaguas Road.
Range: Vicinity of the type-locality.
Quinquevittatus-Group.

D. lamasi Morales, 1992. *Caribbean J. Sci.*, 28: 191.
PASCO POISON FROG
Peru, Dept. Pasco, Prov. Huancabamba, Bosque Castilla, NW of Iscozacin.
Range: Central Peru.
Quinquevittatus-Group.

D. lehmanni Myers & Daly, 1976. *Bull. Amer. Mus. Nat. Hist.*, 157: 240.
LEHMANN'S POISON FROG
Colombia, Dept. Valle, about 13 km west of Dagua, upper Rio Anchicaya drainage.
Range: Vicinity of the type-locality.
Histrionicus-Group.

D. leucomelas Steindachner, 1864. *Verh. Zool. Bot. Ges. Wien*, 14: 260.
YELLOW-BANDED POISON FROG
Colombia.
Range: Northern South America above the Amazon.
Tinctorius-Group.

D. mysteriosus Myers, 1982. *Amer. Mus. Novitates*, No. 2721: 18.

Variants on a theme: Dyeing Poison Frogs, *Dendrobates tinctorius*. Many subspecies have been proposed for this species, but none currently is accepted. The frog at the top left is from French Guiana, that to the top right a female from Villa Nova, Brazil.

In the center are two male *D. tinctorius* from Surinam. Notice the swollen vocal pouch of the frog at the left. In poison frogs there are two separate openings to the vocal pouch, but often only one develops fully. The male *D. tinctorius* to the bottom left is from Villa Nova, the one at the bottom right from central French Guiana. It really is hard to find any two populations of this species that are alike in details of coloration. All photos by A. v. d. Nieuwenhuizen.

CHECKLIST OF POISON FROGS

MARANON POISON FROG
Peru, Dept. Cajamarca, vicinity of Santa Rosa, upper Rio Maranon drainage.
Range: Vicinity of the type-locality, Cordillera del Condor.
Captivus-Group.

D. *occultator* Myers & Daly, 1976. *Bull. Amer. Mus. Nat. Hist.*, 157: 244.
LA BREA POISON FROG
Colombia, Dept. Cauca, La Brea, on the Rio Patia.
Range: Vicinity of the type-locality.
Histrionicus-Group.

D. *pumilio* Schmidt, 1857. *Sitzungsber. Akad. Wiss. Wien, Math. Naturwiss. Kl.*, 24: 12.
STRAWBERRY POISON FROG
Panama, road between Bocas del Toro and Vulcan Chiriqui.
Range: Atlantic lowlands of Central America from Nicaragua to Panama.
Histrionicus-Group.

D. *quinquevittatus* Steindachner, 1864. *Verh. Zool. Bot. Ges. Wien*, 14: 260.
RIO MADEIRA POISON FROG
Brazil, upper Rio Madeira, Salto do Girao.
Range: Rio Madeira drainage, western Brazil.
Quinquevittatus-Group.
Note: This species appears not to be present in the terrarium hobby; the species incorrectly bearing this name is *D. ventrimaculatus*, itself a species complex.

D. *reticulatus* Boulenger, 1884. *Proc. Zool. Soc., London*, 1883 [1884]: 635.
RED-BACKED POISON FROG
Peru, Yurimaguas, Huallaga River.
Range: Vicinity of Loreto, Peru.
Quinquevittatus-Group.

D. *sirensis* Aichinger, 1991. *Herpetologica*, 47(1): 1.
SIRA POISON FROG
Peru, Dept. Huanuco, Serrania de Sira, Rio Llullapichis drainage.
Range: Vicinity of the type-locality.
Quinquevittatus-Group.

D. *speciosus* Schmidt, 1857. *Sitzungsber. Akad. Wiss. Wien, Math. Naturwiss. Kl.*, 24: 12.
SPLENDID POISON FROG
Panama, road between Bocas del Toro and Vulcan Chiriqui.
Range: Western Panama.
Histrionicus-Group.

D. *tinctorius* (Schneider, 1799). *Historiae amphibiorum naturalis et literariae*, 1: 175. [In 1982 in *Bull. Zool. Nomenclature*, 39(4): 264-267 and 267-278, Lescure and Dubois reviewed the early history of the name *tinctorius* and the type species of *Dendrobates*. Among other things, they suggested that the species *tinctorius* be cited as Cuvier, 1797. See their papers for the rather intricate details.]
DYEING POISON FROG
French Guiana, Bruynzeel lumber camp, lower Matarony River.
Range: Guianas and adjacent Brazil.
Tinctorius-Group.

D. *truncatus* (Cope, 1861). *Proc. Acad. Nat. Sci. Philadelphia*, 12: 372.
YELLOW-STRIPED POISON FROG
Colombia.
Range: Northern and central Colombia.
Tinctorius-Group.

D. *vanzolinii* Myers, 1982. *Amer. Mus. Novitates*, No. 2721: 9.
BRAZILIAN POISON FROG
Brazil, Acre State, Porto Walter on the Rio Jurua.
Range: Western Brazil and adjacent Peru.
Quinquevittatus-Group.

D. *variabilis* Zimmermann & Zimmermann, 1988. *Salamandra*, 24: 132.
ZIMMERMANN'S POISON FROG
Peru, Dept. San Martin, Tarapoto-Yurimaguas Road.
Range: Vicinity of the type-locality, but probably widely distributed in Amazonian Peru and Brazil.
Quinquevittatus-Group.

D. *ventrimaculatus* Shreve, 1935. *Occas. Pap. Boston Soc. Nat. Hist.*, 8: 213.
AMAZONIAN POISON FROG
Ecuador, Prov. Pastaza, Sarayacu.
Range: Much of northern and central South America, from Colombia and French Guiana through Brazil to Ecuador and Peru. Almost certainly a complex of several very similar species.
Quinquevittatus-Group.
Note: This (at least in the broad sense) is the species usually called *quinquevittatus* in the terrarium literature.

Summary of Group assignments in *Dendrobates*:
Captivus-Group: *captivus, mysteriosus*
Histrionicus-Group: *arboreus, granuliferus, histrionicus, lehmanni, occultator, pumilio, speciosus*
Quinquevittatus-Group: *biolat, castaneoticus, fantasticus, imitator, lamasi, quinquevittatus, reticulatus, sirensis, vanzolinii, variabilis, ventrimaculatus*
Tinctorius-Group: *auratus, azureus, galactonotus, leucomelas, tinctorius, truncatus*

EPIPEDOBATES Myers, 1987 (type-species: *tricolor*)

E. *andinus* (Myers & Burrowes, 1987). *Amer. Mus. Novitates*, No. 2899: 2.
LA PLANADA POISON FROG
Colombia, Dept. Narino, Reserva Natural La Planada, Municipio Ricuarte.
Range: Vicinity of the type-locality.
Pictus-Group.

E. *azureiventris* (Kneller & Henle, 1985). *Salamandra*, 21: 62.
SKY-BLUE POISON FROG
Peru, Dept. San Martin, Tarapoto-Yurimaguas Road.
Range: Vicinity of the type-locality.
Pictus-Group.

E. *bassleri* (Melin, 1941). *Goteborgs K. Vetensk. Vitterh. Samh. Handl.*, (B)1: 65.
PLEASING POISON FROG
Peru, Dept. San Martin, Roque.
Range: Amazonian Peru.
Trivittatus-Group. Placed by Zimmermann & Zimmermann, 1988 (*Salamandra*, 24: 136) in their

CHECKLIST OF POISON FROGS

new genus *Phobobates*, considered to be a synonym of *Epipedobates*.

E. bilinguis Jungfer, 1989. *Salamandra*, 25: 86.
ECUADOREAN POISON FROG
Ecuador, Prov. Sucumbios, Puerto Francisco del Orellana (=Coca).
Range: Napo, Putumayo, and Aguarico drainages of eastern Ecuador.
Pictus-Group.

E. bolivianus (Boulenger, 1902). *Ann. Mag. Nat. Hist.*, (7)10: 397.
BOLIVIAN POISON FROG
Bolivia, La Paz, San Carlos.
Range: Amazonian Bolivia.
Petersi-Group.

E. boulengeri (Barbour, 1909). *Proc. Biol. Soc. Washington*, 22: 89.
MARBLED POISON FROG
Colombia, Dept. Narino, Gorgona Island.
Range: Choco of Colombia.
Femoralis-Group.

E. cainarachi Schulte, 1989. *Bol. Lima*, 63: 41.
CAINARACHI POISON FROG
Peru, Dept. San Martin, Valle del alto Rio Cainarachi, N Tarapoto on road to Yurimaguas.
Range: Vicinity of the type-locality.
Petersi-Group. Includes *E. ardens* Jungfer, 1989 (*Salamandra*, 25: 89) as a synonym.

E. erythromos (Vigle & Miyata, 1980). *Breviora (Harvard)*, No. 459: 2.
PALENQUE POISON FROG
Ecuador, Prov. Pichincha, Centro Cientifico, Rio Palenque, S Santo Domingo de los Colorados.
Range: Vicinity of the type-locality.
Pictus-Group.

E. espinosai (Funkhouser, 1956). *Zoologica (New York)*, 41: 76.
ESPINOSA POISON FROG
Ecuador, Prov. Pichincha, Hacienda Espinosa, W Santo Domingo de los Colorados.
Range: Choco of northwestern Ecuador.
Femoralis-Group.

E. femoralis (Boulenger, 1884). *Proc. Zool. Soc., London*, 1883 [1884]: 635.
BRILLIANT-THIGHED POISON FROG
Peru, Yurimaguas, Huallaga River.
Range: The Guianas and the Amazon drainages of Brazil, Peru, Ecuador, and Colombia.
Femoralis-Group. Type-species of the generic name *Allobates* Zimmermann & Zimmermann, 1988 (*Salamandra*, 24: 136), considered to be a synonym of *Epipedobates*.

E. flavopictus (A. Lutz, 1925). *Compt. Rend. Soc. Biol. Paris*, 93: 139.
LUTZ'S POISON FROG
Brazil, Minas Gerais, Belo Horizonte.
Range: Vicinity of the type-locality.
Pictus-Group.

E. ingeri (Cochran & Goin, 1970). *Bull. U. S. Natl. Mus.*, 288: 16.
NICEFORO'S POISON FROG
Colombia, Caqueta, Aserrio, near Rio Pescado.
Range: Vicinity of the type-locality.
Pictus-Group.

E. macero Rodriguez & Myers, 1993. *Amer. Mus. Novitates*, No. 3068: 2.
MANU POISON FROG
Peru, Dept. Madre de Dios, Rio Manu across from Coch Cashu Biol. Station, Parque Nac. Manu.
Range: Vicinity of the type-locality.
Petersi-Group.

E. maculatus (Peters, 1873). *Monatsber. Preuss. Akad. Wiss. Berlin*, 1873: 617.
CONFUSING POISON FROG
Panama, Chiriqui.
Range: Known only from the holotype; exact range uncertain.
Maculatus-Group.

The Brilliant-thighed Poison Frog, *Epipedobates femoralis*, gets its common name from the bright orange to ruby red spot hidden in the groin (barely visible here). When the frog moves and stretches the hind leg, the spot is suddenly "flashed" in the eyes of a predator, giving the frog just that extra second to escape. Skin toxins in *Epipedobates* species usually are quite weak and merely distasteful. Photo by P. Freed.

E. myersi (Pyburn, 1981). *Proc. Biol. Soc. Washington*, 94: 67.
MYERS'S POISON FROG
Colombia, near Wacara, Comisaria de Vaupes.
Range: Vicinity of the type-locality.
Femoralis-Group.

E. parvulus (Boulenger, 1882). *Catalogue Batrachia Salientia s. Ecaudata Collection British Mus.*: 145.
RUBY POISON FROG
Ecuador, Pastaza, Sarayacu.
Range: Amazon basin of northern Peru and Pastaza drainage of southern Ecuador.
Pictus-Group.

E. petersi (Silverstone, 1976). *Sci. Bull. Nat. Hist. Mus. Los Angeles Co.*, 27: 37.
PERUVIAN POISON FROG
Peru, Dept. Pasco, Santa Isabel, Rio Nevati, SE Puerto Bermudez.
Range: Amazonian Peru.

CHECKLIST OF POISON FROGS

Petersi-Group.

E. *pictus* (Tschudi, 1838). *Class. Batrachier.* 28.
SPOT-LEGGED POISON FROG
Bolivia, Santa Cruz.
Range: The Guianas and adjacent Venezuela plus the entire Amazon basin and then south to the Paraguay; basically, South America north of 20° latitude except the northwestern corner of the continent.
Pictus-Group. Very variable and perhaps a complex of species.

E. *pulchripectus* (Silverstone, 1976). *Sci. Bull. Nat. Hist. Mus. Los Angeles Co.*, 27: 43.
BLUE-BREASTED POISON FROG
Brazil, Terr. Amapa, Serra do Navio.
Range: Vicinity of the type-locality.
Pictus-Group.

E. *rufulus* (Gorzula, 1990). *Mem. Soc. Cienc. Nat. LaSalle*, 48: 144.
TEPUI POISON FROG
Venezuela, Est. Bolivar, NE edge Amuri-tepui, Macizo del Chimanta.
Range: Vicinity of the type-locality.
Pictus-Group.

E. *silverstonei* (Myers & Daly, 1979). *Amer. Mus. Novitates*, No. 2674: 2.
SILVERSTONE'S POISON FROG
Peru, Dept. Huanuco, Cordillera Azul, NE Tingo Maria.
Range: Vicinity of the type-locality.
Trivittatus-Group. Type-species of the generic name *Phobobates* Zimmermann & Zimmermann, 1988 (*Salamandra*, 24: 136), considered to be a synonym of *Epipedobates*.

E. *smaragdinus* (Silverstone, 1976). *Sci. Bull. Nat. Hist. Mus. Los Angeles Co.*, 27: 44.
EMERALD POISON FROG
Peru, Dept. Pasco, Pan de Azucar, NNE Oxapampa, Iscozazin Valley.
Range: Vicinity of the type-locality.
Pictus-Group.

E. *tricolor* (Boulenger, 1899). *Ann. Mag. Nat. Hist.*, (7)4: 455.
PHANTASMAL POISON FROG
Ecuador, Bolivar, Porvenir.
Range: Southwestern Ecuador and adjacent Peru.
Femoralis-Group. Includes *Colostethus paradoxus* Rivero, 1991 (*Breviora [Harvard]*, No. 493: 20) as a synonym. E. *anthonyi* (Noble, 1921, *Amer. Mus. Novitates*, No. 29: 5, Ecuador, Prov. del Oro, Salvias) currently is considered a synonym but has been treated as valid in the past.

E. *trivittatus* (Spix, 1824). *Spec. Nov. Ranarum*: 35.
THREE-STRIPED POISON FROG
Brazil, Rio Tefe.
Range: Amazon basin and the Guianas.
Trivittatus-Group. Placed by Zimmermann & Zimmermann, 1988 (*Salamandra*, 24: 136) in their new genus *Phobobates*, considered to be a synonym of *Epipedobates*.

E. *zaparo* (Silverstone, 1976). *Sci. Bull. Nat. Hist. Mus. Los Angeles Co.*, 27: 33.
SANGUINE POISON FROG
Ecuador, Prov. Pastaza, W Canelos.
Range: Napo and Pastazas drainages of Ecuador.

Femoralis-Group.
Summary of Group assignments in *Epipedobates*:
Femoralis-Group: *boulengeri, espinosai, femoralis, myersi, tricolor, zaparo*
Maculatus-Group: *maculatus*
Petersi-Group: *bolivianus, cainarachi, macero, petersi*
Pictus-Group: *andinus, azureiventris, bilinguis, erythromos, flavopictus, ingeri, parvulus, pictus, pulchripectus, rufulus, smaragdinus*
Trivittatus-Group: *bassleri, silverstonei, trivittatus*

MINYOBATES Myers, 1987 (type-species: *steyermarki*)

M. *abditus* (Myers & Daly, 1976). *Occas. Pap. Mus. Nat. Hist. Univ. Kansas*, 59: 1.
COLLINS'S POISON FROG
Ecuador, Prov. Napo, E base Volcan Reventador, SW Rio Azuela bridge on Quito-Lago Agrio Road.
Range: Vicinity of the type-locality.

M. *altobueyensis* (Silverstone, 1975). *Sci. Bull. Nat. Hist. Mus. Los Angeles Co.*, 21: 27.
ALTO DEL BUEY POISON FROG
Colombia, Dept. Choco, Alto del Buey.
Range: Vicinity of the type-locality.

M. *bombetes* (Myers & Daly, 1980). *Amer. Mus. Novitates*, No. 2692: 2.
CAUCA POISON FROG
Colombia, Dept. Valle del Cauca, Lago de Calima, SW Puente Tierra.
Range: Vicinity of the type-locality.

M. *fulguritus* (Silverstone, 1975). *Sci. Bull. Nat. Hist. Mus. Los Angeles Co.*, 21: 28.
YELLOW-BELLIED POISON FROG
Colombia, Dept. Choco, Playa de Oro.
Range: Choco of Colombia, also central Panama.

M. *minutus* (Shreve, 1935). *Occas. Pap. Boston Soc. Nat. Hist.*, 8: 212.
BLUE-BELLIED POISON FROG
Panama, Barro Colorado Island.
Range: Central Panama to southwestern Colombia.

M. *opisthomelas* (Boulenger, 1899). *Ann. Mag. Nat. Hist.*, (7)3: 275.
ANDEAN POISON FROG
Colombia, Dept. Antioquia, Santa Ines, N Medellin.
Range: Cordillera Central and Occidental of Colombia.

M. *steyermarki* (Rivero, 1971). *Kasmera*, 3: 390.
DEMONIC POISON FROG
Venezuela, Terr. Fed. Amazonas, Cerro Yapacana.
Range: Vicinity of the type-locality.

M. *viridis* (Myers & Daly, 1976). *Bull. Amer. Mus. Nat. Hist.*, 157: 247.
GREEN POISON FROG
Colombia, Dept. Valle, W Dagua, upper Rio Anchicaya drainage.
Range: Western Cordillera Occidental of Colombia.

M. *virolinensis* Ruiz-Carranza & Ramirez-Pinilla, 1992. *Lozania*, No. 61: 2.
SANTANDER POISON FROG
Colombia, Dept. Santander, Virolin (Inspec. Policia Canaverales), Vereda El Rejoj, Municipio Charala.
Range: Vicinity of the type-locality.

CHECKLIST OF POISON FROGS

The only *Minyobates* presently available to hobbyists is *M. minutus*, the so-called Blue-bellied Poison Frog. Few specimens, however, have much blue on the belly in this species, which is difficult to maintain in captivity. Though the genus *Minyobates* has some sensationally colored species, most have very narrow habitats on isolated mountain ranges and may never be available to the terrarium hobby. Photo by A. v. d. Nieuwenhuizen.

CHECKLIST OF POISON FROGS

Golfodulcean Poison Frogs, *Phyllobates vittatus*, often are available and do fairly well in the terrarium. Because of their tiny range on the Pacific coast of Costa Rica, however, wild-caught specimens could disappear from the hobby at any time. Notice that the stripes on the back extend over the rump to near the vent, not over the posterior lower side into the groin area, a feature of the genus *Phyllobates*. Photo by R. D. Bartlett.

PHYLLOBATES Dumeril & Bibron, 1841 (type-species: *bicolor*)

P. aurotaenia (Boulenger, 1913). *Proc. Zool. Soc., London*, 1913: 1029.
KOKOE POISON FROG
Colombia, Dept. Choco, Pena Lisa, Condoto.
Range: Choco of Colombia.

P. bicolor Bibron *in* Sagra, 1841. *Hist. Phys. Polit. Nat. Cuba, Rept.*: pl. 29.
BLACK-LEGGED POISON FROG
Colombia.
Range: Western Colombia.

P. lugubris (Schmidt, 1857). *Sitzungsber. Akad. Wiss. Wien, Math. Naturwiss. Kl.*, 24: 12.
LOVELY POISON FROG
Panama, road between Bocas del Toro and Vulcan Chiriqui.
Range: Atlantic lowlands of northern Panama and Costa Rica.

P. terribilis Myers, Daly & Malkin, 1978. *Bull. Amer. Mus. Nat. Hist.*, 161: 313.
GOLDEN POISON FROG
Colombia, Dept. Cauca, Quebrada Guangui above junction with Rio Patia.
Range: Vicinity of the type-locality.

P. vittatus (Cope, 1893). *Proc. Amer. Philos. Soc.*, 31: 340.
GOLFODULCEAN POISON FROG
Costa Rica, Puntarenas Prov., Buenos Aires.
Range: Golfo Dulce region of Pacific Costa Rica.

As a General Rule...

Oh, how I hate to start writing this chapter. How can you really write a single chapter that attempts to cover the general behavior, captive care, and raising information on a group like the poison frogs? Actually, I'm just going to try to skim over the basics for you and just hope that any more-detailed questions you might have will be answered by the individual species writeups. I'll continue to ignore rocket frogs and the skunk frog, of course, until later.

As a general rule, poison frogs are day-active (diurnal) animals that spend most or all their adult lives in the leaf litter and under logs and stones, though a few are notorious for living in bromeliads and other epiphytes on trees many meters up. Most of the species are found from near the coast to about 1000 meters in elevation, but a few species are found in higher cloud forests up to 2000 meters. Most species are notoriously active and difficult to collect once found—imagine how many holes an animal only 20 mm long can find to duck into. In some species males definitely are territorial, defending a small spot of litter, a leaf, or a piece of log from other males of the same species and calling at regular intervals to let other males know the preferred spot is claimed. This type of call, an "advertisement call," sometimes is not meant to attract the interest of females. Often the advertisement call is given for an hour or two after sunrise and before sunset, which may be the best time to try to collect or record them—but you won't get females this way. A few species have been reported to be somewhat ventriloquial and difficult to find even when calling, much like many treefrogs.

In nature poison frogs tend to actively hunt down small insects as food (*Colostethus*, on the other hand, seem to be "sit and wait" predators, sitting quietly under cover and waiting for ants to come to them) and they are especially fond of the multitude of ants typical of tropical rainforests. The larger species that have teeth (some *Phyllobates* and *Epipedobates*) can take larger and tougher prey (such as pinhead crickets and moth larvae) than the toothless species and thus may be a bit easier to care for in the terrarium. Tiny beetles and their larvae also are common inhabitants of the leaf litter in the tropics, and they are found in the bellies of many poison frogs. Free-living mites also are eaten by many species. Probably poison frogs actively hunt for anything of appropriate size that moves and doesn't bite back too hard. Several species that often occur in shrubs and other situations a meter or two above the ground may feed on mosquitoes more than you would think. Froglets feed on the tiniest insects of the litter, the springtails or collembolans, which also are abundant in American and European backyards.

The skin toxins of poison frogs apparently have developed to discourage predators. Human researchers experienced with these frogs can develop a "taste test" for the toxin level in a frog, learning how to judge the toxins by how much tingling and numbness or bitterness they feel when they "kiss" the back of a poison frog. This is not a safe procedure for hobbyists, as tasting a frog in the toxic level of *Phyllobates terribilis* or even *P. bicolor* could result in death—no exaggeration. Leave the business of relative toxicity of frogs to the experts with biochemical laboratories. A poison frog housed in a small terrarium with other frogs, however, can lead to the death of the other frogs, as can a poison frog in a collecting bag with other frogs.

When a predator such as a small snake attacks a poison frog, it immediately releases the frog and then tries to scrape its mouth against the ground, obviously trying to remove toxic mucus. Depending on the snake and frog combination, the snake may then writhe for minutes or hours before recovering or may even become semicomatose for several hours. It would appear that such brief encounters seldom or never lead to the death of the predator, and even a frog that has been bitten several times seems to recover without problems. One incident of this type should serve to fix the frog as inedible in the mind of the snake, preventing future attacks by a "learned" snake against similarly patterned frogs. Bright spots of color in the armpits and groin or on top of the thigh that are exposed only when the frog moves generally are called "flash marks" and probably serve to startle potential predators for just the split second necessary to make an escape. Studies on various salamanders with bright "flash marks" show that birds are confused by suddenly appearing patterns, and it is likely that birds would feed upon poison frogs on the jungle floor. Most birds probably can recognize colors, another evolutionary incentive for small prey with toxic skin secretions to develop bright colors to let potential predators know they are protected. These predator-warning color schemes, by the way, often are called aposematic coloration in technical papers, so our poison frogs may be called "aposematic dendrobatids" in the scientific literature—just so you'll know what that means if you ever run across it again.

Poison frogs are creatures of humid, usually wet, habitats, and their skins are not waxy enough to prevent evaporation in dry air. Thus the need for humid surroundings in captivity and the presence of tiny frog mummies if any are allowed to crawl out of the tank. Speaking of crawling, I should mention that although most species move by short hops as you would expect of a small frog, the short-legged species (such as *D. ventrimaculatus* and relatives) often appear to walk or crawl more than hop. Species

AS A GENERAL RULE...

In the species that have been studied, male poison frogs tend to occupy a constant territory, often a particular leaf layer on a shrub or a moist spot on a fallen tree, for weeks or months at a time. Males of *Dendrobates* species may call constantly during the day, but in *Epipedobates* calling may be restricted to a few hours in the morning or late afternoon. This calling male *D. lehmanni* has the silvery white toes typical of the species. Photo by A. v. d. Nieuwenhuizen.

AS A GENERAL RULE...

of genera with greatly expanded finger and toe discs (*Dendrobates, Minyobates*) are more likely to climb than are those with smaller discs (*Phyllobates, Epipedobates*), something to keep in mind when decorating the terrarium. Several *Dendrobates*, in fact, are found only in the trees, 10 or more meters above the ground, living in bromeliads and other vegetation on the trees. Some of the *Epipedobates*, on the other hand, seem to have never been found more than a few centimeters above the ground.

Male poison frogs usually are at least 1 to 3 millimeters shorter than females of the same species at the same locality. In many species (aren't you getting tired of that phrase, "many species"? But what else can I do, there are so many exceptions) males can be recognized by indications of a vocal sac, wrinkled grayish skin across the back of the throat (which doesn't help in the many species with largely black throats). If you could see into the back of the mouth of a male poison frog, you would see two tiny slits, one at each lower back corner, that let air into the vocal sac. The presence of the vocal slits is hard to see, and even experts examining preserved material commonly have made mistakes. Additionally, in at least a few species a good percentage of males never develop both slits, only one opening in the adult. Female poison frogs may call, but not as elaborately or persistently as males, and they don't have vocal sacs. Proper sexing often is one of the major obstacles to successfully breeding poison frogs and one of the reason many specialists suggest colonial breeding using two or three presumed males and double that number of presumed females.

As a great generalization, courting males produce a call that is meant to interest females. To humans the calls of most poison frogs are weak chirps and buzzes that do not carry far and often are hard to hear unless you concentrate. Some males (as in *Phyllobates* and *Epipedobates femoralis*) produce long, loud, harsh calls that carry and can even become annoying, but they are exceptional. Several scientific studies of poison frog vocalizations have been started, but so far no one has been able to do a really comprehensive study of the group. There are indications that technical aspects of the calls may be useful taxonomically, but so far the data are too scattered to be useful. Anyway, most hobbyists don't carry around the equipment necessary to record and analyze frog calls.

Regardless, female poison frogs hear males calling and come to them or a male sees a likely female and devotes several hours calling to her trying to attract her attention. Assuming the female is receptive, eventually she approaches the male and does something to increase his ardor. Often this involves stroking his head or snout or dancing in place in tiny circles while drumming her feet. This female courtship behavior may continue for hours, but usually it leads to the male moving from the calling spot and trying to get the female to follow him to the spot he has determined is best to lay the eggs. Often he moves a bit, the female follows, he moves, the female follows, etc., or he may actively try to push the female along. Eventually they reach the male-determined laying spot or bower, usually a leaf on or near the ground and readily defended by the male. Here the courtship dancing may resume or increase in intensity, or mating may occur with few preliminaries.

In most frogs clasping or amplexus is necessary so the male can be positioned over the female's vent while she lays the eggs. In this way his sperm are sure to cover the eggs and yield a high fertilization rate. In poison frogs, perhaps because the clutches of eggs are so small (usually only two to a dozen eggs at a time per female) and thus easier to fertilize than the thousands laid by most frogs, clasping is absent or of questionable presence. In some species of *Epipedobates* and *Minyobates* cephalic amplexus has been observed, but this rather unusual clasping method (the male's arms lie along the head of the female so this hands, palms down, are under her throat) also features in fighting between frogs of all sexes, so it is hard to interpret as a useful taxonomic character. Also, it seems that even within a species cephalic amplexus may not be practiced by all individuals. Because mating itself usually occurs under cover, there still is controversy as to exactly what happens. In at least *Dendrobates pumilio* and *D. granuliferus* the frogs mate vent-to-vent, but more typically the male fertilizes the eggs after the female lays them and moves away a bit. Sometimes the male lies across the female's back as she lays and then fertilizes the eggs. Females lay several clutches per year (sometimes one clutch per week for several months in a row) with the same or different males—males can care for more than one clutch at a time—and there is a high hatching and apparently metamorphosis success rate, thus the abundance of poison frogs in some localities even though there are only a few eggs laid at a time.

The male (usually, but sometimes both parents) tends the eggs for approximately two weeks, wetting them with water from the bladder or transported on the skin if the humidity drops. Whether males in nature actually guard the eggs, i.e., chasing off intruders, is uncertain in most species. As soon as the eggs hatch, the parent (usually the male, but the female in the case of some species) lowers the rear end of the body onto the clutch and the tadpoles (from one to several at a time) climb onto the back and fasten themselves to the parent's mucus. At this point the tadpole may still contain a large amount of yolk in its gut, and studies have shown that some species can survive for days on the parent's back and may even grow a small amount. The parent may carry only one or two tads at a time or the entire clutch, probably depending a lot on individual circumstances, such as humidity, availability of water bodies, predators, physiological condition of the parent, etc. It would seem that two to four tadpoles is a typical number, and they may be carried around for one to seven (very exceptional) days. If the parent has to go back to the clutch for more tadpoles (which would be the case in species with larger clutches), obviously tads must be able to survive for several days while still in the bower. The tadpoles are carried to usually individual small water bodies, where they slip off the back and swim away.

Dendrobates tinctorius. The male at top right shows the notched scutes of the toes especially well. Though the greatly widened toe tips of this species (and *D. azureus*) with practice can be used to sex the frogs, they are not always distinctive.

The calling male Dyeing Poison Frog at center left initiated an attack on another male in the terrarium. Poison frogs of both sexes fight, though they seldom injure each other. All photos by R. Bechter.

AS A GENERAL RULE...

Though normal amplexus is absent in poison frogs, fighting animals often assume postures resembling amplexus in normal frogs. These two *D. tinctorius*, for instance, almost appear to be mating rather than fighting. Photo by R. Bechter.

AS A GENERAL RULE...

When two larger poison frogs, like these Dyeing Poisons, fight, things can get rough. Because almost all dendrobatids fight, many keepers feel it is safer to not keep the frogs in breeding colonies. Another point to remember is that fighting frogs might be injured by being thrown against spiny plants or sharp rocks—and fungal infections of frog skin often are deadly. Photo by R. Bechter.

Often utilized are water-containing funnels of bromeliads, holes in palm stems, holes in logs, and even small puddles in the ground, especially if heavily moss-covered.

Tadpoles tend to fall into three basic groups. Some have heavy beaks with strong serrations and are carnivorous, feeding on mosquito larvae and other tadpoles. Others have weaker beaks and tend to feed on small detritus of various types, including algae and organic debris. A third type, especially species related to *Dendrobates histrionicus*, requires unfertilized frog eggs, food eggs, for complete development. This third type seems the most frustrating to hobbyists yet these are among the most colorful species and those that most fascinate advanced hobbyists. There seems to be quite a bit of difference in hardiness of tadpoles both from species to species and from clutch to clutch, so most hobbyists prefer to raise each tadpole separately so its feeding can be more carefully controlled and there are fewer acts of cannibalism. Detritus feeders (especially *Phyllobates* and *Epipedobates* species) have been raised on a variety of foods, from powdered fish flakes (high quality, especially with added algae) and yeast cultures to boiled lettuce. More carnivorous species will take brine shrimp nauplii, bloodworms (crushed, freeze-dried, or frozen), tubifex, whiteworms, beefheart, and similar fish foods. It probably is best to start with natural foods before trying prepared foods such as flakes.

Food egg specialists such as *Dendrobates histrionicus, granuliferus, pumilio,* and allies in nature are visited on a rotating basis by the female parent. In these species it is the female that moves the

Photos to right & below: When I said almost all dendrobatids fight, I meant it. Size is no problem to these little animals, as displayed by the calling male *Dendrobates pumilio* attacking a male *Dendrobates tinctorius* that came a bit too close to his territory. Notice again the similarity between combat or aggressive displays and amplexus in more typical frogs. Photos by R. Bechter.

AS A GENERAL RULE...

tadpoles from the bower to the water body, and she apparently can remember where she placed the tadpoles. Of course, since the area that one poison frog can cover in a reasonable period of time is small and the number of available water bodies in that area is limited, this probably is no great feat. As the female enters the bromeliad funnel or similar water body, she goes down tail-first and the tadpole (usually only one per funnel) comes to the surface and shows a lot of agitation. She lays one or two fully formed eggs in the funnel and then moves on. Over the development of the tadpoles she may visit each tad over a dozen times. Chicken eggs seem to lack a vital ingredient found in frog eggs, and even egg mixtures with added vitamins and calcium or mixed with cottage cheese seldom produce successful results in the terrarium.

There is quite a bit of scattered literature on poison frog tadpoles, but no real synthesis is available. Usually the head is oval and depressed, the eyes dorsal (as would be expected of animals that live in small water bodies). The tail fin usually is low. *Epipedobates* tads tend to be rather elongated, while some *Dendrobates* species have short, stubby tails. Often brown splotches are present on the tail, and the tail tip may be brown; some species have gray or golden markings as well, but others may be entirely black. The dorsal pattern of the adult often is indicated long before metamorphosis, making it possible to associate some wild-taken tads with their adults. The mouthparts are not especially modified in poison frog genera, usually with two rows of fine teeth (one split) above the beak and three rows below. Beaks may be thin and weak to heavy and serrated, depending on feeding habits of the species. Species that feed on food eggs often have large oval papillae around the mouth and have reduced rows of teeth. The corners of the oral disc may be continuous or indented (a generic character to some extent), but in reality the indentation may be so subtle as to be called imaginary by the casual observer. The anus may point to the right (dextral) or center (median), a generic character, but the number of times experienced observers have argued in print over the condition in a specific group of tadpoles means it is a difficult character to observe.

Metamorphosis usually takes place after about two to three months in the water body, but there is a lot of variation in the species for which there are data. Unfortunately, the life cycle in nature is unknown (or at least unpublished) for over two-thirds of the species of poison frogs, and probably fewer than half the poison frogs have been bred even by accident in the terrarium, so details are known for few species. It is fairly certain that tadpoles raised in the terrarium take longer to mature than those raised naturally, and those raised on artificial food egg mixtures are much slower to mature.

Most poison frogs are 10 to 15 mm long when they transform, and they obviously require small invertebrate foods. In nature the leaf litter is loaded with all types of little insects and mites, so this is no great problem. The transformed young of many poison frogs have much plainer color patterns than the adults, and bright yellow patterns often take several weeks or even months to develop. This, in a general way, should give you enough background information to be able to keep poison frogs. I hope you don't think much of the above is just verbiage, because you have to understand how these frogs work to be able to keep them successfully. As I said earlier, we'll go into a bit more detail with a dozen common species, but I still haven't told you the general rules about keeping poison frogs in captivity. This chapter already is too long to start going into more detail about actual captive care, so I guess I'll have to give you another chapter just on captive care.

Though most *Dendrobates* species carry only one or two tadpoles at a time and have small clutches of only three to six eggs, the species of *Epipedobates*, such as this *Epipedobates trivittatus*, tend to have larger egg clutches and carry most or all the tadpoles at one time. Photo by P. Freed.

AS A GENERAL RULE...

This Panamanian *Dendrobates pumilio* female is carrying two tadpoles at once, an uncommon occurrence both in nature and in the terrarium. It is possible that the mother already has scouted out the suitable tadpole depositories in the terrarium and knows the location of two spots. Photo by R. Bechter.

AS A GENERAL RULE...

Various dendrobatid tadpoles and their mouthparts (oral discs), redrawn from the literature.

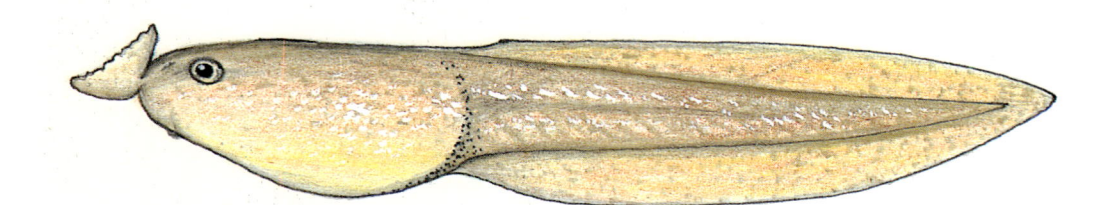

Colostethus nubicola, the mouth modified for feeding at the water surface

Dendrobates auratus, usually a solid black or smoky gray tadpole

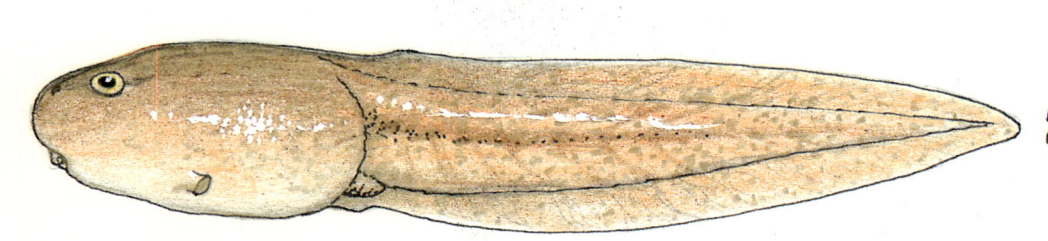

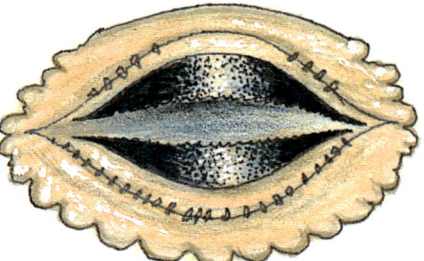

Dendrobates pumilio, showing the large papillae on the edge of the disc and the reduced teeth

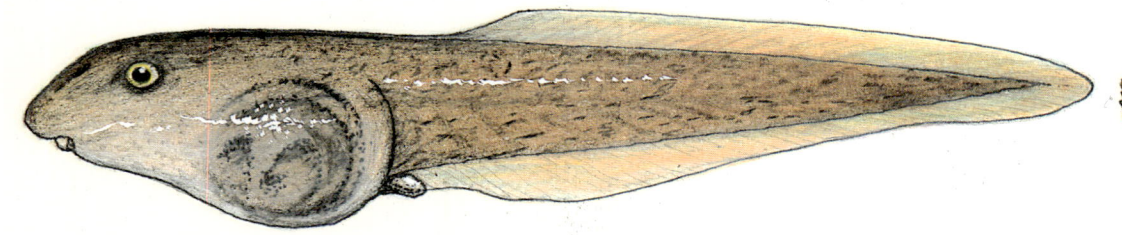

Above: *Minyobates opisthomelas*, showing the notch at the center of the posterior disc edge typical of its genus
Below: *Minyobates minutus*, which lacks a notch on the posterior disc, is the type species of *Minyobates*; it seems likely that the genus is an artificial group of dwarfed species

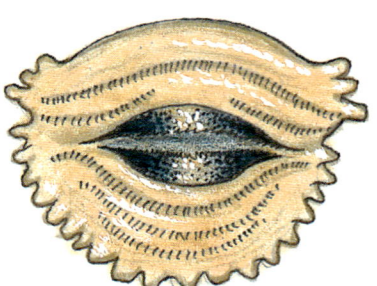

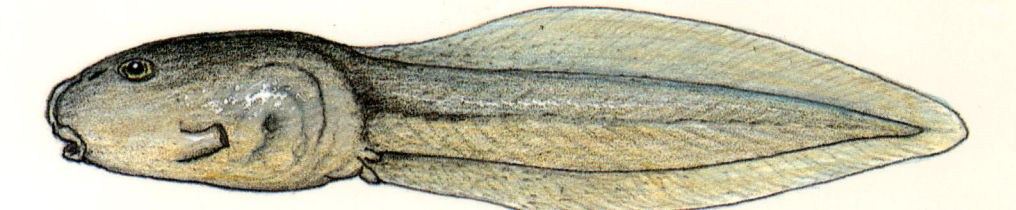

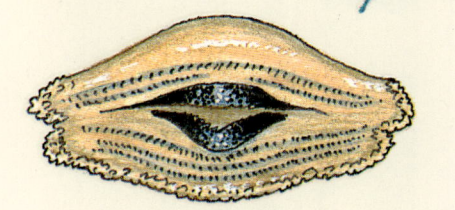

AS A GENERAL RULE...

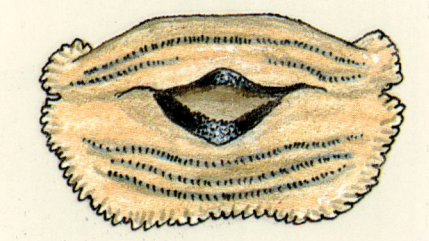

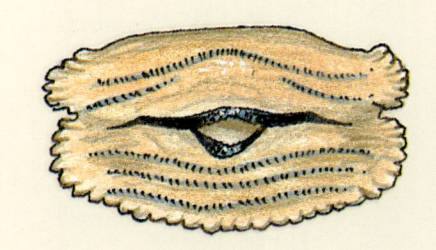

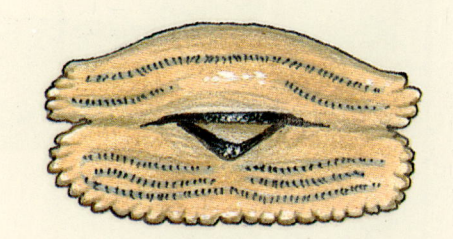

Phyllobates vittatus

Epipedobates boulengeri

Epipedobates espinosai

Epipedobates femoralis

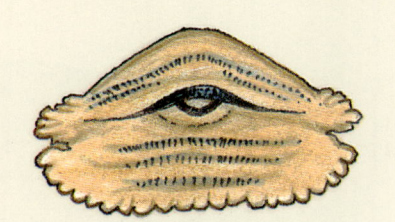

Epipedobates smaragdinus

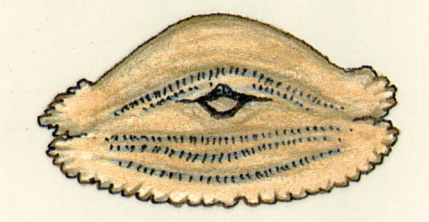

Epipedobates petersi

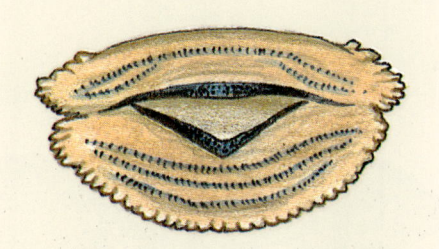

Epipedobates pictus

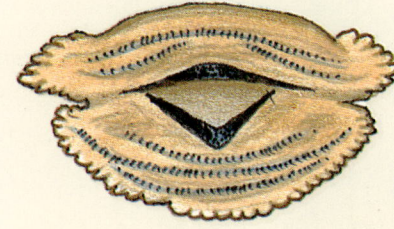

Epipedobates trivittatus

AS A GENERAL RULE...

Phyllobates lugubris

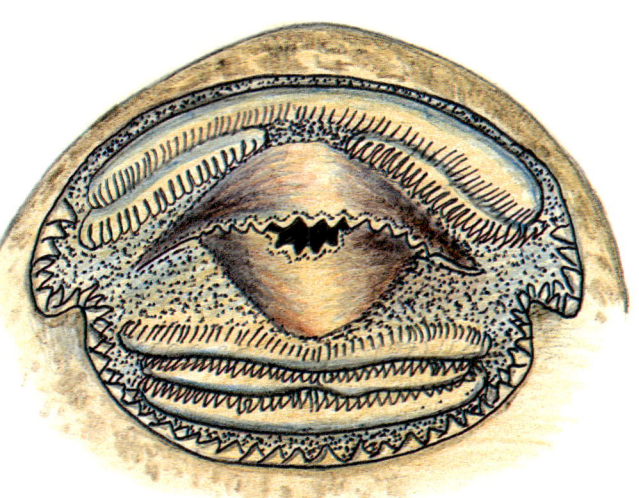

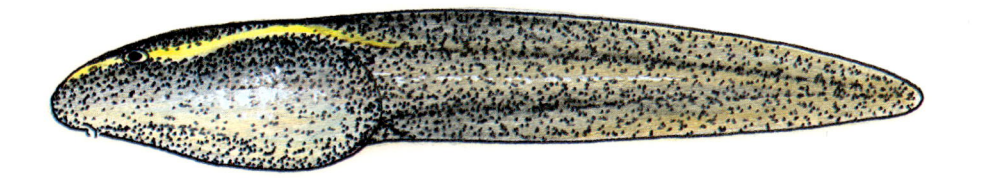

Dendrobates ventrimaculatus, French Guiana form

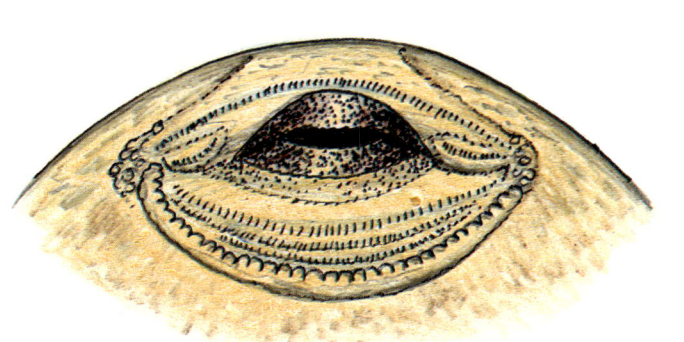

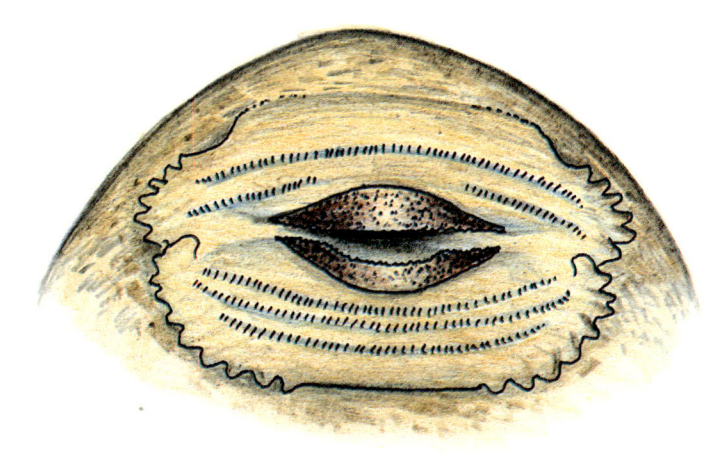

Mouthparts of *Minyobates bombetes*

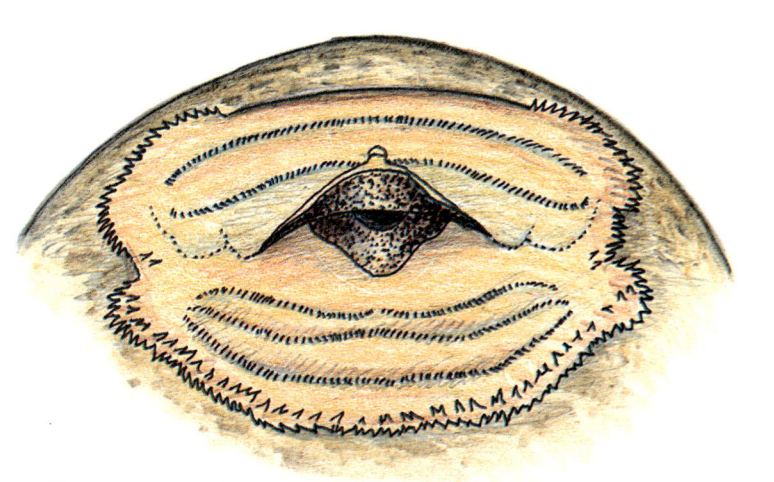

Mouthparts of *Aromobates nocturnus*, the Skunk Frog

Minyobates virolinensis

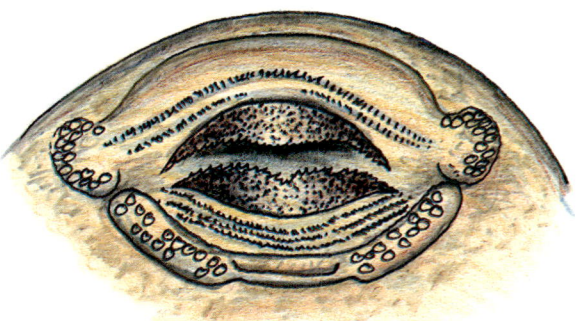

AS A GENERAL RULE...

Late stage froglets (just before completing metamorphosis) of the Dyeing Poison Frog, *Dendrobates tinctorius*. The color pattern, though not the adult colors, develops early in this species. Notice the weak front legs of the top froglet, which may be suffering from spindly leg syndrome. Photo by R. Bechter.

AS A GENERAL RULE...

This late stage froglet of the Red-headed Poison Frog, *Dendrobates fantasticus*, clearly shows the black "crown" on the head that often is developed in this species. In species of the *Quinquevittatus*-Group (as far as known) the adult pattern and colors develop during the froglet stage. The black spots may fuse or break up later in life, depending on the species, but the basic pattern is present very early. Photo by R. Bechter.

AS A GENERAL RULE...

In contrast, newly metamorphosed *Epipedobates*, such as the *E. tricolor* above, often lack all traces of the adult colors (compare below) and may even lack most of the color pattern of the species. It seems possible that some of the variation in coloration of the Phantasmal Poison Frog may be the result of environmental effects after the froglet has metamorphosed. Photos by P. Freed.

AS A GENERAL RULE...

Like other amphibians, poison frogs regularly shed their skin. Also like many other amphibians, they commonly eat the shed as it is pulled off the body. Skin and the mucus on it can be quite high in proteins and other biochemicals that may be necessary for the health of the frogs. Photo of *Dendrobates histrionicus* (notice the black toe tips) by R. Bechter.

The View from the Terrarium

I'll tell you now that this chapter will not satisfy the specialist poison frog keeper. Anyone who has kept and bred five or six species of poison frogs will have his or her own techniques and opinions on how to do things and anticipate problems. This chapter will attempt only to give beginners the basics—my interest is more in taxonomy and natural history than captive care, so you might as well recognize my deficiencies at the beginning. Another problem is that almost any article on breeding poison frogs presents information that appears to conflict with all other articles. Obviously a lot of success or failure depends on the skill and luck of the individual keeper.

TERRARIA

Preferences differ, of course, but most keepers feel that a roomy terrarium is essential for keeping poison frogs. Successful breeding often requires a colony of two or three males and at least three or four females, so you are talking 13 to 15 cm total of animals in a tank, each individual territorial and often aggressive in its own way. Two hundred liters is not too small for a typical 25 to 35 mm species that lives on the ground. There must be an abundance of hiding places of various types, from bark pieces and chunks of living moss to overturned small flowerpots. Each frog must have a place to sit, preferably out of sight of the others in the colony. Species that climb should have tall terraria (placing the cage on end and modifying the top may work) so they can get above the ground to establish territories. Arboreal species should be given bromeliads to feel most at home. If you can't get bromeliads, black film canisters tied to branches and filled with water may help the frogs' sense of security.

Because you will need high humidity in the terrarium, a glass or plexiglass tank is essential—at least you have to use a material that will not warp with humidity. For a substrate try a thick layer of charcoal covered with a couple of centimeters of small gravel, and cover the whole thing with a good layer of living sphagnum moss or something similar. This will allow for better drainage than normal terrarium setups. (A piece of slotted plastic "egg crate," sold to cover fluorescent light fixtures, on the bottom will improve drainage even more.) If possible, put a drain hole and fittings in a lower corner of the terrarium to make later adding of water supply systems easier.

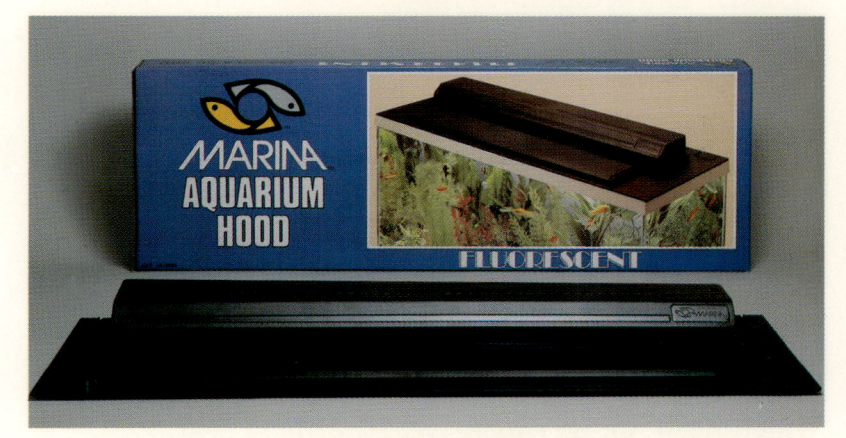

Cover the layer of moss with pieces of bark (leaves rot faster and may promote fungus, but they are more natural if you can keep abreast of the problems). The back of the terrarium should be sculpted with bark to hold a few epiphytic plants such as bromeliads both for looks and to promote more natural breeding. Other plants, such as philodendrons, pothos, and spider plants, can be placed in hidden pots over the base of the terrarium. Use a uniform pot size so the plants can be switched and allowed to relax outside the terrarium every two weeks or so. Poison frogs are active during the day but don't need to bask, so provide only enough light for the plants.

HUMIDITY AND HEATING

You need to maintain both a high temperature (25 to 27°C will work well for most species, lower at night and lower for species from high-elevation cloud forests) and a high humidity, which is asking for

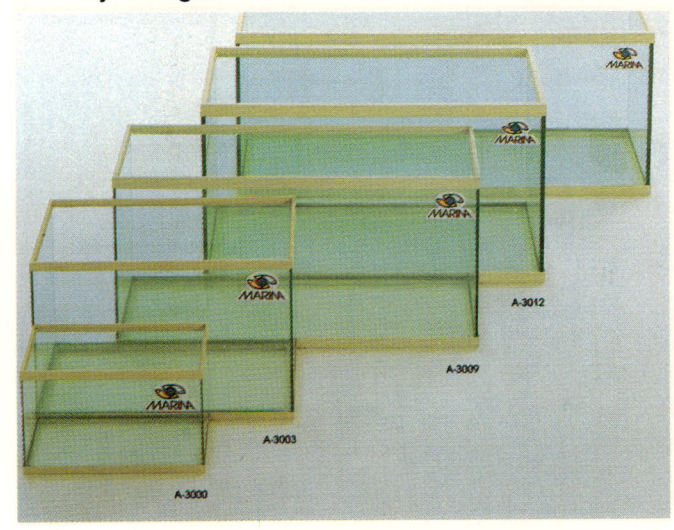

Small plastic aquaria can be used as holding or quarantine cages for adults or, if fitted out with floating cups, rearing containers for tadpoles. Photo courtesy of Hagen.

Though poison frogs need little in the way of special lighting, the plants that most hobbyists use with them do need lighting. An appropriate lighting fixture and bulbs can be purchased in your pet shop. Remember that poison frogs can climb and be sure the lid is secure at the corners. Photo courtesy of Hagen.

Though special terraria for rainforest frogs may be purchased, the old basic all-glass aquarium remains the easiest container for your poison frogs. You may want to create a special mesh inner bottom and have a drain installed, but neither step really is essential. Photo courtesy of Hagen.

45

THE VIEW FROM THE TERRARIUM

Every terrarium must have at least one thermometer, preferably two. The simple liquid crystal stick-on type of thermometer is perfectly satisfactory for all general usages. Photo courtesy of Hagen.

trouble. A high humidity without ventilation will lead to stagnation and fungal growth. In nature even little animals in the leaf litter have constant access to fresh air, and it must not be different in the terrarium. However, poison frogs have thin skins and dry out quickly, so too much ventilation can lead to death. Species with large toe discs can easily climb out of a partially open terrarium.

At a minimum, the terrarium must be misted daily, preferably twice a day. Many advanced hobbyists install automated misting systems that can be set to maintain a constant 85 to 100% relative humidity. Other hobbyists use a small pump to produce a flowing stream that reuses the same water constantly. If you use either of these systems you will need the drain hole and fittings I suggested earlier. Your pet shop should be able to provide you with more detailed information about these systems, which need not be expensive. Heating is best accomplished by using an outside heating plate. If desperate you could try the old "fish tank heater in the can of water" trick, which will provide both some heat and some humidity, but this low-tech device currently is not considered very efficient.

If you put a sheet of plastic over the lid to increase the humidity, small plastic terraria can be used as temporary holding containers for poison frogs. An even better use is to house crickets between trips to the pet shop. Photo courtesy of Hagen.

BREEDING STATIONS

Your final piece of terrarium equipment should be breeding stations, usually called "honeymoon huts." In nature poison frogs usually lay their eggs on leaves on or near the ground (the bower) or on some other relatively moist substrate. Very few keepers allow the eggs to be tended by the parents, so they use artificial substrates. The "classic" honeymoon hut is a halved coconut shell with a notch cut in the base. This is placed over a petri dish containing about 10 to 15 mm of clean water that is replaced daily until it is used for breeding. (Any open water in which a poison frog bathes should be considered potentially toxic and replaced as often as possible. Some keepers report that bathing water eventually will kill the very frog that bathed in it before.) A plastic leaf is wired to the outside of the dish so it overhangs the petri dish with just its tip touching the water. This will be the egg-laying spot and where the male (usually) will sit when allowed to tend the eggs. It must be kept dark. Provide at least one hut for every female in the terrarium, as it is possible for a male to care for more than one brood at a time.

A high quality tropical fish flake food can serve as the staple food for tadpoles of many poison frogs, especially *Epipedobates* species. Never stint on quality, however, and be sure that the flakes are pulverized into tiny flecks before feeding. Photo courtesy of Hagen.

THE FOOD PROBLEM

Most failures in keeping and breeding poison frogs are due to the inability of the hobbyist to maintain a constant supply of the proper foods. Although the larger poison frogs will take small crickets, wax moths, and even tiny mealworms, there is no doubt that fruitflies are the simplest and most suitable artificial food. Fruitfly cultures can be obtained from many pet shops and mailorder dealers. A colony of poison frogs will need several colonies of fruitflies constantly producing adults in order to survive. You also need to maintain several backup fly colonies for when your main colonies weaken or have an accident. The true problem is that as you garner more poison frogs, you have to maintain more fly colonies, so you could end up spending more time raising flies than raising frogs. Additionally, fruitfly cultures always weaken and tend to disappear when you go on vacation, and frogs die if not fed every day or two. Scientists hire people to maintain their fly colonies—you probably can't.

THE VIEW FROM THE TERRARIUM

BREEDING CYCLES

Many poison frogs breed in response to arrival of the rainy (wet) season, as do many other tropical animals. (A few species, such as *Epipedobates femoralis* and its relatives, breed all year at least at some localities.) This is the time of a profusion of insect reproduction and no shortage of small water bodies for the tadpoles. Increasing the incidence of misting in the terrarium should help initiate calling in the males if they have not been cooperative before. A male will attract a female to his hut, where a small clutch of eggs will be laid on the leaf. Remember that females of at least some (if not all) species lay several times during the year, so small clutches still can lead to large numbers of frogs in a short time.

Virtually all keepers remove the egg clutch to separate housing as soon as the male leaves the hut. (Remember that males often fertilize the eggs *after* the female lays them and that the female may leave the hut before the male does his job, so give the male a few hours with the eggs just to be sure.) It is not at all uncommon for competitive females to eat egg clutches of other females if given the opportunity. Female poison frogs often are very aggressive with each other, and eating a competitor's eggs helps assure that your offspring and genes will be a larger part of the population, plus it helps free males for mating. Anyway, remove the eggs, with or without their leaf, to a new petri dish of fresh, dechlorinated water. There should be only enough water in the dish to moisten the edges of the clutch and not let them dry out. Cover the dish to be sure they remain moist, and maintain the water level. Some keepers recommend adding a drop of antifungal chemicals to help prevent problems, but caution is advised before using any chemicals if you do not really need them.

Plastic plants of many different types are available at your pet shop. They are excellent for supplementing living plants to give the terrarium a "fuller" appearance with a minimum of troublesome living plants. Photo courtesy of Hagen.

In the heavily planted poison frog terrarium, a nice colorful backdrop scene can do wonders for the appearance of the terrarium. Photo courtesy of Creative Surprizes.

TADPOLES

Eggs hatch in some 10 to 14 days in the typical terrarium species (unknown for many species, however). The tadpoles should be moved to separate containers as soon as they hatch. Though some species are purported to not be cannibalistic, there really is no reason to take chances. Plastic cups make suitable containers, as long as the water is changed daily. Zoos and commercial breeders use mass-production methods to reduce the chores involved in daily cleaning, but they are not necessary for raising a batch or two of poison frogs. Try to feed the most natural foods you can before resorting to powdered flake foods and other artificial concoctions that might be short of essential nutrients. Bloodworms are a favorite of many species (especially of *Dendrobates*) and always worth a try. Boiled lettuce has worked well with *Phyllobates* species and others that probably feed mostly on detritus in nature. Expect losses, however, under even the best of conditions. Beginners should not start with food egg feeders unless they are looking for frustration.

FROGLETS

Typically the tadpole stage lasts for some two and a half or three months, and not all tadpoles of a clutch transform at the same time. In some species traces of color patterns similar to those of the adult (though usually not as well developed) can be seen a few weeks before metamorphosis. In all amphibians this is a time of high mortality because all the organs of the little animal must change. Froglets must have access to land so they will not drown or exhaust themselves trying to float and breathe. Transfer transforming tads to shallower water levels and give them a ramp so they can leave the water when necessary. Froglets may not feed until two to ten days after leaving the water, so at least you have a little time to make sure your feeding colonies are up to snuff. Though froglets can be caged together (they are not cannibalistic), it might be easier to control feeding if each is given a separate small container where food will be within easy reach without having to search

47

THE VIEW FROM THE TERRARIUM

through lots of litter. Again, a plastic cup with a basic bark bottom might work well. Remember to keep up the humidity and temperature.

Spindly leg syndrome, the number one problem of raising poison frogs, will become obvious just before transformation. Affected tadpoles have underdeveloped front legs that are smaller than normal, lack developed musculature, or even may fail to break through the skin. The resulting froglets flop around with little control of their movements and seldom feed. Spindly leg syndrome appears to be the result of an improper diet somewhere along the line, either for the tadpole or perhaps for the mother even before she lays her eggs. There is no treatment and no sure way of preventing the problem. Additionally, it is unpredictable in occurrence and may vary from clutch to clutch from the same parents.

Small poison frogs tend to have really small froglets that cannot take fruitflies for the first several weeks of life on land. The traditional food here is springtails collected in the backyard leaf litter or compost pile. Springtails can be bred by just putting a few handfuls of litter containing the tiny insects in a plastic box and maintaining the temperature and humidity to which they are accustomed while removing obvious predators such as beetle larvae and small centipedes. In nature poison frogs feed heavily on ants, but in the terrarium ants are more likely to feed on poison frogs—the tables are just too easily turned to take a chance. Mosquitoes and midges are smaller and more delicate than fruitflies, not that hard to breed, and are eaten by small poison frogs in nature, so they might be worth the effort of cultivating. Common mosquito species from the temperate zones usually won't feed on cold-blooded animals such as frogs (but some species will). The whole matter is worth investigating.

Most poison frogs seem to mature in about a year, and there is evidence that many species (certainly the larger ones) live a minimum of three to five years in nature, and perhaps could double this in the terrarium. There are persistent reports of ten-year-old poison frogs in the terrarium. Just because they are small does not mean they are expendable pets.

So there you have it. With modifications and experience, most poison frogs available in the pet shop and from commercial dealers can be kept by following these general schemes. However, do not expect that you will successfully breed wild-caught specimens. The species most often imported in numbers belong to the *Dendrobates histrionicus* group of species, notorious food egg feeders. Wild-caught poison frogs often are damaged or severely stressed and are likely to die within weeks of being caught. Stick with captive-bred stock for the most successful experiences in keeping these little guys.

Though ants such as this *Solenopsis* species are the major food of most poison frogs in nature, they usually are not taken in captivity. This common refusal to take ants in the terrarium is one of the small mysteries of poison frog keeping. In nature the frogs appear to not be selective in the type of ant they take, basically gulping anything in the right size range with the correct type of movement. Photo by S. Minton & Indiana Univ. Med. Center.

One of the reasons gravel makes a poor base for poison frog terraria. Remember that these frogs have very delicate skin, and any break in the skin can lead to infections that probably will be deadly. These frogs must be treated with kid gloves if you want to successfully keep them. Photo of *Dendrobates histrionicus* by W. P. Mara.

THE VIEW FROM THE TERRARIUM

Potential foods for poison frogs are easy to get but may not always be available in the correct sizes and quantities. Waxworms (M. Gilroy photo), vestigial winged fruitflies (M. Gilroy photo), ants (P. Freed photo), and small leafhoppers (P. Freed photo) all have been tried, but only the fruitflies have proved convenient and reliable food.

49

THE VIEW FROM THE TERRARIUM

In the rainforests mosquitoes of many types, some beautiful and fascinating insects (like the metallic plume-legged type from Guyana above left) in their own right, share the habitats of poison frogs from tadpole to adult stages. Mosquitoes are easily collected as egg rafts (top right) and raised in the home with proper precautions, and they might make excellent poison frog food to replace more traditional fruitflies and crickets. Photos by P. Freed (left), R. Schreiber (right).

There are thousands of species of crickets known from tropical forests, many of them very small as adults, only 6 or 7 millimeters long. Crickets provide the food for many adult poison frogs in nature and, as pinheads or microcrickets, in the terrarium. Photo by M. Smith.

50

THE VIEW FROM THE TERRARIUM

Two good tadpole foods are available at least seasonally at most pet shops. Living bloodworms (top) and phantom midges (bottom) can be presented either whole or crushed depending on the size and robustness of the tadpoles. Photos by D. Untergasser.

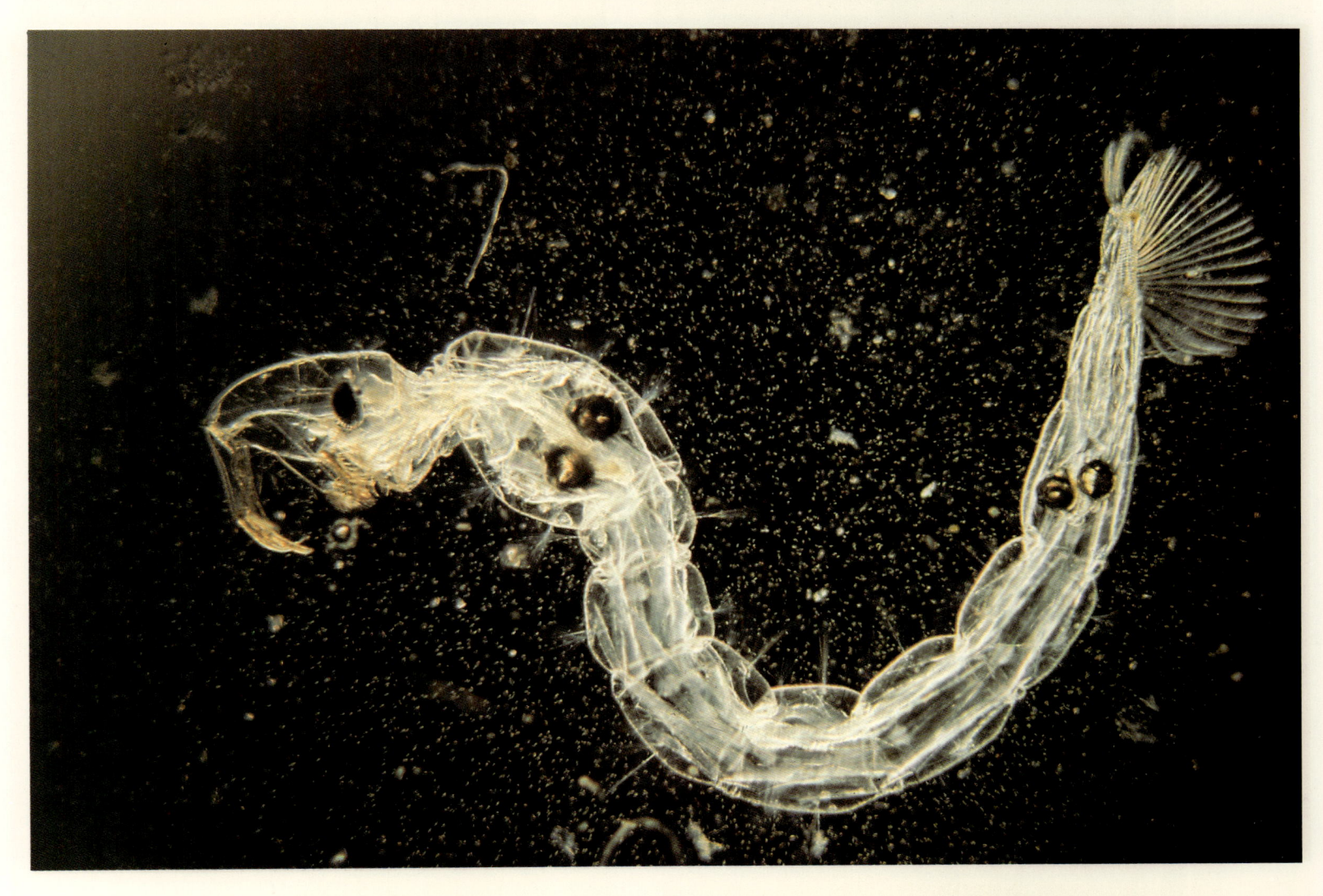

Above: Bloodworms are midge larvae that are relished by many poison frog tadpoles whether alive, frozen, or freeze-dried. They have the advantage of being easy to buy and cheap. Photo by M. Gilroy. *Below:* Mosquito larvae probably should be used more often in feeding poison frog tadpoles. They are a very natural food that is easy to obtain in a variety of sizes. Photo by D. Untergasser.

THE VIEW FROM THE TERRARIUM

A variety of potential poison frog (and tadpole) foods. Clockwise from top left: tubifex worms (photo by R. Schreiber); wild-collected phantom midges (*Chaoborus*) contaminated with dangerous beetle larvae (photo by M. P. & C. Piednoir); blowflies (photo by B. Kahl); crickets—the mainstay (photo by W. P. Mara); a moth (photo by G. Dingerkus).

Most advanced poison frog hobbyists prefer large terraria that are heavily planted with bromeliads, tropical vines, and other hardy plants that tolerate heat and humidity well. Cork often is used for the back wall, and lighting is provided to accommodate the plants, not the frogs. Photos by R. Bechter.

THE VIEW FROM THE TERRARIUM

In a typical professional poison frog colony terrarium, bromeliads (air plants) provide not only decoration but territorial calling spots for males. Keep the major part of the vegetation to the back of the tank for the best impression. Photo by R. Bechter.

THE VIEW FROM THE TERRARIUM

Though most of your plants probably will be purchased from a local nursery, some pet shops now are starting to sell bromeliads of various types. Avoid air plants with spines at the tip or edges of the leaves as they could cause serious accidents. Photo by R. Bechter.

THE VIEW FROM THE TERRARIUM

A view of the habitat of *Dendrobates ventrimaculatus* in French Guiana. Broad-leaved trees and large shrubs provide most of the cover in such a habitat and obviously cannot be adapted for the average poison frog terrarium. Remember that you are trying to simulate a habitat, not duplicate it. Photo by R. Bechter.

THE VIEW FROM THE TERRARIUM

A planted terrarium suitable for more arboreal poison frogs, such as *Dendrobates ventrimaculatus* and relatives. The abundance of bromeliads at all levels of the terrarium should keep many different species of frogs happy. The locking closure keeps out unwelcomed hands—remember that some poison frogs are quite dangerous and others are very expensive. Photo by R. Bechter.

THE VIEW FROM THE TERRARIUM

Successfully growing a variety of bromeliads is something of an art in itself, and you probably will need some advice from either an experienced hobbyist (either herpetologist or horticulturist) or a nursery that specializes in such plants. There are special tools and techniques necessary for putting the plants in place, and they must be given a substrate on the branch that is suitable for each species. Photo by R. Bechter.

THE VIEW FROM THE TERRARIUM

A rearing tank arrangement used for poison frog tadpoles that must be fed on egg foods. Though a few hobbyists have become quite adept at raising such tadpoles, even they have trouble producing healthy froglets. Egg foods spoil quickly and must be replaced on a regular basis, meaning a great deal of attention to sanitation is required. Photo by R. Bechter.

Dendrobates auratus, the Green and Black Poison Frog

The Green and Black Poison Frog is the first species we'll discuss in some detail, just because it comes first alphabetically of the dozen primary terrarium species. Actually, we could not make a better choice for the first frog to be discussed, as this is a large, colorful, popular, common, and easily bred species that is the best choice for the beginner. It also is one of the most variable of a notoriously variable genus and has been heavily studied both in nature

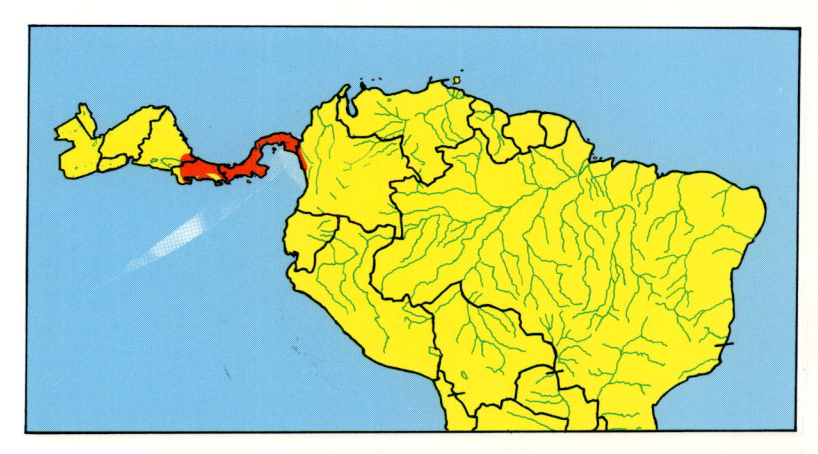

General distribution of the Green and Black Poison Frog, *Dendrobates auratus*.

and in the terrarium. *Dendrobates auratus* is a close relative of *Dendrobates truncatus* and *D. tinctorius*. In fact, there are suggestions that it may hybridize or intergrade with *truncatus* in Colombia where their ranges are in contact. Found throughout Panama in a multitude of color varieties, it ranges north into the southern borderlands of Nicaragua and also is common on the Atlantic slope of Costa Rica. It enters Colombia for a few hundred kilometers along the western Choco. This is not a highlands frog, many populations being found at sea level or only a few meters, but it has been taken up to 800 meters in elevation. Adults vary tremendously in size from about 25 mm to well over 40 mm (there are reports of 60 mm females). Males generally are a bit smaller and slimmer than females and have a barely distinct wrinkled vocal sac under the skin of the throat. Most specimens seen in the terrarium are about 30 to 32 mm in body length. Structurally it has smooth skin on the back, lacks the tarsal tubercle, but has an omosternum (a bone of the sternum that is visible only by dissection or clearing and staining). Its usually larger size and absence of distinct narrow yellow stripes on the back and sides should distinguish it from *D. truncatus*, while the absence of red should distinguish it from the often similarly patterned *D. histrionicus*. *D. histrionicus* lacks an omosternum and has specialized tadpoles with reduced teeth and large papillae around the oral disc; generally it appears more slender and agile than typical *D. auratus*.

It is virtually impossible to describe the color pattern of *D. auratus* in any comprehensive way, but the most common variety (from western Panama,

A "typical" Green and Black Poison Frog, *Dendrobates auratus*, from Costa Rica. This typical form is one of the most colorful of the poison frogs, one of the easiest to maintain in terraria, and also one of the cheapest. Captive-bred specimens, though often less colorful than this specimen, are excellent choices for hobbyists just beginning in poison frogs. Photo by R. D. Bartlett.

Costa Rica, and Nicaragua) is bright glossy black or deep brown. A pair of broad irregular metallic green stripes runs from the lower back forward to meet over the snout, while similar green bands are on the lower sides and on the tops of the arms and legs. Across the middle of the back is a wavy green band that intersects the dorsal stripes and usually breaks them, leaving about three large oval black spots covering the back and irregularly joined to the stripes on the lower sides. The belly is heavily marbled with bright green, blue, or yellow-green on black. Sometimes the belly marbling takes the form of spots, circles, or narrow curving stripes, and usually there is a curved

DENDROBATES AURATUS

bright line on the chin. In some specimens the entire back glows with a golden or silvery sheen that is the origin of the scientific name (auratus = golden).

Over a dozen major pattern variations exist, some seemingly restricted to small populations and others typical of major portions of the range. On the Pacific coast of Panama and in Colombia the green often is replaced with a dull to brilliant blue, while a population from near Panama City is brown with dull tan markings. Some specimens from the Panama Canal Zone may be tan with scattered round yellowish green spots, very similar to some patterns of *D. histrionicus* at first glance. Basically, this frog varies from brown through blue to green on a brown to black background. It seems to have never been determined if the various color forms are genetically distinct, but it appears that at least most of them will interbreed without problems in the terrarium and display similar behavioral patterns.

In nature, the Green and Black Poison Frog usually is a common and readily found frog of the leaf litter both in forests and in partially developed areas such as plantations. However, contrary to statements in some hobbyist literature, it is far from being a strict ground-dweller, as it is not uncommonly active in trees at up to 10 to 15 meters height. In fact, in Panama it seems to show a distinct propensity for placing its tadpoles in tree holes well above view from the ground. Ants are the preferred food in nature, though small beetles and their larvae as well as mites are eaten. Feeding may occur while high in trees and even while carrying tadpoles.

Calling and courtship seem to be limited to the ground level. Males ready for breeding call almost continuously during the day from preferred spots in the litter, often near the bases of trees or logs. Males do not have constant territories but usually are separated by at least 5 meters from the nearest other calling male. Their call has been described as a "slurred cheez-cheez-cheez" of fairly high pitch and fairly musical. Males may fight over females, though this is not common. They wrestle while standing on their hind legs and try to push each other down. Females are much worse fighters than males and in the terrarium can be quite aggressive.

Courtship is extended in *D. auratus*, often lasting a couple of hours. Females are slowly attracted to a calling male and approach him over a period of several minutes to an hour. When they finally are in contact, the male continues to call and seems to ignore the female. She physically pushes herself on him, often first touching snouts and then moving behind him to stand on his back, tap dance with her hind feet on this back, and generally push and shove. Eventually the male moves on a bit and the female follows. The "chase" may extend over an hour before the pair selects (or returns to the spot selected by the male) a suitable dark spot in the leaves to lay eggs.

A typical Green and Black, Dendrobates auratus. These relatively large frogs may be very territorial in the terrarium but generally are problem-free. Photo by R. D. Bartlett.

DENDROBATES AURATUS

After laying the eggs, the female leaves, but the male remains to tend the eggs. Clutch size varies from just two or three eggs to a dozen, but four to six probably is about average for most frogs. Over the next 10 to 14 days the male returns repeatedly to the hidden egg clutch, often after soaking his body in small puddles and then sitting on the eggs to help keep them moist. He also works the clutch so the eggs spread out and the jelly mass around them increases in size. While he is attending the one clutch, he continues to call and may mate several more times. It is not uncommon for one male to be caring for two or even more clutches simultaneously. Females can produce eggs about every two weeks, and since males often are at least partially occupied with clutches, females ready to lay must greatly outnumber males with time to breed in any population, perhaps one of the causes of female-female aggression and female eating of egg clutches not her own.

The male can sense when the eggs are about to hatch and will be present. He assumes a rather odd stance with the hind legs partially extended over the clutch to form a rough trough that the tadpoles can use to wriggle up onto his back. Usually he transports only one tadpole at a time, often to tree holes over 10 meters above the ground. (Tadpoles contain a large amount of yolk and will survive in the jelly of the clutch for days while waiting for their father to return for them.) Many different males may introduce tadpoles into the same water hole, which can be almost anything that holds a few milliliters of water, from bromeliad funnels to holes in logs on the ground. The tadpoles are up to 40 mm long, usually uniformly black above and below (some are brown, paler below), and have nearly uncolored fins. The beaks are strong and serrated, and there are two rows of teeth above the beak (the lower one incomplete in the middle) and three full, long rows below the beak, a rather primitive arrangement for the family. The oral disc is edged on three sides by a double row of small papillae (absent from the front or top edge). This whole arrangement is very similar to the mouthparts of *D. tinctorius* and very different from that of *D. histrionicus*. The spiracle is sinistral, as usual for the family.

The tadpoles seem to feed on whatever they can get. Stomachs have shown rotifers and protozoans as well as woody detritus, but in captivity they will eat lettuce, bloodworms, and other tadpoles. Though a dozen or more tads often are found in a single tree hole (representing tads from several males and clutches), they often are of greatly different sizes and exhibit varying growth rates, so it seems likely that larger tads may feed on smaller tads at least on occasion. In the terrarium, it is safest to house each tadpole separately to ensure their safety. Metamorphosis occurs anywhere from nine or ten weeks to 15 weeks after hatching, each tadpole seeming to be on its own schedule. A lifespan of four years is common, and there are reports of specimens living 12 or even 15 years.

This is a very affordable poison frog, and your pet shop should have no problems getting a captive-bred pair for you. Highly recommended for beginners, as long as you do not try wild-caught specimens.

The Hawaiian form of *Dendrobates auratus* often is more subdued in color than the typical Costa Rican form, with the green more yellowish and the black pattern less well-defined. Photo by M. Panzella.

A group of *Dendrobates auratus*, Green and Black Poison Frogs, from the Atlantic Coast of Panama. The two frogs in the center and the one at lower right are from Taboga Island, the type-locality and also the source of the Hawaiian population. Photos by A. v. d. Nieuwenhuizen.

DENDROBATES AURATUS

A Hawaiian specimen of *Dendrobates auratus*. Though sometimes locally common, the Green and Black Poison Frog never has spread very far from its release point in Hawaii and the introduced population still is considered unstable after more than 60 years. Photo by R. Bechter.

DENDROBATES AURATUS

Most blue specimens of the Green and Black Poison Frog, *Dendrobates auratus*, **come from the Pacific Coast of Panama. Structurally these specimens seem identical to green Atlantic populations. Photo by A. v. d. Nieuwenhuizen.**

Green and Black Poison Frogs, *Dendrobates auratus*. Above are a clutch of embryonated eggs and a male guarding an egg clutch on a wet bromeliad leaf in the terrarium.

Another view of egg care is to the left center (in the terrarium these frogs often fail to nest in the usual bower on the land), and a rather dull brown and gold Hawaiian specimen on the right center. At the bottom left is a brown and gold Hawaiian specimen as contrasted to a typical green and black Costa Rican specimen on the right. All photos by R. Bechter.

DENDROBATES AURATUS

Most keepers seem to prefer bright blue and black specimens from Panama to the normal green and black Costa Rican form, but blues are much harder to obtain. The color forms do not differ in terrarium requirements. Photo by R. Bechter.

At one week of age—actually after metamorphosis (left), *Dendrobates auratus* has little to indicate the bright colors of adults. Even when four months old (right), it still is far from a beautiful frog. All photos by A. v. d. Nieuwenhuizen.

At left center is a Green and Black with just weak tints of green. To the right is a hybrid of *Dendrobates leucomelas* and *D. auratus*. At the bottom are two views of a hybrid *Dendrobates leucomelas* X *D. auratus*. This interesting and attractive hybrid was produced in the terrarium. There are few records of hybrid poison frogs in nature, as would be expected because of the method of mating and brood care.

DENDROBATES AURATUS

Not all *Dendrobates auratus* from the Pacific coast of Panama are blue. Notice that in this specimen just the limbs are tinged with blue. Photo by A. v. d. Nieuwenhuizen.

DENDROBATES AURATUS

A terrarium hybrid of *Dendrobates auratus* X *Dendrobates azureus*. This relatively unattractive frog has few of the better features of its parents. Hobbyists should not randomly hybridize poison frogs, and if hybrids are produced (perhaps by accident), they always should be labeled as such to prevent accidental crossing with the parent species. Once two genetic lines are mixed, both lines may suffer if breeding is not strictly controlled. Photo by A. v. d. Nieuwenhuizen.

Above are back and belly views of a bright blue Panamanian *Dendrobates auratus*. At center left is a truly dull color form of *Dendrobates auratus* from the former Panama Canal Zone. Such brown specimens appeal only to specialists. To center right is a hybrid *D. auratus* X *D. azureus* feigning death.

Below are two oddly colored *Dendrobates auratus* from Panama. The specimen to the left has a strange blue-green color, while the one to the right (from Taboga Island) has a greatly reduced green color pattern. All photos by A. v. d. Nieuwenhuizen.

DENDROBATES AURATUS

A very pale green, almost creamy, Green and Black Poison Frog, *Dendrobates auratus,* from Pacific Panama. Photo by A. v. d. Nieuwenhuizen.

Dendrobates azureus, the Blue Poison Frog

At first glance, the southernmost portions of Surinam near the Brazilian border look like anything but rainforest. This region is technically called the Sipaliwini Savannah, and it is a relatively dry, prairie-like zone that looks like a poor spot for poison frogs. Actually, the region is more complex than it seems, and it harbors several "forest islands" of relict rainforest at moderately low elevations (often called mountains by the Dutch who first explored and named the region). These isolated forest islands stand out from the surrounding drier regions but are difficult to reach and collect in. In 1969 the Dutch

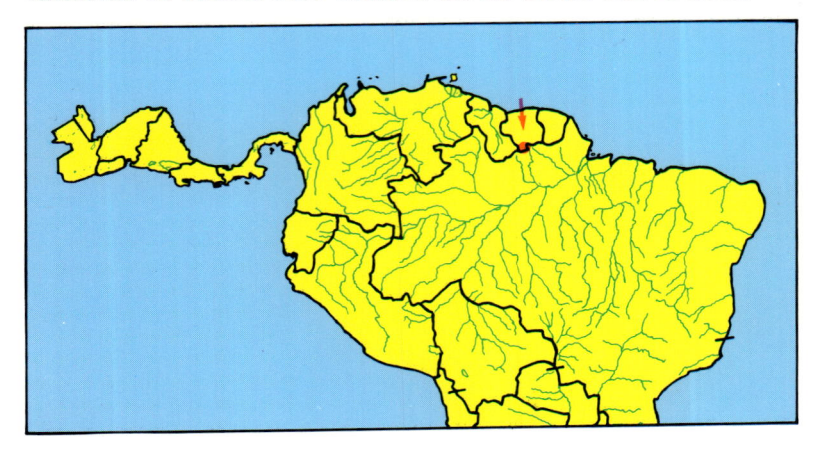

General distribution of the Blue Poison Frog, *Dendrobates azureus*.

herpetologist Hoogmoed described a poison frog from this area that immediately took hold of the imagination of terrarium hobbyists, the Blue Poison Frog, *Dendrobates azureus*. Though closely related to *D. tinctorius* (the two species have been hybridized in the terrarium), there are both color and structural differences between the species.

The Blue Poison Frog is about 38 to 45 mm long in adults, within the size range of the Dyeing Poison Frog. As in the Dyeing Poison Frog, the male has obviously widened finger discs compared to the female, easily seen when the two sexes are compared. Relaxed specimens sit in a distinctly hunch-backed position (not a constant character, obviously) compared to the more upright *D. tinctorius*. The tympanum (eardrum) of *D. azureus* is relatively small (about a third the diameter of the eye), oval, and has indistinct edges compared to the larger (half the eye diameter), round, and more distinctly edged tympanum of *D. tinctorius*.

The most obvious differences between the two species are in color, however. While *D. tinctorius* often is bright blue (almost black) at least on the sides and legs, it almost always has a yellow or white saddle down the middle of the back and usually has broad white or yellow stripes or spots on the sides. In the Blue Poison Frog the bright blue-black arms and legs contrast with the paler, more sky-blue, almost unmarked sides and a similarly colored head and back covered with a reticulation of large and small round black spots (actually the black background

A fairly typical Blue Poison Frog, *Dendrobates azureus*. The details of the black spotting on the back and sides of this species vary considerably, as does the shade of blue on the limbs. Still, this is considered to be the most desirable poison frog by many advanced hobbyists. Photo by P. Freed.

color showing through). The belly is paler blue with a variable arrangement of round black spots especially on the breast and sometimes a darker blue midbelly stripe. Though not nearly as variable as the Dyeing Poison Frog (but of course it has a much more isolated and much smaller overall distribution), there is considerable variation in details of both pattern (size of black and number of black spots and their distribution) and intensity of blue coloring. There are indications that color fades with increasing generations in captivity.

As mentioned, the range of *D. azureus* is very limited and hard to access. The relict forests in which the species is found are relatively cool (22 to 27°C, cooler at night) humid forest, always with running rocky streams. The frogs are found under rocks and other cover, especially moss, near but not in the streams. They are mostly terrestrial but have been seen up to 5 meters high in trees, so they probably climb like *D. auratus* (perhaps to deposit tadpoles in tree holes?). Ants and termites have been found in their stomachs.

DENDROBATES AZUREUS

These frogs are relatively easy to breed. Males are quiet callers from a position in the leaves or on a rock. Females are attracted to the call and draw the male's attention by stroking his snout and back in a typical poison frog courtship sequence. A female follows the male back to a hidden spot to lay a small clutch of two to six eggs that are tended by the male and probably also by the female in some instances. Hatching takes about 14 to 18 days. Both parents have been found carrying tadpoles.

The tadpoles are much like those of *D. tinctorius*, with a strong, serrated beak, an oral disc edged with a double row of small papillae except at the front (top) of the disc, and five rows of teeth, two above the beak (one spilt) and three below (one split). The spiracle is sinistral. In the terrarium the tadpoles are raised individually to prevent cannibalism. They transform in about 70 to 85 days.

This frog fetches a high price and is greatly in demand, but it is considered greatly threatened because of its small range and illegal collecting. I've heard stories of European collectors smuggling in dozens of frogs to the Netherlands and Germany and actually selling them to clients waiting for them in the passenger lounges of the airlines. Because their export from Surinam has never been legal, some experts have suggested that all specimens currently in the hobby trade are the offspring of illegally obtained parents and thus themselves illegal to hold. Perhaps this air of intrigue about the specimens makes them just as desirable as their coloration to some hobbyists—but this is certainly an attitude that is not to be promoted.

Assuming they are legal to purchase and own (please check all your local laws—breaking international treaties and being discovered might lead to an unpleasant future), these are perhaps the premium poison frog—large, colorful, exotic, expensive. What more could you ask?

The hunch-backed stance of these Blue Poison Frogs, *Dendrobates azureus*, is real and one of the features that will help distinguish the species from *Dendrobates tinctorius*. Photo by A. v. d. Nieuwenhuizen.

Notice the differences in number and size of black spots over the center of the back in these two *Dendrobates azureus*. Photo by B. Kahl.

DENDROBATES AZUREUS

In the top photo, notice the hunched position of the Blue Poison Frog and the fact that it is hard to clearly discern the tympanum. Pure blue specimens of *Dendrobates azureus* like this one are most desired by hobbyists. In the bottom photo, notice that the frog on the flat rock has an extensive dorsal pattern of large black spots that are partially fused, even on the upper side, while there are distinct black spots on the limbs. Such specimens either serve as links to *Dendrobates tinctorius* or are evidence of hybridization between the two species in the terrarium with later crossing to the parental lines. Photos by R. Bechter.

A rare sight sure to set the heart of the confirmed poison frog fanatic aflutter. Most hobbyists will never see even one Blue Poison Frog, let alone seven in one terrarium. The species is not that difficult to breed in captivity, however, but there are many legal questions about the status of all specimens in captivity. This is considered an endangered species under some regulations, and you must not take the chance of purchasing a specimen until you are absolutely sure that it is legal and it is legal for you to own it in your area. Photo by R. Bechter.

DENDROBATES AZUREUS

Fighting males of *Dendrobates azureus*, the Blue Poison Frog. Notice the very wide finger tips. Photo by R. Bechter.

77

Various views of *Dendrobates azureus*, the Blue Poison Frog. Contrast the finger tips of the female to the above left with the male at bottom left. Note also the duller pattern of the juvenile at the above right. At center left is a juvenile shaming death. Contrast its dull colors to the adult female at center right.

The greatly widened finger tips (below left) are typical of males of this species and *Dendrobates tinctorius*. In the Blue Poison Frog the tadpole (below right) obtains its color pattern before completing metamorphosis and also shows greatly widened finger tips early on. All photos by A. v. d. Nieuwenhuizen.

DENDROBATES AZUREUS

A typical gorgeous male Blue Poison Frog, *Dendrobates azureus*, from the Sipaliwini Savannah of southern Surinam. Photo by A. v. d. Nieuwenhuizen.

DENDROBATES AZUREUS

Two male Blue Poison Frogs about to enter combat over territory in a terrarium. Notice that the sitting specimen lacks almost all black spotting. Photo by R. Bechter.

DENDROBATES AZUREUS

A very dark Blue Poison Frog, *Dendrobates azureus*. Often it is difficult to distinguish this species from *Dendrobates tinctorius*, and it often is suggested that *azureus* should be considered part of *tinctorius*. Photo by A. v. d. Nieuwenhuizen.

DENDROBATES AZUREUS

An attractively marked *Dendrobates azureus* with nice contrast of the bright blue legs (unspotted, by the way) to the paler blue back and sides. Photo by R. D. Bartlett.

DENDROBATES AZUREUS

In contrast, this *Dendrobates azureus* is almost uniformly violet in tone, with little contrast in limb and side coloration. Pigmentation in poison frogs probably is due both to genetics and food as well as other environmental agents. Photo by A. v. d. Nieuwenhuizen.

Dendrobates granuliferus, the Granular Poison Frog

A stunning little poison frog with a distinctive color pattern, the Granular Poison Frog is restricted to the Golfo Dulce region of the Pacific coast of Costa Rica, especially the area around Puntarenas. This is an area of humid, relatively low altitude rainforest (0 to 700 meters), the heaviest rains coming from September to November, while the months from January to March are relatively dry. The area is somewhat developed but not extensively so. Here the frogs still are common, especially in areas of dense vegetation along streams. The only other poison frogs that occur in the area are *Dendrobates auratus* and *Phyllobates vittatus*. The Puntarenas region has been a popular research area for a couple of generations of graduate students, so the Granular Poison Frog is a fairly well-known little species.

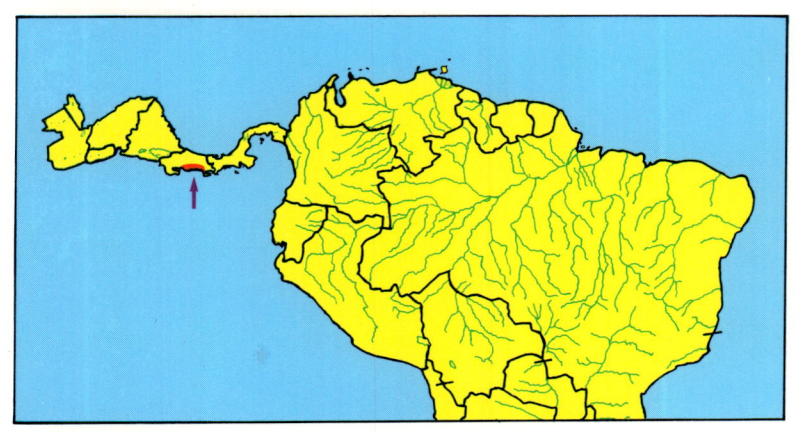

General distribution of *Dendrobates granuliferus*, the Granular Poison Frog.

A typical Granular Poison Frog, *Dendrobates granuliferus*, has obviously bumpy orange skin on the back and sides and has the back legs at least partially blue-green (in this individual more blue than green), usually of a pale shade. This species shows rather little variation in color. Photo by A. v. d. Nieuwenhuizen.

Dendrobates granuliferus is a small (19 to 22 mm long) relative of *D. pumilio, speciosus,* and *histrionicus* (among others) distinguished by its very granular back (actually, the whole skin is granular except the throat) that is bright orange in color without black spots. The upper arm also is orange, while the belly, lower arm, and hind legs both above and below are bright green to blue-green. In males the vocal pouch is black, making it possible to recognize sexes easily in this species. The tarsal tubercle is absent or nearly so. The granular back in combination with the simple color pattern, especially the green hind legs contrasting to the orange back, make this one of the easiest poison frogs to recognize. There is relatively little variation in the Granular Poison Frog, though a few specimens from the northern edge of the tiny range were yellow-olive on the back and sides. It is most closely related to the Strawberry Poison Frog, which occurs on the Caribbean coast of Costa Rica south into Panama.

This is not really a ground-dwelling frog. Though feeding generally occurs on the ground (ants are the usual food, as might be expected), calling and even mating generally occur at heights of 1 to 1.5 meters. Males have small territories on large leaves or branches that they will defend from other males by wrestling. They regularly call through the morning hours, producing a low insect-like buzzing. Males call

Though this poison frog has the skin texture of *Dendrobates granuliferus*, its leg color is extensively red for the species. Probably it is just a minor color variant, but supposedly it was collected near the Rio Chiriqui, Panama, an area from which the species is unknown, and might represent an undescribed form. Photo by A. v. d. Nieuwenhuizen.

DENDROBATES GRANULIFERUS

Because the Granular Poison Frog, *Dendrobates granuliferus,* still is common in a very small area of Costa Rica, it often is collected for the terrarium market and appears in pet shops. It is not easy to keep, and it is very difficult—perhaps impossible for most hobbyists—to breed in captivity. Photo by A. v. d. Nieuwenhuizen.

DENDROBATES GRANULIFERUS

Most specimens of the *Dendrobates granuliferus* are essentially two-colored animals, bright red above, paler blue-green below and on the limbs. It would seem that this species is very closely related to the Costa Rican *Dendrobates pumilio*, which has smoother skin (usually with some dark dotting on the back) and usually darker back legs in the typical Costa Rican form. Photo by A. v. d. Nieuwenhuizen.

Like most members of its species seen in captivity, this *Dendrobates granuliferus* comes from the Puntarenas area of Pacific Costa Rica. The similar color varieties of *Dendrobates pumilio* come from the Atlantic slope (versant) of Costa Rica and Panama (as well as Nicaragua), while the very smooth-skinned *Dendrobates speciosus* comes from the highlands of Panama. Photo by P. Freed.

continuously both to let other males known they own their spot and to attract females. Males seem to space themselves about 3 to 5 meters apart and can reach high densities in favorable habitat.

As usual, a female comes to a calling male (usually a meter or so above the ground) and then hesitantly follows him to the selected laying spot. This seems to be a shaded leaf either in the ground litter or even a meter or more above the ground on a fallen log. The female strokes the male's snout repeatedly in their bower and presents her vent to him. He also may dance in place a bit, but most of the activity is on the part of the female. Eventually, often after an hour of stroking and circling, the frogs mate vent-to-vent, a clutch of only three or four eggs being laid. The male and female both stay in the vicinity of the eggs during the two weeks it takes for them to hatch.

After hatching, the female transports the tadpoles to suitable small bodies of water. Bromeliads, broken palm branches, and the axils of many other types of plants serve for raising the tads. Each tad is placed in a separate small water body. Larger bodies of water that might hold tadpoles of *Dendrobates auratus* are avoided, perhaps because the *auratus* tadpoles are "known" to eat other tadpoles. The female lays one or two unfertilized (obviously, since the male is not present) eggs in the water body with each tadpole. This serves as their only (or at least main) food, food eggs. Yes, like the other species related to *D. histrionicus*, the Granular Poison Frog lays food eggs for its tadpoles, making it virtually impossible to raise in captivity and a poor investment if you plan on breeding poison frogs.

The tadpoles are about 25 mm long, have pointed tails and low fins, and are splotched with gray. The head is depressed, as usual. Also as is typical of food egg eaters, the oral disc is edged (except at the front or top) by large papillae, the beaks are strong, and the tooth rows are greatly reduced, one broken row above the beaks and one row below. Assumedly development to metamorphosis in nature takes two to three months.

Hobbyists would be well-advised not to purchase *Dendrobates granuliferus* unless they have considerable experience with poison frogs. The species occupies a very small range and though currently common, the area could be developed at any time. Excessive collecting of this frog for the pet market may already be occurring, though few specimens that are wild-collected survive to make good pets. Usually wild-caught specimens are damaged and stressed and die within a month or two of being purchased. In the future it is likely that trade in this species will be legally restricted. If you can find captive-bred specimens (but be sure it can be *proved* they are captive-bred, not just *said* to be captive-bred) you might have a better shot at keeping and breeding them. Natural breeding of a colony of two males and four to six females might work best, letting the females take care of their own tadpoles under semi-natural conditions. Remember that this is a climbing poison frog, so it needs a high terrarium with lots of plants. Pretty it may be, but certainly not recommended.

DENDROBATES GRANULIFERUS

A close view of the granular skin of *Dendrobates granuliferus.* In some specimens the color of the sides, belly, and limbs is much brighter, but it never is blue-black as in *Dendrobates pumilio.* Photo by A. v. d. Nieuwenhuizen.

DENDROBATES GRANULIFERUS

The Granular Poison Frog is almost constant in size, color, pattern, and skin texture, an unusual consensus in this group of frogs. Ecotours visit its home in Costa Rica, where the species still is easy to see in nature. Photo by A. v. d. Nieuwenhuizen.

Dendrobates histrionicus, the Harlequin Poison Frog

This is undoubtedly the most confusing poison frog when it comes to trying to describe color patterns and separate it from related similar species. Technically, the species lacks the omosternum of the pectoral girdle skeleton, has smooth skin, and lacks a tarsal tubercle. In these features it agrees with another familiar species, *D. leucomelas*, which is readily distinguished by colors, being yellow-orange with two black bands on the body and numerous small black spots within the yellow-orange areas. Two other species, *D. lehmanni* and *D. occultator*, have patterns that fall just to the "edges" of color pattern variation in *D. histrionicus*, the first being regularly banded with black and orange or red, the other being red above with bright yellow spots on the sides and belly. These two species differ from *D. histrionicus* in details of the skin toxins they have or do not have, a character that can be determined only by chemical analysis.

I really cannot tell you what is a "typical" pattern of the Harlequin Poison Frog, *Dendrobates histrionicus*, but this certainly is not one of the more commonly seen forms. This mottled brown and dull red frog would appeal only to a specialist, but it may be immature. Photo by R. D. Bartlett.

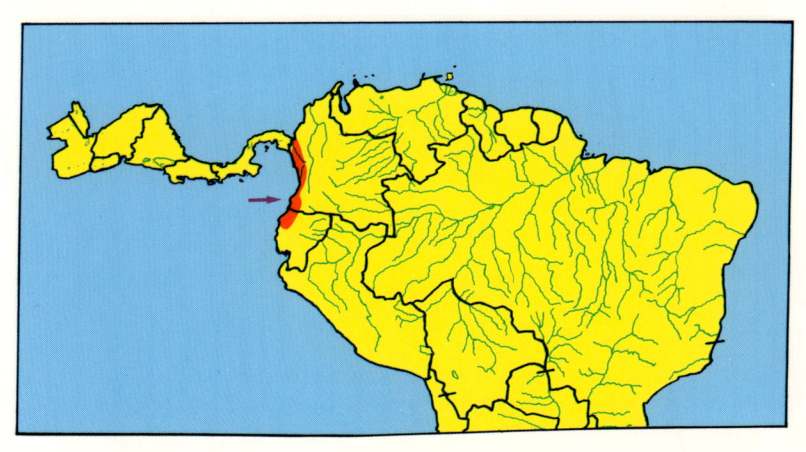

General distribution of the Harlequin Poison Frog, *Dendrobates histrionicus*.

Yellow snout and yellow bracelets—along with a yellow vocal sac—are obvious features of this little male *Dendrobates histrionicus* of the bull's-eye morph. Photo by R. D. Bartlett.

In a general way, the Harlequin Poison Frog can be called a black and red poison frog. Though almost any locality within its broad range in the lowland rainforests (from almost sea level to usually 300 or so meters, but extending to over 1100 meters in some areas) of Colombia and Ecuador will include several different patterns, most (but not all) fall into some variation of a black or brown background covered with one to many red, orange, or yellow spots. The spot may be just a gigantic central spot on the back or perhaps three spots in a line down the center of the back, combined with orange sides and bright orange bands around the limbs, or the back and sides may be covered with a dozen to two dozen or more spots, the pattern continuing onto the sides. Sometimes the bright spots fuse and break in irregular ways to produce a network over much or all the back and sides, occasionally with the snout or rump area still showing a regularly spotted pattern. When the spots fuse sufficiently, they may produce an almost solid red to yellow frog with only traces of a black or brown reticulation on the back or even two irregular black stripes, one on each side of the back. Occasional individuals and populations may be grayish or tan with little in the way of bright colors, while rare individuals have faint traces of greenish in the reticulations. Generally, however, green and blue colors are absent in this species. The belly color and pattern usually reflect at least somewhat the pattern of the back and sides. The toes seldom are bright silvery white as in most *D. lehmanni*.

This is a fairly large poison frog, about 25 to 38 mm in adult length, unusual in that the male is as large or larger than the female. The sexes are virtually impossible to distinguish externally, as the faintly grayish vocal pouch seldom is a good character. The finger discs are broadly expanded but not wider in males than females. Males often wrestle with each other in apparent attempts to protect their territory. The male's call has been described as like a small saw cutting wood or (single notes) like the quack of a duck.

Males tend to call from low perches, a meter or less high, and probably defend relatively stable territories. They often call from the sides of standing trees and from fallen logs. A broad variety of ants has been taken from the stomachs of wild-caught specimens, along with the usual smaller numbers of tiny beetles and mites. Foraging usually occurs on the ground during the day. Calling and mating have been noted especially during the afternoon hours but probably occur all day. Over much of its range there is no dry season, and it has been suggested that its range is restricted by increasingly arid habitats both to the north and especially to the south, where it is replaced by species that can cope with a dry season that may last for three months. Females are attracted to calling males as in other poison frogs, but then behavior begins to differ. In most poison frogs that have been studied, the male leads the hesitant female toward a pre-chosen egg-laying site (which I've been calling a bower for convenience). In the Harlequin, however, the male may follow the female or the female may follow the male, or they can switch position during the trip. It appears that the bower is not chosen in advance and is not chosen only by the male. Additionally, the male often touches the back of the female and sits on her back on the way to egg-laying. At the bower the male and female may spend two or three hours in a sequence of various sitting, bowing (female only), crouching, and touching behaviors. One of the most interesting behaviors is circling, in which one of the frogs slowly circles the other in a jerky and irregular fashion, sometimes while slightly kicking the feet or shaking the head. Often the male sits on the female's back at various angles and positions, his vent, however, not in a position to fertilize the eggs. Amplexus does not occur and actual fertilization has not been seen. Clutches of three or four eggs (to nine in captivity) have been found attached to bromeliads as much as 3 meters above the ground.

Though tadpole-carrying adults apparently are rare in nature, it would seem to be the female that cares for the tadpoles and places them in bromeliad water funnels and similar small water bodies in various plants. This is a food egg feeder and as such is virtually impossible for the typical hobbyist to breed in captivity. The tadpoles are grayish with tan tails and low fins that end in a rounded point. The

The bull's-eye morph of *Dendrobates histrionicus* is distinguished, at least in theory, by the presence of a single bright round spot in the middle of the back. Usually such specimens also have bright bracelets as well. The color of the sides may vary tremendously, as we will see in later photos. Photo by R. D. Bartlett.

DENDROBATES HISTRIONICUS

oral disc is edged by large papillae except to the front (top), and the teeth are reduced to only two rows, the row above the beaks often indicated by only a few teeth. The beaks are heavy and serrated. Presumably the female visits each tadpole every few days throughout its growth and provides it with unfertilized eggs as its only (or major) food. Attempts to reproduce the food eggs with mixtures of chicken egg yolk and cottage cheese generally have failed or been only marginally successful. Natural metamorphosis probably takes about 80 to 100 days, much longer in captivity on the replacement diet.

Almost any Harlequin Poison Frog you see in the pet shop and on dealers's lists will be wild-caught in Colombia and probably will represent one of the more colorful brown and orange-spotted color phases. (Drug activities in Colombia recently stopped most exports temporarily, but a few dealers currently are bringing in large numbers again.) Limited studies have suggested that unless their habitat is under stress from development, large numbers of Harlequins can be collected regularly from a relatively small area with no reduction in the number of frogs in the population from year to year. Remember that females probably can produce a clutch of eggs every two weeks or at least every month over much of the year (there is no dry season in much of the natural range of the species) and reproductive success (i.e., number of eggs that result in adult frogs) may be very high because of parental care and limited predators, and it is not hard to understand how the species can replace itself very quickly. On the other hand, wild-collected frogs usually are stressed and have been poorly handled during shipping, so large mortalities occur and most wild-caught specimens do not thrive in captivity. A few captive-bred specimens are beginning to appear on lists and would be much the better specimens on which to base a breeding colony. There is no doubt that some Harlequin Poison Frogs are incredibly colored animals and there always will be a market for them. Remember that they need constantly high relative humidities and temperatures and large amounts of vitamin-fortified fruitflies at all times. These are relatively delicate frogs, their large size to the contrary, if not cared for with a skilled hand.

Until recently, most Harlequin Poison Frogs, *Dendrobates histrionicus,* in the terrarium hobby were small-spotted forms. In such specimens the dark color (often red or black) of the back is heavily invaded by bright yellow in the form of irregular spots of various sizes. Occasionally the back may be largely yellow with just traces of the black or red background, or, as in this specimen, the black may dominate. Many small-spotted specimens also have bright orange heads that give them a very distinctive appearance. Every valley in western Colombia that is suitable for Harlequins may be home to two or three distinctive color patterns, only one or two of which may be shared with the next valley down the road or river. Photo by R. D. Bartlett.

Various colors of bull's-eye morph Harlequin Poison Frogs, *Dendrobates histrionicus*. Most specimens of this group are amazingly symmetrical in markings. All photos by A. v. d. Nieuwenhuizen.

DENDROBATES HISTRIONICUS

A stunning red and yellow Harlequin Poison Frog, *Dendrobates histrionicus*. Such heavily spotted patterns are not uncommon in the terrarium trade, but like most members of their species they fare poorly in captivity. Photo by A. v. d. Nieuwenhuizen.

DENDROBATES HISTRIONICUS

Two bright yellow males of a small-spotted pattern of the Harlequin Poison Frog. There are no indications that the various color patterns of *Dendrobates histrionicus* are genetically sorted. If you were to breed (or find breeding in nature) a red and black bull's-eye with a small-spotted yellow, you might get offspring of totally different patterns, intermediates, or like the parents. Photo by A. v. d. Nieuwenhuizen.

DENDROBATES HISTRIONICUS

Harlequin Poison Frogs, *Dendrobates histrionicus,* often are found in and near the axils of bromeliads, and it is here that they raise their tadpoles if given the choice. Like the other poison frogs that feed their tadpoles food eggs, the tadpoles are almost impossible to raise in the terrarium. Photo by A. v. d. Nieuwenhuizen.

Assorted bull's-eye morph *Dendrobates histrionicus* with some differences. Notice here that there is no correlation between the spotting pattern on the back and the color of the sides, though usually the color of the back spots and the side spots (if present) match.

I find specimens with three spots on the back (plus the snout spot) especially attractive, but the symmetry of spotting as in the specimen at the lower right also is very interesting. All photos by A. v. d. Nieuwenhuizen.

A variety of Harlequin Poison Frogs, *Dendrobates histrionicus*. Bright orange and black (above left) make a truly eye-catching combination. All photos by A. v. d. Nieuwenhuizen.

Above: Notice the difference in length of the large yellow side spots in these two frogs. *Below:* The bright red-orange form with black reticulations has been called the "Valley" form and has been said to be from Ecuador.

Still more Harlequin Poison Frogs. The bright yellow and black specimen on the above right and the two below are a pattern recently imported and noted for not only bright colors but large size and robust shape. All photos by R. Bechter.

Below: Also newly imported is the bright red-orange and black reticulated "Valley" form.

DENDROBATES HISTRIONICUS

Close-up view of the "Valley" form of *Dendrobates histrionicus*. Photo by A. v. d. Nieuwenhuizen.

DENDROBATES HISTRIONICUS

The Harlequin Poison Frogs, *Dendrobates histrionicus*, on this and the facing page look quite different at first glance, but it is not hard to imagine how the patterns are related to each other and to some of the patterns shown on previous pages. It seems to be a matter of just how the bright spots are related to the dark background colors rather than a matter of any pattern being absolute. Photo by A. v. d. Nieuwenhuizen.

DENDROBATES HISTRIONICUS

If you look closely at the skin of this Harlequin Poison Frog you will notice that what at first appears to be virtually smooth skin actually is comprised of numerous glandular spots just below the surface. Photo by A. v. d. Nieuwenhuizen.

DENDROBATES HISTRIONICUS

This oddly marked Harlequin Poison Frog, *Dendrobates histrionicus*, is supposed to be from Ecuador, at the southern edge of the range of the species. Similar specimens, however, occur in various localities in Colombia. Photo by A. v. d. Nieuwenhuizen.

DENDROBATES HISTRIONICUS

A classic bull's-eye pattern *Dendrobates histrionicus*. Photo by M. Panzella.

DENDROBATES HISTRIONICUS

The large black and red-orange Harlequin Poison Frogs, *Dendrobates histrionicus*, recently imported from Colombia (and perhaps Ecuador) are striking animals sure to draw the attention of any hobbyist. Though they can be maintained with difficulty in a properly equipped terrarium, do not expect to be able to breed this frog. Photo by A. v. d. Nieuwenhuizen.

DENDROBATES HISTRIONICUS

Red-headed Harlequin Poison Frogs always are popular when available. The continuing conversion of Colombian forests into drug fields, plus all the political intrigue associated with the drug trade and anti-drug enforcement, makes the continued importation of *Dendrobates histrionicus* unlikely. Photo by A. v. d. Nieuwenhuizen.

DENDROBATES HISTRIONICUS

Sometimes the differences between a black background color and a brown one are matters of mood and background lighting. Regardless, the pattern of this frog is interesting and attractive. Remember that even a small Harlequin Poison Frog will eat large numbers of fruitflies every day. Photo by A. v. d. Nieuwenhuizen.

A variety of color patterns of *Dendrobates histrionicus*, the Harlequin Poison Frog. Notice the small egg clutch in the lower left photo and the reticulated specimen (supposedly from Ecuador) at center right. All photos by A. v. d. Nieuwenhuizen.

DENDROBATES HISTRIONICUS

A "saddlebags" variation on the bull's-eye variety of *Dendrobates histrionicus*. Here instead of one large central spot we have a pair of spots on the upper sides. Photo by A. v. d. Nieuwenhuizen.

The three major groups of patterns most commonly available in the Harlequin Poison Frog, *Dendrobates histrionicus*. At the upper right is a small-spotted specimen that also has a red head. The two photos in the center represent a very open-spotted phase of the "Valley" form, also noted for its robust build. At the bottom are two patterns that loosely fall into the bull's-eye form. All photos by A. v. d. Nieuwenhuizen.

DENDROBATES HISTRIONICUS

And saving the best for last—a bright yellow reticulated form of the Harlequin Poison Frog with the dark background reduced to minor remnants. It's a pity *Dendrobates histrionicus* is so difficult to breed in captivity, or it might be possible to select for even more stunning versions of this pattern. Photo by A. v. d. Nieuwenhuizen.

Dendrobates leucomelas, the Yellow-banded Poison Frog

The common name says it all—bright yellow bands on black is a good description of this rather large (31 to 38 mm in adults) ground-living poison frog. The three (over the head, the midbody, and rump) broad, bright orange-yellow bands contain large or small black spots of irregular size and distribution, a sure mark of the species. Intensity of the colors varies, but not a great deal. The belly is black, usually without any other color, while the arms and legs are heavily spotted and mottled with bright yellow like the body. The finger discs are expanded, there is no omosternum, and the tarsal tubercle is absent or weakly indicated.

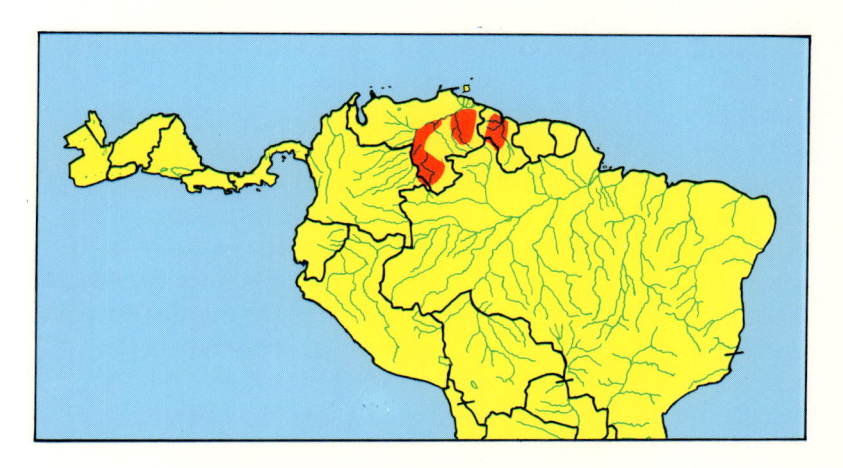

General distribution of the Yellow-banded Poison Frog, *Dendrobates leucomelas.*

In a typical *Dendrobates leucomelas* there are broad black bands behind the head and over midbody, as well as a black area around the vent, all on bright yellow. The number and size of the smaller black markings vary greatly, however. Photo by R. D. Bartlett.

This probably is a juvenile Yellow-banded Poison Frog, *Dendrobates leucomelas*, because the black bands are almost continuous across the back and not yet broken into smaller spots and blotches. Photo by P. Freed.

This is one of the poison frogs that is rather poorly known in the wild but is not uncommon in the terrarium. Because the omosternum is absent, this species traditionally has been considered a close relative of *D. histrionicus*, which also lacks the omosternum. Interestingly, it would be the only member of the *Histrionicus*-Group of *Dendrobates* known to lack tadpoles that need food eggs. In many respects its life history in the terrarium is very similar to that of *D. auratus*, including the behavior of the tadpoles, and I have to wonder if the lack of an omosternum in *leucomelas* is misleading. I've run across no detailed description of the tadpole, though one might exist, and a breeder of *leucomelas* might do well to carefully preserve some tadpoles after the popping of the hind legs and before the front legs come out. Myers and his colleagues have removed *leucomelas* from the *Histrionicus*-Group because of differences in the call, but so far I haven't seen it reassigned to another group (though I could have missed it). In size, tadpole behavior, and some aspects of color pattern it resembles *D. auratus* and *D. tinctorius*, so just to have a working relation I've put it in the *Tinctorius*-Group. This placement should not be considered in the scientific literature, however, and is just a convenient spot to put the species to help make identifications easier. Interestingly, in the terrarium it has been hybridized with *D. tinctorius* and *D. truncatus*, which would seem to strengthen its relationships with the *Tinctorius*-Group.

Unlike the species of the *Histrionicus*-Group, which occur in Central America and western South America in Colombia and Ecuador, *D. leucomelas* is a species of northeastern South America, Guyana and adjacent Venezuela and Brazil. Because it is relatively secretive, spending much of its time in the litter, it might have a somewhat broader range, but still it seems to be separated from *D. histrionicus* by a quarter of a continent. It is a species of typically very humid rainforests from about 50 to 800 meters in elevation. It is the only poison frog known to estivate during the dry season (S. Gorzula, pers. comm.). Specimens in captivity generally had ancestors imported from southern Venezuela.

Males call from the leaf litter in the shade (rarely from low perches on the sides of trees and shrubs), producing a long musical trill that can be quite loud. Sexes cannot be told externally except by breeding behavior. As in some other poison frogs, most calling activity (and probably feeding as well, on the usual ants) occurs for an hour or two after sunrise and before sunset. Breeding in nature may be restricted to the wet season, as there are hints that terrarium animals breed for only a few months a year. Females are attracted to calling males and one follows him to a bower, where she strokes his back and snout. The animals also may slowly circle each other and stamp the feet. Actual mating apparently has not been seen as these frogs are quite shy, but the female seems to deposit her eggs first, while the male is outside the bower. He returns to fertilize the clutch. Clutches of five to six eggs are typical, with occasionally eight or nine eggs produced at a time. In captivity the parents usually do not care for their eggs, which are removed for rearing. Hatching may take over 18 days, and in nature the male does not return until the eggs are ready to hatch.

The tadpoles are generalized feeders much like those of *D. auratus*, accepting almost any foods. Some keepers say their pets prefer a good plant-based tropical fish flake food, but bloodworms and other tadpoles are not ignored. Because of their broad diet, they are best raised separately to prevent cannibalism, though some keepers swear they have never had a problem of this type. The tadpoles are more delicate than those of some other species, and the water must be kept absolutely clean if fungus and other diseases are to be avoided. Metamorphosis occurs after some 70 to 90 days, producing a little froglet that looks like an adult but with much duskier yellow bands. The bands brighten up in only a few days and get brighter over the next month, gradually acquiring the black spots typical of the species. One small problem with the froglets is that they require large amounts of food at all times. Any break in the feeding for even 48 hours might lead to death. They will take pinhead crickets as well as the usual fruitflies, by the way. Adults often seem to have a "sweet tooth" for small caterpillars of various types.

Its large size, bright colors, and ready availability at moderate prices (for captive-bred specimens, yet) make this a great poison frog for beginners, though its relative shyness, common aggression between adults, and the tendency of adults to abandon their eggs are small disadvantages. It is an excellent choice that should not be passed up if you run across one or two in your local pet shop—or (if you have the money) a half dozen from a dealer's list.

Yellow-banded Poison Frogs, *Dendrobates leucomelas*, are not especially good climbers and in nature usually are found near the ground, but this does not mean that they cannot climb well in the terrarium. Photo by B. Kahl.

DENDROBATES LEUCOMELAS

Recent research has shown that the Yellow-banded Poison Frog, *Dendrobates leucomelas*, estivates during the dry season. This perhaps is one of the reasons it can survive in areas that are marginal at best for poison frogs. Photo by A. v. d. Nieuwenhuizen.

DENDROBATES LEUCOMELAS

This rather distorted appearing poison frog is a terrarium hybrid between *Dendrobates leucomelas* and *D. auratus*. Whether such artificial creations would survive in nature is uncertain, but that they can successfully breed in the terrarium appears to be true. Photo by A. v. d. Nieuwenhuizen.

A variety of patterns in the Yellow-banded Poison Frog, *Dendrobates leucomelas*. Top left and bottom left: Specimens from Canaima, Gran Sabana, Venezuela. At top right is a male and below him is a female from Colombia, while at center left is a male and bottom right is a female from Brazil.

Pattern variation in this species does not appear to be strongly connected to geography. All photos by A. v. d. Nieuwenhuizen.

DENDROBATES LEUCOMELAS

In this specimen of *Dendrobates leucomelas*, the Yellow-banded Poison Frog, from Venezuela, only one complete stripe crosses the back, increasing the resemblance to *D. auratus*. Photo by A. v. d. Nieuwenhuizen.

Dendrobates pumilio, the Strawberry Poison Frog

Without doubt, this is the most extensively studied species of poison frog. Found over a rather large range in lowland (0 to 960 meters) rainforests of the Caribbean coast of Central America from Nicaragua to Panama, it is a common to abundant amphibian in many places and one that never fails to draw attention. Its natural history has been studied from many different aspects, though terrarium hobbyists tend to notice it mostly for its color and the odd color variations that occur on small islands off the coast of Panama.

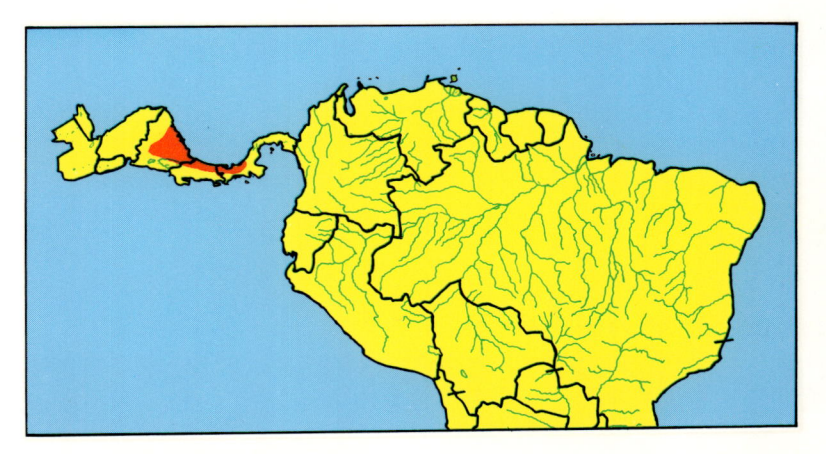

General distribution of the Strawberry Poison Frog, *Dendrobates pumilio*.

One of the prettiest color phases of the Strawberry Poison Frog is that of bright red specimens with distinct rounded dark spots over the back and legs. Such specimens occur in several areas of Panama. Photo by R. S. Simmons.

The spotted phase of *Dendrobates pumilio* found in several areas of Panama once was called *D. galindoi*, and one certainly could make an argument for its continued recognition as a subspecies. Photo by P. Freed.

This is a small species, 18 to 24 mm (usually 19 to 22 mm in Costa Rica) adult length, with bright red back, relatively smooth skin, and black to dark blue hind legs. The belly usually is some shade of red, occasionally red and blue, but can vary toward tan and white in some Panamanian localities. Usually the back has some small black specks scattered over it, but they may be absent or sometimes become distinct round spots. The tarsal tubercle is absent or nearly so. The closest relatives of the Strawberry Poison Frog are *D. granuliferus*, from the Pacific slope of Costa Rica, which has an obviously granular back skin and greenish to blue-green hind legs; and the uncommon *D. speciosus* of the Panamanian highlands, which has very smooth skin and is entirely red above and below as well as maturing at sizes over 27 mm. Specimens from Isla Bastimentos, Isla Shepard, Isla Colon, and other Panamanian areas have attracted the attention of scientists and collectors because they differ greatly from typical Strawberry Poison Frogs. Once they were called *D. galindoi* Trapido, a name now relegated to the synonymy of *D. pumilio* because there is a continuous chain of variants leading back to typical *pumilio*, there are no structural differences, and several different patterns and colors may occur in a single population. These atypical Panamanian populations occur in at least the following spectrum of colors: blue above and below, without spots; green above and yellow below with small spots; green above and white below with small spots; red above and white below with small spots; olive green above and

DENDROBATES PUMILIO

yellow below with black flecks. Other even more strangely patterned individuals also are found on occasion. Like other poison frogs, Strawberries feed mostly on ants, and they also eat a large number of mites, with other small insects and their larvae being eaten when available. Foraging is mostly in the ground litter, and activity is mostly in the pre-noon hours.

Males can be distinguished externally from females by their tan to grayish vocal pouch under the throat. They establish territories on leaves, logs, and standing trees about half a meter to a meter about the forest floor and defend these territories from intruding males. The frogs station themselves about 3 meters apart and respond to males that come within about 2 meters of their calling position. Males in an area often call in synchrony. When removed from their territory, males are able to home, probably by using a combination of visual and scent clues. The call is a low buzz or ticking note and serves both as a territorial advertisement call and to attract females.

When a female is attracted to a calling male, he drops to the ground and she follows him to a bower. The courtship is extremely simple for a poison frog, with little contact between the sexes other than some stroking of the back. The eggs usually are laid in leaves on the ground. The male first deposits sperm on the leaf and then the female deposits her clutch of two to five eggs over the sperm. For the next seven or so days the male tends the clutch, moistening the eggs as required and probably chasing away small predators and eating fungused eggs. At the time of hatching the female returns to the clutch, stretches her hind legs over the hatching eggs, and allows the tadpoles to creep onto her back. One to four tadpoles are carried at one time to the funnels of bromeliads or other water-filled plant stems.

Dendrobates pumilio is a typical food egg feeder. The tadpole is tan, with low fins that end in a rounded point. The oral disc has large papillae around the edge except for the front (top) edge, the beaks are heavy and serrated, and there are only two rows of teeth, a broken row with few teeth above the beaks and a single well-developed row below the beaks. Occasionally the anterior tooth row may be

A bronzy green color pattern of the Strawberry Poison Frog, *Dendrobates pumilio*. Photo by R. D. Bartlett.

DENDROBATES PUMILIO

Typical specimens of the Strawberry Poison Frog, Dendrobates pumilio, from Costa Rica are bright red above with only traces of dark spots or specks. Usually the arms and legs are a deep blue or even blue-black in color. Photo by R. D. Bartlett.

lacking entirely. The mother visits all her tadpoles on a regular basis, looks in each funnel, lowers her rear end into the funnel, and deposits one to five unfertilized eggs. The tadpoles react actively to the presence of their mother. Experiments seem to show that the tadpoles feed only on food eggs and die without this source of nutrition. Over the about 50 days that they grow before transformation, each tadpole receives an average of 28 food eggs from the mother. They must receive an egg meal before they have been in the funnel for three days or they will die. At metamorphosis the froglets are about 11 mm long, the size to some extent depending upon how many food eggs they received. Curiously, not every visit by the mother leads to feeding, even though the mother goes through the entire ritual including lowering her rear end into the funnel. Also, other females commonly look into the funnels (apparently while checking for their offspring) and the tadpoles react to them as well, but only the mother feeds her offspring. Apparently the mother can recognize her children and distinguish them from seemingly identical tadpoles of other Strawberry Poison Frogs in the area. Rearing this species in captivity is difficult, perhaps impossible for the non-specialist. Chicken egg yolk and cottage cheese mixtures yield some froglets, but development is very slow and many tadpoles die. Captive-bred specimens are not commonly offered for sale, most specimens seen being wild-collected. The frogs are extremely abundant in some areas and often do well in rainforests converted to plantations, and they also may be very common on some of the small Panamanian islands. Mortality in wild-caught specimens often is high.

DENDROBATES PUMILIO

A fairly typical (if there is such a thing) *Dendrobates pumilio* from Bastimentos Island (or Isla Bastimentos), Panama. Such frogs really don't fit the common name Strawberry Poison Frog very well. Photo by A. v. d. Nieuwenhuizen.

DENDROBATES PUMILIO

The variability of the Strawberry Poison Frog, *Dendrobates pumilio*, over its rather small range has led to its being named several times in the scientific literature. This specimen from northeastern Costa Rica, for instance, displays more spotting and a more varied color pattern on the limbs than do specimens from further north. Photo by A. v. d. Nieuwenhuizen.

DENDROBATES PUMILIO

A "moss green" pattern of *Dendrobates pumilio* from near Colon, Panama. Notice the isolated yellow spot on the side. Such misplaced pattern elements are common in Strawberry Poison Frogs of many eastern populations. Photo by A. v. d. Nieuwenhuizen.

DENDROBATES PUMILIO

Another of the spotted *Dendrobates pumilio* from Bastimentos Island, Panama. These frogs may be extremely abundant locally and tolerate quite a bit of collecting, but they fare so poorly in the terrarium that they cannot be recommended for the general hobbyist. Photo by A. v. d. Nieuwenhuizen.

123

DENDROBATES PUMILIO

A blue phase individual from the Bocas del Toro area (probably not really from near the type locality) of Panama. Such odd individuals are highly prized by specialists but, like other Strawberry Poison Frogs, are difficult to maintain. Photo by A. v. d. Nieuwenhuizen.

Panamanian Strawberry Poison Frogs, *Dendrobates pumilio*. The three photos on the left represent specimens from Colon Island, while the three on the right represent specimens from Bastimentos Island. Remember that such specimens are selected from large and variable populations that are much more variable than shown by just a few photos. All photos by A. v. d. Nieuwenhuizen.

DENDROBATES PUMILIO

Notice the distinctly ringed or ocellated brown spots on the back of this greenish Bastimentos Island, Panama, specimen of *Dendrobates pumilio*. Photo by A. v. d. Nieuwenhuizen.

Some extremes in coloration of the Strawberry Poison Frog, *Dendrobates pumilio*. The top two specimens are from Siquirres, extreme eastern Costa Rica, and are rather heavily patterned compared to the two more typical Costa Rican specimens at the bottom of the page. The blue specimen in the photos at the center is from the Bocas del Toro area of Panama. All photos by A. v. d. Nieuwenhuizen.

DENDROBATES PUMILIO

Oddballs from the Bocas del Toro area of Panama. These *Dendrobates pumilio* have a relatively coarse skin texture and lack the typical dark coloration on the limbs. To the best of my knowledge, little has been published on the genetics of color inheritance in this or any other poison frog. Photo by A. v. d. Nieuwenhuizen

More Strawberry Poison Frogs, *Dendrobates pumilio*, from Bastimentos Island, Panama, plus the bright green variation most common on Shepard Island. Bastimentos (Island or Isla) is one of many small islands in the Lago de Chiriqui at the northwestern corner of Panama south of Siquirres, Costa Rica. All photos by A. v. d. Nieuwenhuizen.

DENDROBATES PUMILIO

A greenish and spotted male specimen of *Dendrobates pumilio* from Colon, Panama. Colon is at the Atlantic mouth of the Panama Canal many kilometers east of the Lago de Chiriqui and its many small islands. Photo by A. v. d. Nieuwenhuizen.

Guess where these Strawberry Poison Frogs, *Dendrobates pumilio*, came from. Right...the frog with large spots is from Bastimentos, the two greenies in the center are from Shepard Island, and the red (to orange) ones are from Costa Rica. All photos by A. v. d. Nieuwenhuizen.

DENDROBATES PUMILIO

Like the other poison frogs that feed food eggs to their young, the female carries the tadpoles to their water spot. In the Strawberry Poison Frog, *Dendrobates pumilio*, typically only one tadpole is carried per trip, but this Bastimentos mother is carrying two. Photo by R. Bechter.

Compared to the reddish Costa Rican specimen at the upper right, all these *Dendrobates pumilio* appear a bit different. However, all but the middle pair came from Bocas del Toro Island next to Bastimentos Island (the home of the middle pair). All photos by A. v. d. Nieuwenhuizen.

DENDROBATES PUMILIO

If properly maintained in the terrarium, it is not all that hard to get the Strawberry Poison Frog to lay eggs and even watch over them until they hatch. The problem is adequately feeding the tadpoles. Photo by R. Bechter.

The Panamanian varieties of *Dendrobates pumilio*: top pair, Bastimentos; center left, Colon; center right, Shepard; lower left, Cayo Nancy; lower right, Slit Hill. The photographer assures me that the Nancy specimen is indeed *pumilio*, not *speciosus*, but I really would find this photo hard to identify. All photos by R. Bechter.

Activities of Panamanian Strawberry Poison Frogs: top left, controlling access to a bromeliad funnel for tadpole deposition; top right, dominance fight; center left, fighting while carrying a tadpole; center right, carrying a tadpole; bottom left, carrying two tadpoles; bottom right, late tadpoles with full color patterns and (left) spindly leg syndrome. All photos by R. Bechter.

Another lineup of Strawberry Poison Frogs. Top left, Costa Rica (very pale and with little dotting on back); top right and bottom right, Panama; center left, Cayo Nancy (compare with the solid orange specimen of a few pages ago); center right, Bastimentos; bottom left, unusual yellow specimen from Bocas del Toro. All photos by A. v. d. Nieuwenhuizen.

More varieties of *Dendrobates pumilio*. Top and center photos are, as you might expect, of specimens from Bastimentos, the center right being the "Gold Dust" variety. Bottom two photos are a bright red form with little limb coloration from eastern Costa Rica, very similar to *D. speciosus* in appearance. All photos by A. v. d. Nieuwenhuizen.

Dendrobates tinctorius, the Dyeing Poison Frog

No, no—look at the spelling of the common name, *dyeing*, not *dying*. This actually is one of the hardier poison frogs and also one of the largest and most bright colored. Adults are 34 to 50 mm long (supposedly reaching 60 mm in the terrarium), smooth-skinned, and lack a distinct tarsal tubercle. We'll get to the origin of the common name shortly, but suffice it to say that this species has been in the literature for over 200 years, being the first poison frog known to Europeans. Its nomenclature is messy, and there currently is a minor controversy as to whether it was officially named by Cuvier or Schneider, but it makes little difference since neither of these workers actually saw a specimen and just applied a name (*tinctorius* of course refers to a tincture and has it origin in a legend leading to the common name) to an illustration in an older book. Currently this species is considered the type-species of *Dendrobates*, and its characters thus define the basis of the generic name.

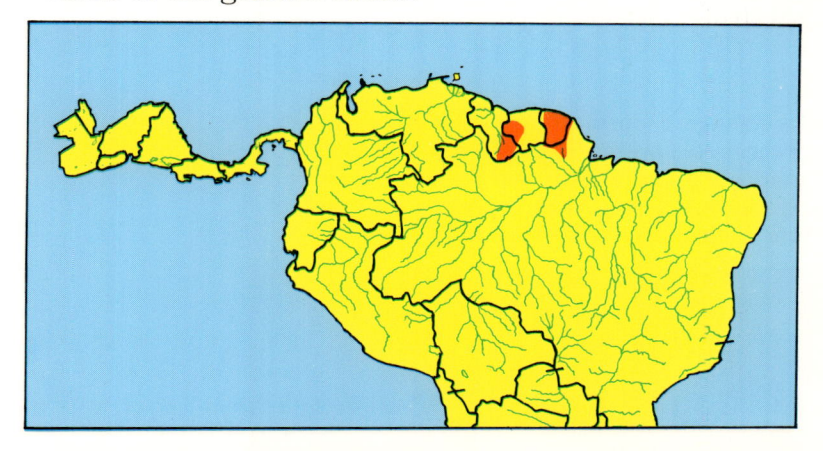

General distribution of the Dyeing Poison Frog, *Dendrobates tinctorius*.

This is a species of relatively low (0 to 300 or 400 meters) humid forests of the Guianas, being found in French Guiana, Surinam (Dutch Guiana), and Guyana (British Guiana) on the northeastern shoulder of South America. There are a few records from Brazil just to the south of these countries, but the species does not range south to the Amazon basin. Because of the unusual nature of forests in the Guianas, often relatively small "islands" of forest being isolated by relatively dry savannahs or high mountain plateaus, no two populations of *D. tinctorius* are exactly alike. There is a real problem defining this species because on one hand it grades into the yellow *D. galactonotus*, and on the other it becomes virtually indistinguishable from *D. azureus*. Typical specimens are blue-black frogs with strong yellow, yellow-white, or blue-white patterns. Usually the back from the snout to over the tail is yellow, the sides are black, and the belly is either black or yellow, with or without a dark or light spotted and reticulated pattern. The second common pattern exhibits a yellow stripe on each side of the back, usually joining with its partner over the vent and over the snout; a second stripe fills much of the side.

A fairly typical Dyeing Poison Frog, *Dendrobates tinctorius*, from Surinam, of the white or pallid type. Photo by R. D. Bartlett.

Often the two dorsal stripes and even the side stripes are connected by narrower bands of yellow, isolating one to three black spots down the midback. In either typical pattern the limbs tend to be deep blue to black with or without black or even yellow spotting. In the third common pattern the yellow is reduced to a

A brilliant yellow specimen of *Dendrobates tinctorius*. The swollen belly may indicate a female (as do the narrow toe pads)—or it may indicate recent heavy feeding. Photo by R. D. Bartlett.

narrow network on the blue-black background. In many specimens seen in the hobby today the limbs show a reticulated pattern rather than the spots and stripes typical of older specimens.

From the Blue Poison Frog, which is very closely related and has been hybridized with the Dyeing Poison Frog in the terrarium, *D. tinctorius* should be easily distinguished by its yellow stripes or stripe remnants. As mentioned, the two species are not always clearly told apart by color pattern (especially captive-bred specimens of questionable parentage), and structure must be looked at as well. The Dyeing Poison Frog has a typical erect posture and a distinct, round tympanum about half the diameter of the eye. The Blue Poison Frog has a humpbacked posture because of small differences in its backbone and pelvis and has a small tympanum that often is indistinct and hard to tell from the surrounding skin. *D. galactonotus* also is very similar to bright yellow specimens of *D. tinctorius* but *tinctorius* usually has a more complex pattern showing yellow stripes on the back. Additionally, *D. galactonotus* is one of the few large poison frogs with a well-developed tarsal tubercle.

There are many indications that the taxonomy of the Dyeing Poison Frog is far from settled and that a thorough modern review may lead to the recognition of several species within it. Either that or the Blue and the Spash-backed Poison Frogs will be shown to be extreme variants of *D. tinctorius*. More research obviously is necessary, but the isolated populations of all three of these species are under threat from development and overcollecting.

Though at home in protected spots in the leaf litter and usually quite secretive, the Dyeing Poison Frog has greatly expanded finger discs and is a good climber. Often it is found on the sides of trees and in heavy vines 1 or 2 meters above the ground, where its bright yellow stripes stand out in the darkness of the forest. The bright color obviously advertises its poisonous nature, and it has few predators. Like other poison frogs, it feeds mostly on ants.

In theory, males can be distinguished from females by having larger finger discs that are cut straighter across the tips, but this does not always work. Additionally, males are somewhat territorial and may wrestle, but so do females on occasion. Of course, only males call.

The courtship and breeding are of the relatively simple type. A female attracted to a calling male follows him to a bower of his choice on the forest floor, usually dead leaves in a hidden spot. The female

A direct comparison of two closely related poison frogs: *Dendrobates tinctorius* (bottom) and *Dendrobates azureus*, the Blue Poison Frog (top). There is little doubt that these two frogs share a common ancestor, though there is quite a bit of doubt whether they are worth recognizing as full species. The more hunch-backed posture and poorly defined tympanum of *D. azureus* argue for species rank, while the variability of color patterns and the ability to hybridize in captivity argue for subspecific rank. Photo by B. Kahl.

DENDROBATES TINCTORIUS

A typical Dyeing Poison Frog, *Dendrobates tinctorius*, probably a male, showing the greatly expanded toe pads with distinct scutes separated by a valley. Photo by M. Panzella.

Variations of the Dyeing Poison Frog. Top left, northern Brazil, female; center left, French Guiana; bottom left, Table Mountains, Surinam, male; top right, coastal French Guiana; center and bottom right, a female from French Guiana. All photos by A. v. d. Nieuwenhuizen.

strokes the male's back on occasion, but there seem to be no complicated dances or other behaviors. The female lays rather large clutches of eight to ten eggs, occasionally even 15, that are fertilized later by the male. In fact, the female may have left the bower for several minutes before the male fertilizes the eggs. The male tends the eggs for the 14 to 18 days before hatching, keeping them moist and probably fighting off small predators. When the tadpoles emerge they climb onto the father's back, usually by one's and two's, and are taken to the water body in which they will live for over two months. Like *D. auratus*, many tadpoles from several different clutches and fathers may be deposited in a rather large raising hole, often a tree hole or even pieces of human junk such as cans and plastic pots. The tadpoles are non-selective feeders that take algae, detritus, mosquito larvae, and probably each other on occasion. In the terrarium they often feed on brine shrimp nauplii (remove all salt) and bloodworms, among other things. The tadpoles transform in about ten weeks if they are fed continually. This is one of the species in which the adult color pattern, and even some of the colors, are visible in late stage tadpoles. The froglets need tiny food for the first few weeks but soon graduate to fruitflies and pinhead crickets.

Large, colorful, and relatively inexpensive, this is a hardy species in the terrarium and one that can be recommended to beginners. Most available specimens are captive-bred, but get a guarantee from the dealer that they are not wild-caught just to be sure. Because of their relatively large clutches and the fact that females may lay every ten days or so for several months in a row, this is one of the few species that has been bred commercially. Remember that it likes to climb, likes it warm and humid, and needs lots of food and you should have few problems.

Oops, almost forgot—*dyeing*. Both the common and scientific names of this frog come from an old story introduced into Europe along with the first preserved specimens of the frog. For over two centuries there have been legends that Amerindians of various tribes in the Guianas and the Amazon use animal concoctions of various types to change the plain green feathers of parrots into red feathers. Frankly, I've no idea why this would be a desirable thing to do, and doubt that any Amerindians would really want to do it either, but that is the story. *Dendrobates tinctorius* was pinpointed in these legends as the frog used in the Guianas to produce the color change, a technique called *tapirage*. Supposedly the living frog or a tincture of frog skin and blood (thus the scientific name) was rubbed on the selected area of the parrot where a color change was wanted. The parrot had to be young, and its original green feathers had to be plucked. When the new feathers grew in, they would magically be bright red or perhaps yellow. In effect, they would have been dyed (thus the common name). It's a good story and an old one, but needless to say it has never been observed by a "competent observer" or proved in the laboratory under scientific conditions. Of course, some readers with access to both parrots and *D. tinctorius* (not really an unlikely combination) might want to try this at home. Let me know what happens—but don't send me any bills for dead parrots, dead frogs, or finger amputations.

Three variations on the white or pallid color pattern of *Dendrobates tinctorius*. All photos by R. Bechter.

DENDROBATES TINCTORIUS

A male *Dendrobates tinctorius*, the Dyeing Poison Frog, from French Guiana. Photo by A. v. d. Nieuwenhuizen.

DENDROBATES TINCTORIUS

One of the most gorgeous yellow specimens of *Dendrobates tinctorius* I've ever seen pictured. This specimen came from southeastern French Guiana. Photo by A. v. d. Nieuwenhuizen.

145

DENDROBATES TINCTORIUS

This female *Dendrobates tinctorius* from Surinam has unusually pale blue legs that remind one of the reticulum on the legs of *Dendrobates ventrimaculatus*. Photo by A. v. d. Nieuwenhuizen.

DENDROBATES TINCTORIUS

Like most of the larger poison frogs, *Dendrobates tinctorius* lacks "flash colors" in the groin and at the back of the leg. Photo by A. v. d. Nieuwenhuizen.

DENDROBATES TINCTORIUS

An interesting male Dyeing Poison Frog, *Dendrobates tinctorius*, from French Guiana. Notice in this specimen that the legs are metallic blue and very sparsely spotted. It is hard to find any color feature that is constant in this species of poison frog. Photo by A. v. d. Nieuwenhuizen.

DENDROBATES TINCTORIUS

Though it definitely is a fairly typical *Dendrobates tinctorius* from French Guiana, notice the very hunch-backed posture of this Dyeing Poison Frog. Photo by A. v. d. Nieuwenhuizen.

DENDROBATES TINCTORIUS

A colorful yellow and very dark blue male Dyeing Poison Frog, *Dendrobates tinctorius*, from coastal French Guiana. Photo by A. v. d. Nieuwenhuizen.

Dyeing Poison Frogs, *Dendrobates tinctorius*. Notice the spotted belly pattern of the Surinam female at the upper left and its resemblance to the pattern of *Dendrobates reticulatus* and *D. imitator*.

The female at right top and center is from French Guiana; the almost black male at center left is from Surinam, as is the female at lower right. The juvenile at bottom left is a hybrid between *D. tinctorius* and *D. azureus* but looks much like a normal juvenile *D. tinctorius*. All photos by A. v. d. Nieuwenhuizen.

DENDROBATES TINCTORIUS

A male yellow-headed pallid phase Dyeing Poison Frog, *Dendrobates tinctorius*, from the Emperor Mountains of Surinam. Photo by A. v. d. Nieuwenhuizen.

Male-male combat in *Dendrobates tinctorius* can be rough though specimens seldom are injured. These are relatively large poison frogs and a couple of fights can seriously disrupt a terrarium. All photos by R. Bechter.

Believe it or not, all these Dyeing Poison Frogs but one are from French Guiana. The oddball is at center left, a specimen from Villa Nova, Brazil. Few Brazilian poison frogs make it to the terrarium hobby. All photos by A. v. d. Nieuwenhuizen.

Variations in development of yellow in the pattern of *Dendrobates tinctorius*. Notice also the differences in coloration of the lower sides and the limbs. All photos by R. Bechter.

DENDROBATES TINCTORIUS

Like most other poison frogs, *Dendrobates tinctorius* is diurnal and often easy to see even at midday. Though largely a ground-dweller, it is not afraid to climb and can be found several meters up in trees. Photo by R. D. Bartlett.

DENDROBATES VENTRIMACULATUS

Dendrobates ventrimaculatus, the Amazonian Poison Frog

Trying to write-up this species has simply driven me crazy. The biology as far as known is not too complicated—repeat, as far as known—but the taxonomy is utterly confused and I am not able to make any sense of the various conflicting stands in the scientific papers. For this reason you must consider this chapter to be questionable because we may be dealing with five or more almost identical species rather than one, and the possibility exists that in the terrarium each might be significantly different in behavior.

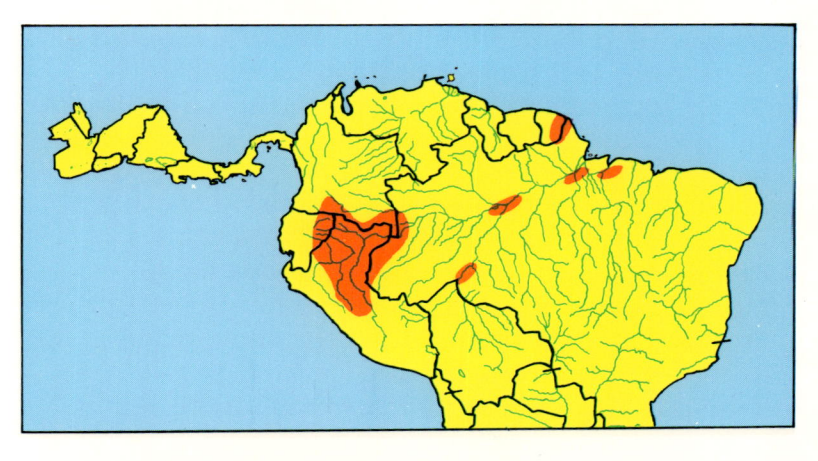

General distribution of the Amazonian Poison Frog, *Dendrobates ventrimaculatus*. The systematic status of many of the populations shown here is very uncertain.

A Peruvian *Dendrobates ventrimaculatus* with a dorsal pattern similar to one of the type specimens of the species. Notice the pair of large black spots on the anterior back and the three black spots across the lower back. Photo by A. v. d. Nieuwenhuizen.

Ventral view of a poison frog of the *Dendrobates ventrimaculatus* complex from Peru. Notice the pattern of colors: yellow throat, blue chest, yellow belly. Photo by J. P. Bogart.

This is the "species" known universally in the hobby as *D. quinquevittatus,* but Myers and his co-workers in recent papers have restricted *quinquevittatus* to a very narrowly defined species with orangish tan arms and legs covered with widely spaced small blackish spots, the base of the arm with a dull golden "flash mark." Myers has been using the name *D. ventrimaculatus* in a broad sense to apply to the frog that is widely distributed in the upper Amazon drainages of Peru, Ecuador, and Colombia, as well as in French Guiana, with a few scattered populations in the Amazon basin proper of Brazil. In this species and most of the remaining species of the complex, the arms and legs are covered with small black spots separated by a fine network (reticulation) of narrow blue-white lines that appear metallic. Usually the back has three yellow lines separating black areas. Four species of this complex have very distinctive color patterns and are readily recognized, while having few intermediates to more typical patterns. *D. castaneoticus* and *D. vanzolinii* are black with small bright spots over the back, *D. reticulatus* has a bright orange-red back, and *D. fantasticus* has the lower back mostly black and the head red, often with a black "crown" between the eyes. In *D. imitator* and *D. variabilis,* species very close to what we here are calling *D. ventrimaculatus,* a yellow stripe runs down the middle of the back from between the eyes and separates two rows of more or less regular squarish black spots; in *D. imitator* there are two large squarish black spots on the snout, while in *D. variabilis* there is one rounded central black spot. *D. lamasi* and *D. biolat* are extremely similar to *D. ventrimaculatus* in the broad sense; see their discussions for distinctions.

For our purposes, any small frog (usually 16 to 21 mm, sometimes less, sometimes a bit more) with heavily reticulated blue-white and black-spotted legs that does not exactly fit any of the patterns above will be called *D. ventrimaculatus.* The last couple of years have seen an increasingly complicated literature develop for this frog as each pattern type is correlated

DENDROBATES VENTRIMACULATUS

with details of belly and throat coloration and structural details of the feet. Frankly, the last word on identifying these species has not been written, and it is virtually impossible to associate many photos with any specific pattern with complete confidence. It seems possible that there may be another dozen or more species still to be segregated from *D. ventrimaculatus* in the sense I am using it here, and I doubt that hobbyists will ever be able to recognize them with certainty.

The Amazonian Poison Frog is a glossy, usually yellow and black little frog that typically is found in the trees and bromeliads several meters above the ground. It often is most common on edges of forests and along small streams and impoundments. Males can be located by their loud, high-pitched rapid clicking calls, but they do not differ from females in color or width of the finger discs. The first finger is very short compared to the second, has two distinct tubercles at its base, and usually lacks a distinct disc, while the first toe is very short (sometimes just a nubbin) and also lacks a distinct disc. The throat is yellow, usually with a pair of spots toward the back, while the breast and belly may be bluish white or yellow (probably variable at the specific level) with swirling black lines. The undersides of the hind legs are bluish white heavily spotted with black spots. The rest of the pattern is variable, but usually there are a pair of bright yellow (sometimes orange or even red) stripes, one on each side of the back, and a row of black spots or a black stripe under each yellow stripe on the side. The middle of the back is most variable, but a yellow stripe usually runs from between the eyes to at least the middle of the back, with black stripes on each side. Toward the back quarter of the body the yellow stripe may be continuous and separate the back part of the same pair of black stripes or may be absent and blocked by a pair or more of black spots. Or the entire middle of the back may be filled with a black Y (the arms ending at the eyes and the stem ending over the vent). The types of *D. ventrimaculatus* had partially connected black spots running from the eyes to midback, with three oval elongated black spots further back; this pattern does not seem to be common in the hobby.

Bromeliads seem to serve as the centerpoints of Amazonian Poison Frog life. A male seems to establish a territory in a favored bromeliad funnel and stays there (at least in the terrarium) for several months. They call constantly each morning and probably have a territorial structure similar to that of *D. pumilio* and *D. granuliferus*. Females are attracted to calling males when they fill with eggs and are ready to mate. It has been suggested that the sight of an egg-filled female is the releaser that initiates mating behavior in the male, so perhaps small differences in color pattern could in nature serve to help related sympatric (found in the same place) species, prevent interbreeding.

As usual, the male leads the female to the egg-laying site, the female following hesitantly but staying in sight of the male. The pair come into contact at the base of a bromeliad leaf over a funnel of water. Here an elaborate mating dance may take place and there is much mutual stroking of the back and snout. The dance involves the male slowly rotating around the female, sometimes stamping the feet in place, then the female rotating around the male. This may continue for over an hour. During and between dances the frogs often move together side-to-side, back-to-back, or vent-to-vent. Finally the male deposits sperm in the selected spot at the base of the leaf and moves off. The female then deposits her clutch of about four eggs (two to six) and leaves. The eggs are untended by a parent, at least in some terrarium breedings.

In specimens from French Guiana (with a black Y down the middle of a yellow back, one of the relatively common terrarium forms) captive males were seen to deposit sperm directly into the water of the bromeliad funnel, and the female laid her eggs in the water containing the sperm. This observation appears to be unique in the genus, but there is no reason to doubt it. Until the taxonomy of this group of frogs is straightened out, conflicting reports about behavior should be expected, as every "real" or biological species (as opposed to morphological species—the kind that humans can distinguish with their eyes) contained within *D. ventrimaculatus* might have many small distinctions in its behavior to help it remain genetically separate from its very similar neighbors.

The eggs take about 12 days to hatch (in the French Guiana specimens studied most closely), and the male returns to the laying-site only two days before hatching. He carries each tadpole to a

This very different color pattern assigned to *Dendrobates ventrimaculatus* probably represents a different species. Coming from the Ucayali region of Peru, the specimen somewhat resembles *D. biolat* but has a different snout pattern. Photo by P. Freed.

DENDROBATES VENTRIMACULATUS

separate bromeliad funnel. One or two tadpoles are taken from the clutch at a time, and they commonly spend one to three days on his back before being put into the water. The tadpoles have heavy beaks and are thought to be cannibalistic, so establishing only one per container prevents accidents. In the French Guiana specimens the tadpoles had two bright yellow stripes on the head connected across the snout. The teeth were well-developed, in two rows in front of the beaks (the bottom row split) and in three full rows behind the beaks. A single row of small pointed papillae edged the back half of the disc, with a slight indentation at the center edges and a broken row of papillae continuing a short distance above the middle on each side; as usual, the anterior edge of the disc lacked papillae. The tadpoles feed well on flake fish food in captivity and also take bloodworms and other animal foods. There are observations that at least some populations depend on food eggs for additional nourishment, but the full complement of oral disc teeth makes it doubtful that food eggs are necessary for survival of the tadpole.

This is not an easy species to keep or breed in the terrarium. Its small size and requirement for bromeliads and other heavy plantings mean it disappears into the furnishings and strong lighting is needed for the plants. The temperature and humidity should be about normal for poison frogs, perhaps 26°C during the day (lower at night) and 80% or more relative humidity. Both males and females fight, and females have a bad reputation as egg-eaters, feeding on the clutches of other females in the same terrarium. Tadpoles have a high mortality rate, often are weak, and produce very weak froglets that may not feed. Perhaps this is one of those species in which mosquitoes would serve as a better food than springtails and fruitflies.

Scientifically this is a fascinating species with great potential for useful terrarium observations. Be sure that you mate only specimens with similar color patterns—in the present state of our knowledge even small differences in pattern may indicate distinct species not yet named or understood. Observations on whether or not the eggs and sperm are deposited in water and if food eggs are supplied by the female would be very interesting, but only if they can be attached to very specific color pattern adults. Specimens in the terrarium are almost always wild-collected and may be difficult to adapt. An interesting but difficult species. Have fun!

Compare this ventral view of a frog of the *Dendrobates ventrimaculatus* complex with the one from Peru shown two pages earlier. Notice that both the throat and the chest are yellow, while the belly is blue; this pattern agrees well with specimens of the French Guiana form. To identify an Amazonian Poison Frog today requires not only a glance at the color pattern of the back, but an analysis of the belly pattern (poorly reported for most described populations) and details of toe structure, as well as records of the calls and even observation of breeding and the tadpole. Photo by R. D. Bartlett.

DENDROBATES VENTRIMACULATUS

In the European terrarium hobby, specimens of the French Guiana form of *Dendrobates ventrimaculatus*, the Amazonian Poison Frog, sometimes are available and even are bred with some regularity, though they are far from common. The forked black stripe down the center of the back, ending on the eyes, is typical of this form, but the actual colors may vary quite a bit. Photo by A. v. d. Nieuwenhuizen.

DENDROBATES VENTRIMACULATUS

This French Guiana specimen of *Dendrobates ventrimaculatus* differs significantly in color from the specimen on the facing page. Notice also the round dark spot on the snout of this specimen, absent on the specimen on the facing page. Photo by A. v. d. Nieuwenhuizen.

DENDROBATES VENTRIMACULATUS

Ventral view of a French Guiana *Dendrobates ventrimaculatus*. Though seemingly constant in specimens from this area, this pattern is very different in many specimens from western South America. Notice the similarities (and differences) to *Dendrobates imitator*, which differs in color. Photo by A. v. d. Nieuwenhuizen.

DENDROBATES VENTRIMACULATUS

Though small (under 25 mm in most cases) and very arboreal, French Guiana *Dendrobates ventrimaculatus* are glossy little frogs that have a certain appeal. Their terrarium care may be very difficult, however, with only the advanced hobbyist having any chance of keeping them alive. All photos by A. v. d. Nieuwenhuizen.

French Guiana specimens of *Dendrobates ventrimaculatus*. The pair shown in the bottom four photos mated in the wet axil of a bromeliad, where the male maintained his territory. The eggs (with late embryos, lower right) were kept moist and protected by the male. All photos by R. Bechter.

In the terrarium, males of French Guiana specimens of *Dendrobates ventrimaculatus* carry the tadpoles to bromeliad funnels for further development, though at least some females feed their tadpoles on food eggs and must be able to find them every few days.

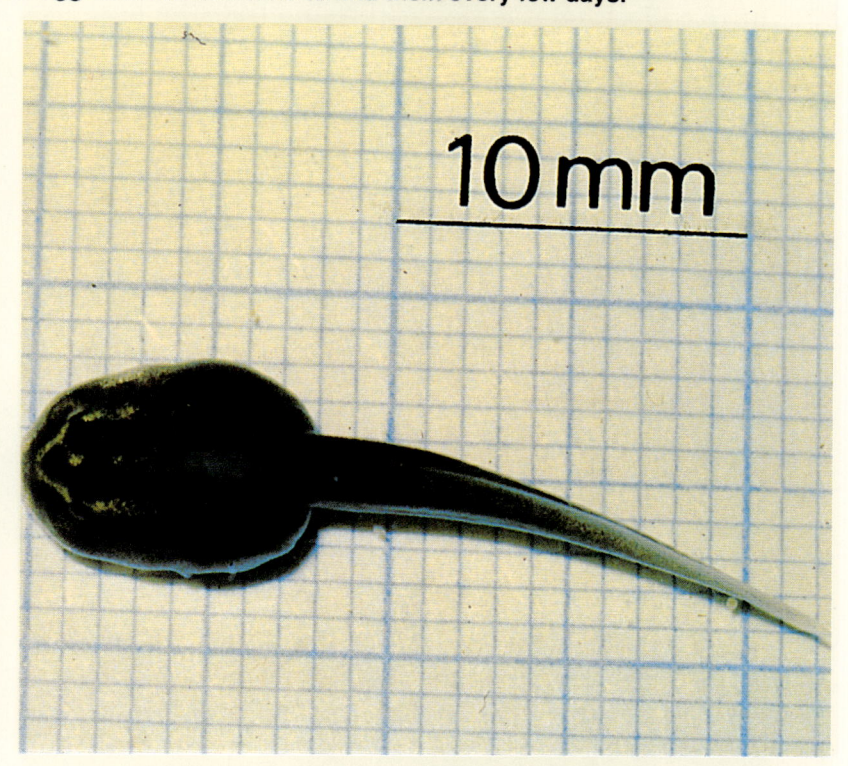

This population has yellow stripes on the head in the tadpole. The metamorphosing and metamorphosed froglets at shown at the bottom. All photos by R. Bechter.

Other Dendrobates

At the time of writing there are some 26 species recognized in the genus *Dendrobates*, eight of which we have discussed in some detail, so here we'll talk a bit about the remaining 18. Though a few of these are kept and bred on occasion, none could be considered common in the terrarium hobby...yet.

Remember that externally most species of *Dendrobates* can be recognized by the combination of greatly expanded toe discs and the first finger shorter than the second. From *Minyobates*, which shares these characters, most *Dendrobates* can be distinguished by larger adult size, usually 20 to 50 mm, though this is not always the case, so color patterns must be relied upon.

POLKA-DOT POISON FROG
Dendrobates arboreus

Tropical frogs that live high in trees always are difficult to collect, so it is not surprising that the first specimens of this arboreal species (an exception

General distribution of *Dendrobates arboreus*, the Polka-dot Poison Frog.

Dendrobates arboreus, the Polka-dot Poison Frog.

among the normally terrestrial poison frogs) were not discovered until 1981, when pipeline construction in western Panama brought the first specimens to the attention of Victor Martinez. Later collecting showed the species to be relatively common in cloud forests of western Panama and even to be present in the Atlantic coastal lowlands. The species lives in association with bromeliad funnels usually more than 10 meters above the ground; it is seldom found on the ground unless its tree has been cut or knocked down. The entire life history probably centers around the bromeliads, though no tadpoles were found in natural situations.

This little (20-22 mm) bronzy-brown poison frog is distinctive in being covered with small, irregularly spaced, round yellow spots both on the back and the belly. (At least some juveniles have the yellow replaced by blue.) The finger discs are greatly expanded, and structurally the species is similar to the Harlequin and Strawberry Poison Frogs. *Dendrobates mysteriosus* has a similar pattern (though the life color is reddish with white spots) but is larger and has white fingertips. *Epipedobates maculatus* also is spotted (perhaps in yellow) above but apparently is brown below; it has a very different hand and many other structural differences. The female seems to display interest in a calling male by stroking his snout and then performing a long (20 minutes) routine of circling in place while drumming with both front and hind feet. In captivity specimens mated vent-to-vent and did not display amplexus. (Aggressive behavior included head-grasping, sometimes interpreted as a remnant of cephalic amplexus.) Clutches of four to eight eggs were laid on bromeliad leaves away from the wet funnel. If not removed, the eggs were eaten by poison frogs other than the parents. The eggs hatched in 14 days, but the tadpoles never fed and died before metamorphosis; they may require food eggs. The grayish tadpoles had a depressed head, low dorsal fin, and an unindented oral disc with only two rows of teeth, one above and one below the beaks. Large papillae around the oral disc seem to support relationship with the Harlequin and Strawberry Poison Frogs.

This is one of the most strikingly colored poison frogs, but it probably will prove difficult to breed in captivity if it really requires food eggs. Though common, it is found in areas that are seldom entered, and though it may be very vocal it is difficult to collect.

BIOLAT POISON FROG
Dendrobates biolat

This split of the frogs usually called *D. ventrimaculatus* seems to be typical of Tahuamanu Province, southern Peru. Like its relatives, the arms and legs are covered with small black spots on a metallic bluish green reticulation. The back has three distinct narrow yellow stripes on black, the center one extending over the snout. The dorsolateral stripes curve toward the center just in front of the eyes and join with the middorsal stripe, so the two resulting rectangular black snout spots curve back under the eyes and continue with the black bands on the upper sides. Basically, the frog gives the appearance of having solid black bands separated by narrow yellow stripes; no dorsal spots are present. The bases of the

OTHER DENDROBATES

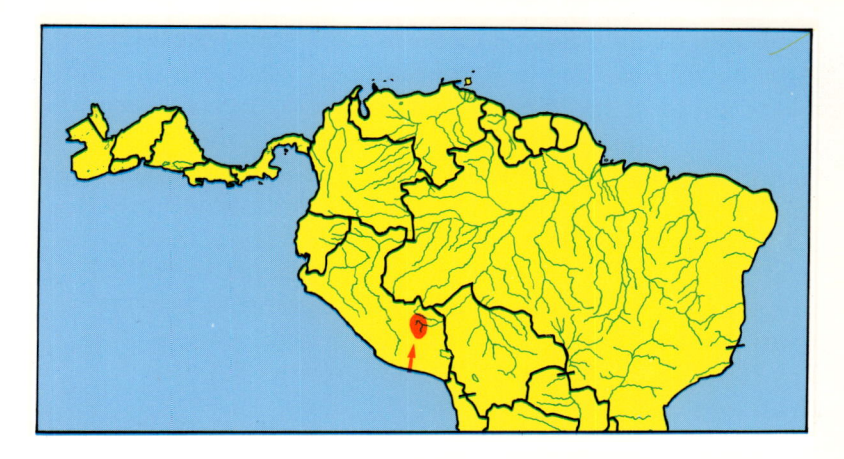

General distribution of *Dendrobates biolat*, the Biolat Poison Frog.

arms and legs are bright yellow (blue in *D. lamasi*). I am not at all sure that it is possible to separate random specimens of this species from variants of *D. imitator, variabilis, lamasi,* and *ventrimaculatus*. The underside is mottled with black as usual, the yellow throat being separated from the yellow belly (bluish white in most other species and populations) by a white chest. The first finger is short and lacks a disc, while the first toe is just a nub. Adults are relatively small, just 15 mm or so in body length.

The Biolat Poison Frog, *Dendrobates biolat*.

Like the other species related to *D. ventrimaculatus*, this is an arboreal species often associated with bromeliad funnels. It is found at about 300 meters elevation and is active during the day. The tadpoles are described as uniformly gray (most other species of this complex have some yellow on the head of the tadpole). The scientific and common names of this species refer to the acronym BIOLAT, standing for the Smithsonian program Biodiversity of Latin America. Photos of terrarium specimens from southern Peru resemble *D. biolat* in many regards, so presumably this species occasionally shows up in the hobby, though virtually impossible to identify. The last word has not yet been written on speciation in the frogs related to *D. ventrimaculatus*, and I am sure that several researchers currently are planning on even more changes in this group.

This Peruvian poison frog bears a close resemblance to *Dendrobates biolat*, though it differs a bit in the pattern on the sides. Photo by A. v. d. Nieuwenhuizen.

RIO SANTIAGO POISON FROG
Dendrobates captivus

Apparently this species has not been seen since the type specimens were taken in the 1920's in the Rio Maranon drainage of Peru. Life colors are not known, but the pattern is quite distinctive. A tiny species, adult males are only 14.6 to 15.4 mm long, while females reach almost 16 mm. The skin of the back is smooth, the first toe is shorter than the second, the finger discs are greatly expanded, and teeth are absent. The hand is considerably smaller overall than most *D. quinquevittatus* complex species, so it presumably is not a frog to be looked for in bromeliads on tall trees. This is a brown frog above and below, with possibly yellowish or white spots (life colors are unknown, as I mentioned, but the possibly related *D. mysteriosus* has white spots and the somewhat similar *D. vanzolinii* and *D. castaneoticus* have yellow and white spots respectively). The spots of the back are round to elongated and tend to form two rows, one on each side of the back. Each row

General distribution of the Rio Santiago Poison Frog, *Dendrobates captivus*.

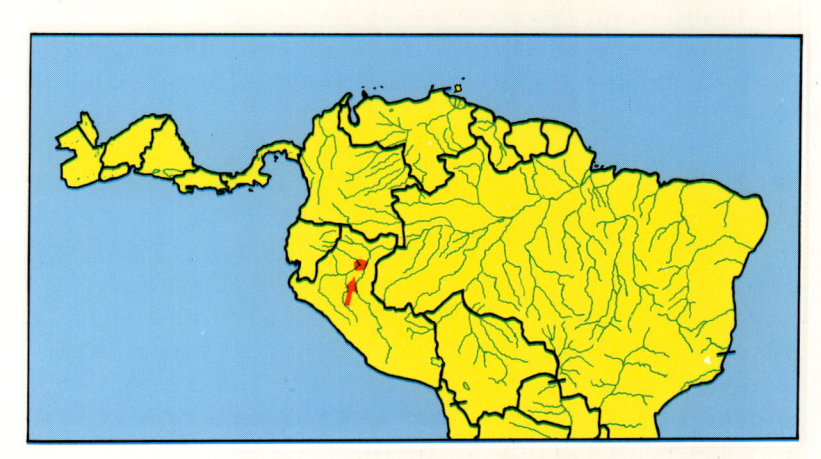

OTHER DENDROBATES

The Rio Santiago Poison Frog, *Dendrobates captivus*. This frog is unknown in life and the colors are a guess based on similar species.

ends in a small spot above the thigh and starts with one in front of the eye. There are conspicuous spots (perhaps bright yellow "flash marks") at the base of the arm and on the top of the thigh. The belly is brown with large irregular bright spots (perhaps yellow or white), including one under the chin and one rather large spot under each thigh. Though this species has been placed in a group with *D. mysteriosus*, a much larger frog with granular skin, it looks a lot like *D. castaneoticus* at first glance, though that species has spots or short bands down the center of the back and has much orange under the legs, including a large spot under the shank. The two species share the presence of bright spots at the arm bases and on the thighs, a bright spot under the chin, and a dorsally spotted pattern, while lacking reticulated arms and legs. *D. vanzolinii* has spots on the back but has reticulated arms and legs. It will be curious to see just what colors are present in living *D. captivus* when it is rediscovered, assuming it is not extinct. Because poison frogs change colors so drastically in preservative, it really isn't possible to do more than guess at life colors, and we know that closely related species often differ greatly in colors even if similar in pattern. The Rio Santiago valley, the type-locality, was described as a level plain with isolated hills. In the 1920's the valley was uninhabited and heavily forested. The frogs were taken with one of the varieties of *D. ventrimaculatus* by the collector, Harvey Bassler (as in *Epipedobates bassleri*).

BRAZIL-NUT POISON FROG
Dendrobates castaneoticus

One of the most striking *Dendrobates* species to be described in recent years, *D. castaneoticus* has a pattern of small scattered white spots on a glossy black back and large bright orange spots at the arm insertions and on the legs. The white spots may appear as remnants of three lines in some specimens, and the orange spots on the hind legs are paired so they appear as a single large orange spot when the legs are folded. The belly is blackish with less distinct white spots or mottling. There is an orange calf spot under the shank of the leg. There is no inner metacarpal tubercle (at the base of the first finger), an unusual character in *Dendrobates*. This small (18 to 23 mm, females about 2.5 mm longer than males) frog appears to be rare or at least difficult to collect but may be widely distributed because it is known from two localities in Para State, Brazil, almost 300 km (180 miles) apart, in the Xingu and Tapajos drainages.

D. castaneoticus is a typical ground-litter dweller in humid rainforest areas. Adults seldom were collected more than 1 or 2 meters above the ground and were active during the day. Clutches of probably one to six eggs are produced. The tadpoles are transferred to any available water bodies for raising, especially the husks of Brazil-nuts (*Bertholletia*) lying on the forest

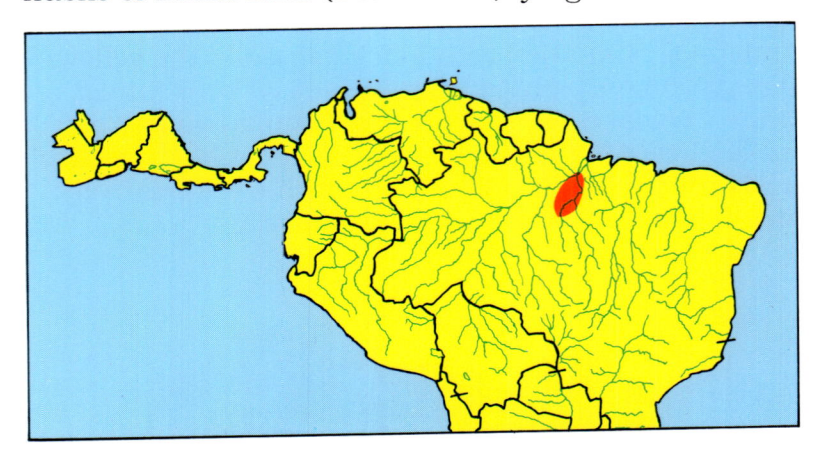

General distribution of *Dendrobates castaneoticus*, the Brazil-nut Poison Frog.

floor, and have been found growing there along with the tadpoles of *E. femoralis* and *Colostethus marchesianus*. All apparently feed on mosquito larvae. The closest relative of the Brazil-nut Poison Frog may be *D. quinquevittatus* in the restricted sense because both lack the inner metacarpal tubercle, but the color pattern is so distinctive that identification should not present a problem. Only *D. vanzolinii* has a similar body pattern of black background with rows of white spots, but it has reticulated arms and legs and lacks the bright orange "flash marks" on the thigh. Possible relationships and similarities to *D. captivus* are discussed under that species.

Dendrobates castaneoticus, the Brazil-nut Poison Frog.

OTHER *DENDROBATES*

RED-HEADED POISON FROG
Dendrobates fantasticus **(see page 174 for distribution map)**

A good alternative name for this poison frog might be Crowned Poison Frog, but certainly Red-headed also is descriptive. This relative of *D. ventrimaculatus* and *D. reticulatus* possesses features of both. In adults the posterior half or so of the back is almost black, being covered by irregular black blotches separated at best by narrow wriggly yellowish to whitish lines. The front half of the back is yellow-orange, usually with a pair of connected black spots between the eyes, the crown. The arms and legs are reticulated with bluish or golden white and black spots, while the belly is typically covered with irregular black spots on a bluish white ground, the throat yellow with black spots. There is a tendency for some males to have only two very large rounded spots on the throat on a pale creamy yellow background, with traces of a yellow-orange spot on the chin. Such males may have the chest and belly spotting enlarged and fused as well. The first finger and toe are short and discless, the back is smooth or nearly so, and teeth are absent.

Only two other species of the *D. ventrimaculatus* complex are orange on the back: *D. sirensis*, which lacks traces of reticulation on the legs and arms; and *D. reticulatus*, which has the entire back bright orange, has the belly finely reticulated, and has the chin with a bright orange spot. There are variants of *D. fantasticus* that seem to grade into more typical *D. ventrimaculatus*, however.

Like most similar species, *D. fantasticus* is a rather small (16 mm or so) species typically found in and near bromeliads in tall trees of the dense Peruvian rainforest. Its range apparently is centered in the Province of San Martin on the eastern slopes of the Andes at 500 to 800 meters elevation. Sympatric with *D. imitator* and several other related species, its natural breeding habits are similar to theirs. Males call from a selected territory near a bromeliad funnel, a female is attracted and then led to a funnel of the male's choice (apparently, though females may refuse his first few choices), where she lays three or four eggs on the leaf. The eggs hatch in about 14 days and are carried by the male to individual bromeliad funnels. In nature the male may tend the bower only for the first few days and return only when the eggs are ready to hatch. The tadpoles are carnivorous and eat almost anything that falls into the funnel, so they will take bloodworms and tubifex in the terrarium. Persistent hobbyist reports that food eggs are necessary for full development may or may not be true, but clutches of tads seem to mature without them. Metamorphosis occurs in about three months. Mortality rates are high, and the tadpoles and froglets do not have a good record in the terrarium. Young froglets are dull orange-bronze in front with separate brownish spots posteriorly, but after about a month they develop the full adult pattern.

These delicate little frogs are not common in the hobby and seldom are imported or bred. They also appear to be uncommon in nature, but this could be a reflection of their tree-dwelling habits. An interesting but obscure species for the specialist.

This Red-headed Poison Frog, *Dendrobates fantasticus*, has the "crown" reduced to two large spots by the eyes and has the head only a deep golden yellow. Photo by R. Bechter.

OTHER DENDROBATES

The very irregular pattern of the lower back of *Dendrobates fantasticus*, the Red-headed Poison Frog, is characteristic of the species and develops shortly after metamorphosis. Photo by R. Bechter.

Specimens of the Red-headed Poison Frog, *Dendrobates fantasticus*, from San Martin, Peru. All lack the red head but have variations of the black crown. Notice the varying development of the broad black band across the midback. All photos by A. v. d. Nieuwenhuizen.

OTHER *DENDROBATES*

Dendrobates fantasticus typically has two large black spots at the lower angles of the throat, a good mark for the species if all else fails. However, the spots are not always present—look at the frog at the upper left on page 171. Photo by A. v. d. Nieuwenhuizen.

OTHER *DENDROBATES*

This San Martin, Peru, specimen of *Dendrobates fantasticus* shows an exaggerated crown with long posterior extensions. Additionally, the black of the lower back is almost solid. Photo by A. v. d. Nieuwenhuizen.

OTHER DENDROBATES

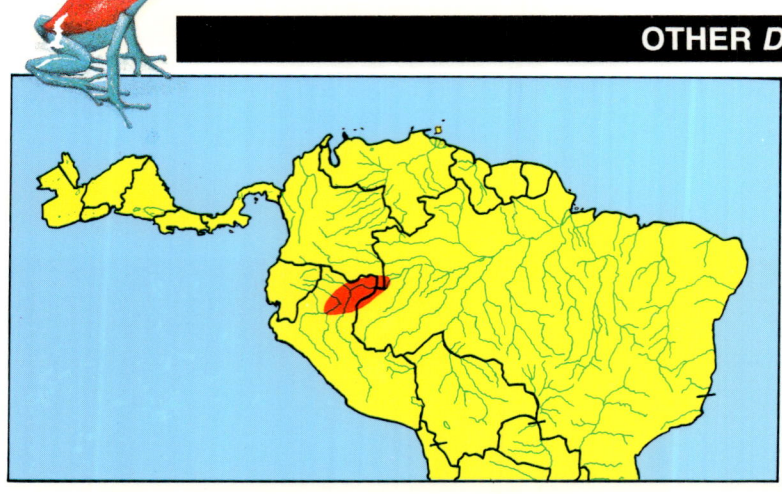

General distribution of the Red-headed Poison Frog, *Dendrobates fantasticus*.

Dendrobates galactonotus, the Splash-backed Poison Frog.

General distribution of the Splash-backed Poison Frog, *Dendrobates galactonotus*.

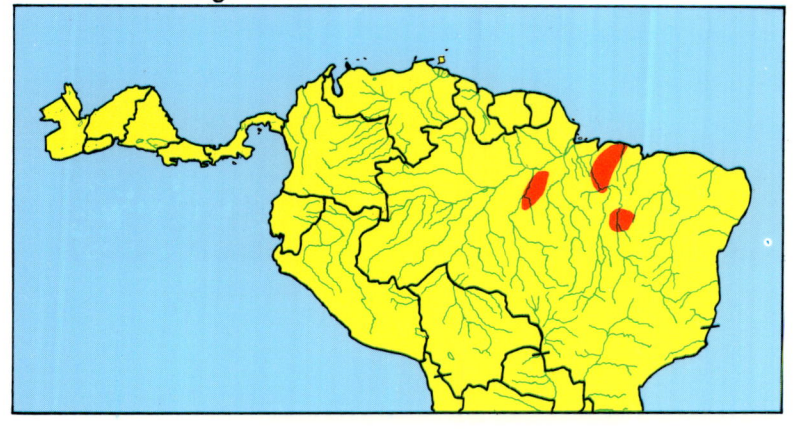

SPLASH-BACKED POISON FROG
Dendrobates galactonotus

At 30 to 40 mm in adult length, the Splash-backed Poison Frog is a moderately large species closely related to *D. auratus* and *tinctorius*. Basically this is a yellow and black poison frog with smooth skin and a well-developed tarsal tubercle (the tubercle is absent in its close relatives). The belly is uniformly glossy black, while the limbs may vary through black, black with yellow spots, and mostly yellow. The back may vary from entirely bright yellow through mostly yellow with large or small black spots to almost all black with irregular yellow spots and splotches. It never has the regularity of pattern seen in *D. tinctorius*, however. Though poorly known, its range seems to be entirely south of the Amazon in Goias, Maranhao, and Para States, Brazil.

A dweller in the ground litter, this species has for some reason not entered the terrarium hobby, though it seems likely that it would be kept much like *D. tinctorius*. It is a resident of lowland humid rainforests and, like most poison frogs, feeds largely on ants, tiny beetles, and mites in nature.

MIMIC POISON FROG
Dendrobates imitator

The Mimic Poison Frog is another in the seemingly endless series of species related to *D. ventrimaculatus* and sharing with it arms and legs covered with black spots on a bluish white to greenish network. In the Mimic the back is covered with relatively large and somewhat squarish black spots on an often metallic green (but also yellow and even pale orange) background. Traces of the middorsal stripe extend forward between the eyes and cut off a pair of rather squarish black snout spots, the major character of the species that distinguishes it from more typical *D. ventrimaculatus* and the form known as *D. variabilis*, which tend to have a single round spot over the snout. *D. biolat* also has a pair of black snout spots,

A very iridescent bronzy specimen of the Mimic Poison Frog, *Dendrobates imitator*. Photo by A. v. d. Nieuwenhuizen.

OTHER *DENDROBATES*

In ventral view *Dendrobates imitator* usually has two very large black spots at the back corners of the throat (as in *D. fantasticus* and some *D. ventrimaculatus*), while the belly often is extensively yellow. Photo by A. v. d. Nieuwenhuizen.

OTHER *DENDROBATES*

Though very variable in color and details of pattern, the regular and squarish spots on the back in combination with two squarish spots on the snout are marks of *Dendrobates imitator*, the Mimic Poison Frog. Photo by A. v. d. Nieuwenhuizen.

but they extend back through the eye and the rest of the back pattern is of long black blotches and not spots. The throat is yellow, the belly yellow or white, both with black spots as usual (the throat spots of *D. imitator* may be very large and paired). The first toe is described as relatively large, longer that that of *D. ventrimaculatus*, but this character varies considerably from species to species of the complex.

Another species of the dense wet rainforests of Peru, especially the northeastern part of the country,

This *Dendrobates imitator* has the yellow of the throat fading rapidly below the chest so the belly is mostly bluish. Also, the central black spot on the throat displayed by the specimen on page 175 is absent. Photo by A. v. d. Nieuwenhuizen.

males are associated with bromeliads as usual. A female attracted to a male's call follows him to a laying site, which in this case tends to be a nearly vertical surface such as a hanging leaf or even the shaded side of the terrarium. This preference for a vertical surface is seemingly unique in the poison frogs. The female lays three to five eggs in an exceptionally tough and adhesive gel that instantly sticks to the leaf so the eggs will not slide off. The male at least sometimes fertilizes the clutch after the female lays, but other times (different populations?) he fertilizes each egg as it is laid. In some spawnings the male and female circle each other repeatedly in slow motion before laying, but in other matings the frogs just do a bit of nudging and stroking. Very elaborate courtships have been described for this species, but they either do not occur in all frogs or require very careful and patient observation to be seen.

The eggs hatch in about two weeks and are taken to individual bromeliad funnels by the male. They are larger than the tadpoles of at least some related species, are carnivorous, and will take the usual bloodworms, etc. Again there is conflict about feeding, as some frogs apparently produce food eggs

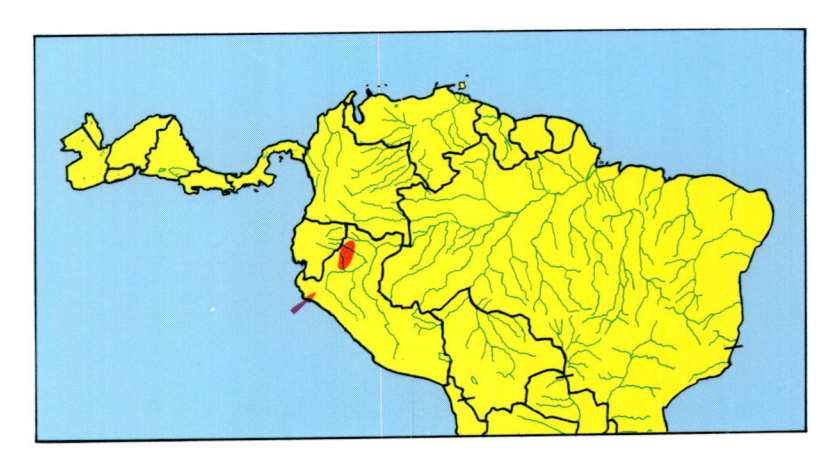

General distribution of *Dendrobates imitator*, the Mimic Poison Frog.

to feed the tadpoles. In these cases the male supposedly stations himself near a tadpole in a funnel and attracts a female with his call, then induces her to lay one or several eggs directly into the funnel. Supposedly he even fertilizes the eggs and if uneaten they may develop into tadpoles. Such behavior seems extremely haphazard and perhaps is more the result of crowding in the terrarium than a natural behavior. Much more research on natural matings and tadpole-raising behavior is required but is difficult because of the habits of the frog. Metamorphosis occurs in about ten weeks in the terrarium. The froglets are quite large relative to the adults and have a fully developed pattern.

The Mimic Poison Frog is quite popular in Germany and often is bred in captivity, but it seldom is available in the United States. Perhaps it is just too small and shy (in a heavily planted tall terrarium it might be seen only if you go looking for it) for American tastes. Additionally, to most hobbyists it looks just like a *D. ventrimaculatus*, so why bother.

Variation and egg care in the Mimic Poison Frog, *Dendrobates imitator*. Notice the differences in spotting pattern and even in general background color from specimens shown on earlier pages. This frog lays highly adhesive eggs attached to vertical surfaces. All photos by R. Bechter.

OTHER *DENDROBATES*

Though probably a variant of *Dendrobates imitator*, this Peruvian poison frog bears more than a passing resemblance to *Dendrobates lamasi* in head and body pattern. However, there are differences in details of spotting pattern and in the yellow versus blue base of the arm. Without call records and knowledge of foot structure as well as ventral pattern, a positive identification probably is impossible. Photo by A. v. d. Nieuwenhuizen.

OTHER *DENDROBATES*

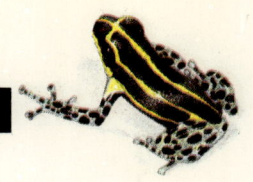

A Mimic Poison Frog, *Dendrobates imitator*, with a very irregular back pattern. Photo by A. Kerstitch.

A head-on view of *Dendrobates imitator* showing a beautiful bronzy green color. Photo by A. v. d. Nieuwenhuizen.

Two fighting specimens of *Dendrobates imitator*. Photo by A. Kerstitch.

Dendrobates lamasi, the Pasco Poison Frog.

PASCO POISON FROG
Dendrobates lamasi

Another "peas in a pod" species related to *D. ventrimaculatus*, the Pasco Poison Frog occurs in the vicinity of Tingo Maria in central Peru east of the Andes. Elevations range from about 300 to 700 meters, and it inhabits the typical dense wet rainforests, frequenting bromeliad funnels. Adults are about 16 to 18 mm long, about typical for most similar species. The legs and arms are covered with black spots on a bluish white or golden white reticulated background, a sign of a species related to *D. ventrimaculatus*. In most species of this group the

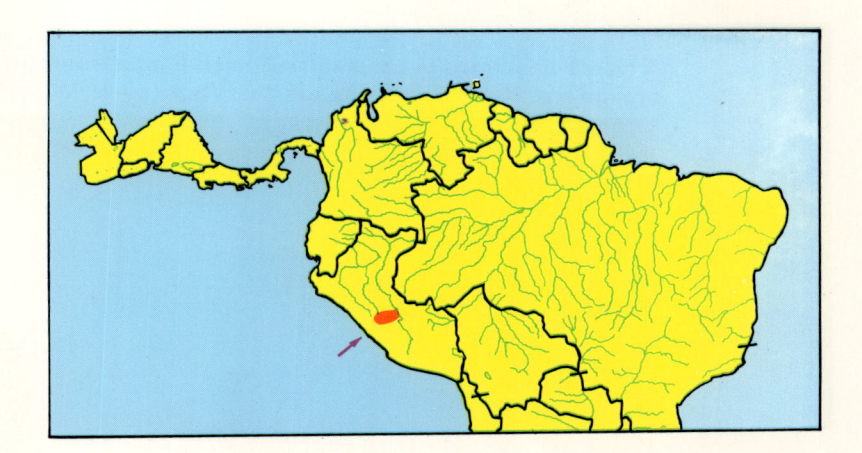

General distribution of the Pasco Poison Frog, *Dendrobates lamasi*.

base of the arm is yellow, but in *D. lamasi* it is bright blue. The back pattern is fairly complex, with two broad black bands running back from the eyes to over the hump of the back, where it is broken by a golden stripe that runs from side to side. The middorsal yellow stripe forms a T just in front of the eyes, isolating a broad black snout spot that is separated from the eyes in front by thin yellow vertical lines. As usual, the underside has black spots and mottling on pale, the throat and belly being yellow, the chest band being white. The first finger is fairly long and lacks a disc, while the first toe is slender but only somewhat shorter than normal and also lacks a disc. The completely black snout is

OTHER DENDROBATES

unusual, as is the blue arm base. In most other species with similar arms and legs the belly is white rather than yellow. Whether the pattern is constant enough to allow the frog to be identified in terrarium specimens from unknown localities is uncertain. Detailed analysis of the calls of the males seems to be necessary for accurate identification of species in this group, so hobbyists are out of luck. Besides, the taxonomy is sure to change again shortly.

Like related species, *D. lamasi* is arboreal and associated with bromeliads, forming territories near the water-filled funnels. The tadpoles have yellow areas on the head. There seems to be no information on raising this species (as compared to the more common Y-backed *D. ventrimaculatus* form).

LEHMANN'S POISON FROG
Dendrobates lehmanni

The Harlequin Poison Frog is one of the most variable of frogs, and there is no doubt that Lehmann's Poison Frog is closely related to *D. histrionicus*. Seemingly restricted to the Anchicaya Valley near Dagua, Colombia, this relatively large (31 to 36 mm, males and female about the same size) black and orange poison frog first came to scientific attention through specimens collected for the pet trade. The skin is smooth, the first finger is slightly shorter than the second, and histrionicotoxins are absent (present in *D. histrionicus*). Basically it is a glossy black frog encircled by two broad bright orange bands, one behind the head and the other over the hump of the back. The orange bands often are irregularly broken by black. The pattern continues across the belly, though it may be quite irregular there. The arms are encircled by orange, as are the legs. Usually the fingertips are shiny silver to white, a good character to distinguish questionable specimens from *D. histrionicus*. Yellow may replace the orange in some specimens.

D. lehmanni will breed with *D. histrionicus* in captivity and produce viable eggs. Other than the difference in skin toxins, Lehmann's Poison Frog actually is no more different from typical Harlequins than are many other populations, and the recognition of *D. lehmanni* as a species has been questioned repeatedly. Tadpoles require food eggs.

At the type-locality it is common but hard to collect because of dense plant growth and rather steep

General distribution of Lehmann's Poison Frog, *Dendrobates lehmanni*.

A typical specimen of Lehmann's Poison Frog, *Dendrobates lehmanni*, showing the broad black banding on bright orange and the brilliant white toe tips. Photo by W. Mudrack.

180

OTHER DENDROBATES

terrain. It is found at elevations between about 850 and 1200 meters and is active during the day. Though usually found on the ground, it has been seen over 2 meters up in the trees and vines. Mating behavior is like that of *D. histrionicus*, and the tadpoles require food eggs or a good substitute to develop. Imported specimens are bad buys and virtually always die after a few weeks. They are delicate and usually injured, and may be parasitized as well. They seldom feed, especially on the adult crickets that some pet shops seem to feel are appropriate food. A species strictly for the specialist if captive-bred specimens are available—not suitable for beginners no matter how beautiful the frogs look or how cheap they may be if wild-caught. Fortunately, during the last few years the species has been imported less and less, so today wild-caught specimens are a rarity.

Though originally known only from a single valley in Colombia, recent importations of Lehmann's Poison Frog, *Dendrobates lehmanni*, have included specimens quite different in color and pattern from typical specimens. Perhaps they are coming from a new locality, or the pattern could be changing in the single described population. Photo by M. Panzella.

181

Often it is difficult to distinguish between *Dendrobates lehmanni* **and** *D. histrionicus* **on the basis of color and pattern. The specimen at the top left definitely is a Harlequin Poison Frog, while the others all appear to be Lehmann's Poison Frog, even the yellow specimens. The froglet at lower right was the first one raised on egg yolk in captivity. All photos by R. Bechter.**

Look at the toe tips! The top four frogs all are *Dendrobates lehmanni* with characteristic white toe tips, while the Valley form of *Dendrobates histrionicus* at the bottom has black toes. The damaged snout of a specimen at upper right is typical of damage inflicted during shipment and may be fatal. All photos by A. v. d. Nieuwenhuizen.

Two specimens of *Dendrobates histrionicus* (top right, center left) compared to typical orange and the new yellow color forms of *Dendrobates lehmanni*. Notice that the lower left specimen is very similar to the bull's-eye morph of the Harlequin Poison Frog. All photos by A. v. d. Nieuwenhuizen.

All six specimens on this page are said to be from a locality between the type-locality of *Dendrobates lehmanni* and one with only typical *D. histrionicus*. They vary from typical large yellow-spotted Harlequins to silver toe tip Lehmann's. Without an analysis of the skin toxins it is not possible to understand the variation in this population. All photos by R. Bechter.

OTHER *DENDROBATES*

Once Lehmann's Poison Frog, *Dendrobates lehmanni*, was imported in large numbers, but almost all died within a few months. This is a very delicate frog that is not suitable for the typical hobbyist and probably not even for the advanced poison frog specialist. Currently they appear to be absent from the market, but who can tell what tomorrow will bring. Photo by M. Panzella.

OTHER *DENDROBATES*

The Maranon Poison Frog, *Dendrobates mysteriosus*.

MARANON POISON FROG
Dendrobates mysteriosus

The mysterious poison frog of the Maranon is no longer a mystery! Described from a single immature specimen taken in 1929 from near Santa Rosa, Dept. Cajamarca, Peru, its life colors were unknown. In 1989, Rainer Schulte and party rediscovered the species near the type locality in the Cordillera del Condor area at 600 to 1200 meters elevation. Surprisingly, it turns out to be a fairly large species (adults to at last 27 mm body length) that is typical of dry scrub forest with numbers of spiny bromeliads of the genus *Aechmea* (relatives of a common houseplant) and is arboreal.

The Maranon Poison Frog is a granular-skinned species that is reddish brown to cinnamon red above and below, covered on all surfaces, including the belly and limbs, with large, relatively regular, shining white spots. The fingers and toes also are shiny white. In color and pattern it is one of the most distinctive poison frogs, and when the coloration is combined with the granular skin and typical characters of the genus *Dendrobates*, it becomes unique. Though placed in a group with *D. captivus*, to me the relationship seems remote now that adults of *D. mysteriosus* are known—the two species differ in size, skin texture, and color pattern. The pattern of the Maranon Poison Frog (and its lack of an omosternum) is matched to some extent by some populations of *D. histrionicus*, though that species never (?) has white spots and white toes (but see *D. lehmanni* for the white toes); however, the oral discs of the tadpoles of the two species are very different and would seem to preclude any close relationship.

As mentioned, *D. mysteriosus* lives in a relatively dry, scrubby forest of the type where most of the plants have spines. The area sees a wide variation in temperatures, from about 13 to 32°C, and the humidity is not nearly as high as in most poison frog habitats. The frog usually is found in the axils of the leaves of the spiny bromeliad *Aechmea*, where it spends its entire life as much as 10 meters above the ground. Tarantulas, crickets, springtails, and ants share its habitat, the ants and springtails serving as food. Males call to receptive females and then lead the chosen mate to spawn on a bromeliad leaf. Courtship may include the frogs slowly circling around each other and much stroking and nudging. Typically fertilization is vent-to-vent, each egg being fertilized as it is laid. Clutches number up to 12 eggs that hatch in about two weeks. The tadpoles survived in captivity on flake fish foods and probably take mosquito larvae in nature, such larvae being common in bromeliad funnels. The oral disc is fringed by a single row of small pointed papillae, with a large gap over much of the anterior edge of the disc and a small gap at the center of the posterior edge. There are two rows of teeth (one split) above the beaks and three rows (one

Tadpoles and oral discs of *Dendrobates histrionicus* (above) and *Dendrobates mysteriosus* (below). Major differences in the oral discs of these two species seem to indicate they are not closely related.

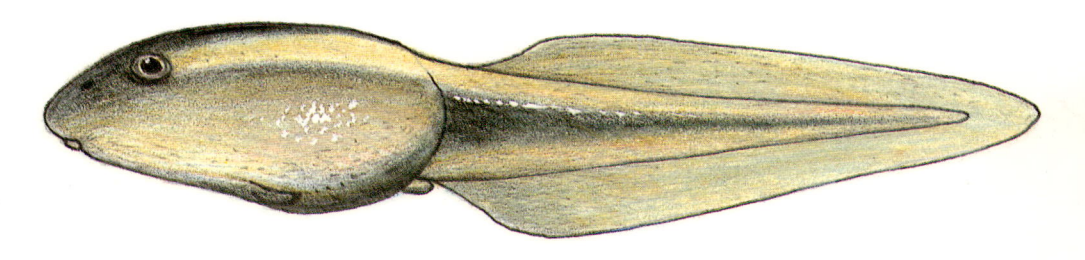

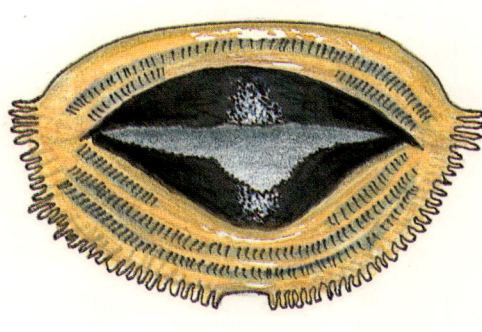

OTHER DENDROBATES

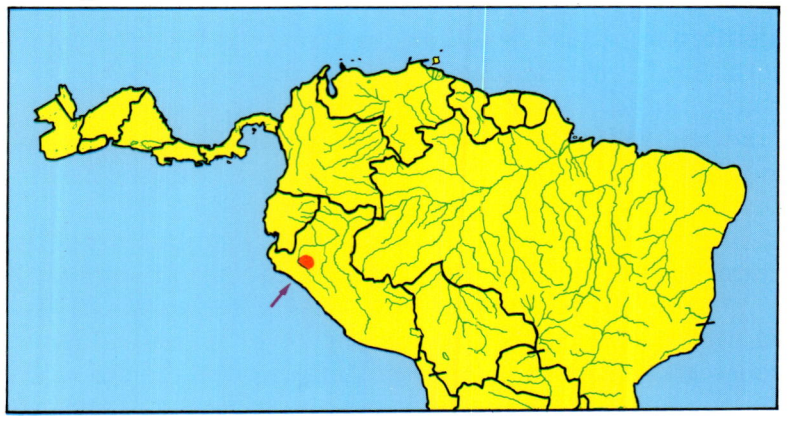

General distribution of *Dendrobates mysteriosus*, the Maranon Poison Frog.

split) below. Metamorphosis occurs about four months after hatching, at least in captivity on artificial foods. Late tadpoles may show hints of the adult color pattern.

D. mysteriosus would seem to make an excellent pet if it were to become available, and it should be very adaptable to terrarium conditions. Its home is much drier than that of almost all other poison frogs and subject to considerable variations in temperature, points in favor of any frog in captivity. The remote and restricted range will limit its availability for a long time, however.

LA BREA POISON FROG
Dendrobates occultator

Known only from the type-locality near the Colombian town of La Brea in the Rio Patia drainage at about 50 meters elevation and from the nearby Quebrada Guangui at 200 meters, *D. occultator* is a shy and poorly understood species that is some 25 to 27 mm long as an adult. It is closely related to *D. histrionicus* in structure (including absence of an omosternum) but has a unique color pattern. The back is uniformly bright red, the red extending into the bases of the arms and legs. The rest of the body, including the belly and limbs, is black, but the sides and belly are covered with a pattern of small (on the sides) to large (on the belly) bright yellow spots. The belly spots may fuse in various ways to produce a nearly solid yellow belly in stark contrast to the yellow-spotted sides and bright red back. The finger

The La Brea Poison Frog, *Dendrobates occultator*.

and toe tips may be somewhat white but not as contrasting as in *D. lehmanni*. This must be a beautiful frog in life, but unfortunately it is not available. *D. occultator* occurs with frogs that definitely can be assigned to *D. histrionicus*, so it cannot be a variety of that species. Additionally, it differs in details of skin toxins from *D. histrionicus*, further proof that it is a full species. The pattern is not matched by any known Harlequin Poison Frog population or, for that matter, any other described poison frog.

The La Brea Poison Frog appears to be more arboreal than the Harlequin, often calling at 1.5 to 3 meters above the ground. The lowland rainforest in which it was found was unusually wet, with swampy areas of standing water. The frogs called from the cover of dense growths of vines and other epiphytes on

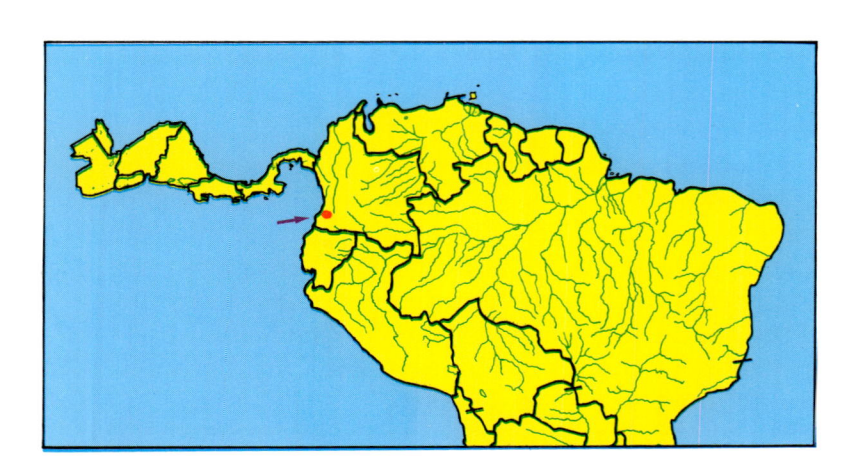

General distribution of *Dendrobates occultator*, the La Brea Poison Frog.

the trees. Two males were found wrestling on the ground. The species appears to be uncommon to rare in the two known localities, and at Quebrada Guangui a party of herpetologists failed to collect any during a two-week stay even though local Amerindians had collected ten specimens previously. Nothing seems to be recorded about its reproduction in nature or captivity, though it is assumed that the tadpoles would require food eggs and would be placed in individual bromeliad funnels or similar water bodies.

RIO MADEIRA POISON FROG
Dendrobates quinquevittatus

The terrarium (and scientific) literature is filled with references to *D. quinquevittatus*, but as currently used that name must be restricted to an uncommon species apparently restricted to the Rio Madeira drainage in Rondonia and probably surrounding areas of western Brazil. At 17 to 20 mm in adult length (females larger than males), this is one of the smaller *Dendrobates* species, well within the size range of *Minyobates* species. Like *D. castaneoticus*, it lacks a tubercle at the base of the first finger (the inner metacarpal tubercle), but the color pattern is quite distinctive. The black back has three narrow bluish white to greenish white stripes and there also is a similar stripe low on each side above the belly. The belly itself is bluish white with large black spots, while the throat and chest stripe are yellow. Most distinctively, the arms and legs are entirely dull orange with a few small,

OTHER DENDROBATES

The true Dendrobates quinquevittatus, the Rio Madeira Poison Frog.

distinct round spots widely scattered over the limbs. Rather indistinct yellow "flash marks" are at the insertions of all four limbs.

A typical poison frog of lowland rainforests, its tadpoles are transported to any available water container on the forest floor, from water-filled holes in logs to the husks of Brazil-nuts. It appears to be uncommon and is difficult to collect though active during the day.

General distribution of Dendrobates quinquevittatus, the Rio Madeira Poison Frog.

There is little doubt that D. quinquevittatus is closely related to D. ventrimaculatus, the species actually present in the hobby, and some specimens intermediate in pattern have been collected. The entire cluster of species with spotted hind legs and striped backs is poorly understood and names are certain to change. See the discussion of D. ventrimaculatus for a more complete survey of the problem. For the moment, the Rio Madeira Poison Frog can be distinguished from its relatives by the sparsely spotted orange legs with traces of "flash marks" at the insertions of the limbs. There is no reason to assume that this frog would be any different from D. ventrimaculatus in keepability if it were to become available.

RED-BACKED POISON FROG
Dendrobates reticulatus

This beautiful little (14 to 16 mm in adults, females a bit larger than males) poison frog is one of the most easily recognized species yet for years it was put as a synonym of D. quinquevittatus. There is no doubt that it is related to the D. ventrimaculatus complex of species, and in many ways it is intermediate between D. fantasticus and D. sirensis. The upper back, including the head, is bright orange, surrounded by a brilliant reticulation of black spots (often fairly large) on a blue-green to greenish white background. This reticulation continues over the rump and the limbs and also occupies the belly. The reticulated or finely spotted belly is a very unusual character is this group of species. There usually are no markings on the orange back, though occasional specimens show small scratch-like black specks and

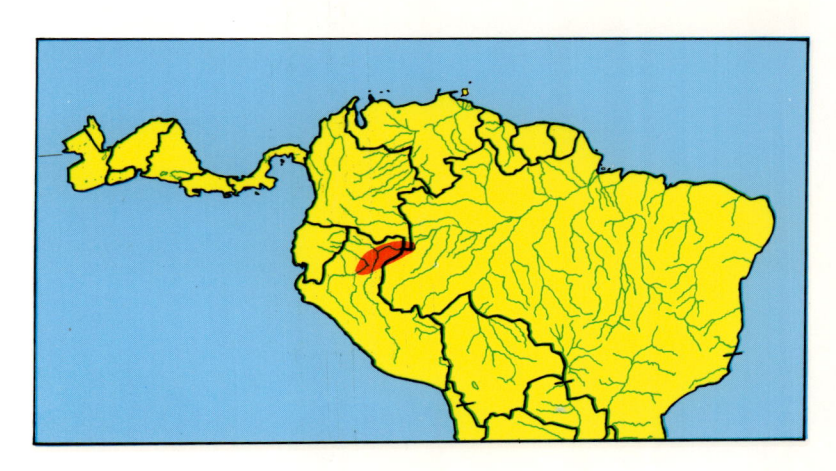

General distribution of the Red-backed Poison Frog, Dendrobates reticulatus.

young frogs may show traces of two black bands. There are no traces of the "crown" of D. fantasticus, which has a more normally patterned and colored belly. As a final touch, the chin of D. reticulatus is marked with a large bright orange spot of nearly the same intensity as the back, a feature shared (to some

The bright colors and tiny size of the Red-backed Poison Frog, Dendrobates reticulatus, make it a true jewel of the rainforest. Photo by R. D. Bartlett.

189

OTHER *DENDROBATES*

A very arboreal species that frequents bromeliads and other epiphytes, the Red-backed Poison Frog, *Dendrobates reticulatus*, long has been a coveted frog among European hobbyists. Though bred in small numbers, it is delicate and not that easy to keep. Recently numbers of captive-bred (apparently) specimens have appeared on the American market, but their small size works against their increased popularity. Photos by R. Bechter.

extent) only by *D. sirensis*, which lacks all traces of the black spots in the network so typical of the Red-backed Poison Frog. Structurally the Red-backed is similar to the average run of *D. ventrimaculatus* species, with short first toe and finger, but the skin of the back often appears more granulate than in typical Amazonian Poison Frogs and relatives. The Red-backed Poison Frog is found with assorted species of the *D. ventrimaculatus* complex and seems to retain its identity, though occasional intermediate specimens of various types are found.

The Red-backed Poison Frog is another species of the wet rainforest of Peru, typically found in the northeastern part of the country at elevations between 400 and 800 meters. It is a tree-dweller, hiding in the dense assemblage of vines, bromeliads, and other epiphytes on tall jungle trees. Specimens usually are found 2 to 6 meters above the ground. Remember this when setting up their terrarium and provide a high cage with lots of cover. Unfortunately, if you provide sufficient cover you will never see your frogs unless you search for them. The humidity should be high and the temperature at the usual 26°C or so during the day, a bit lower at night.

Males call from a selected territory on a leaf or in a bromeliad and attract a female ready to lay. As usual, the female follows the male to a selected laying spot, usually in the axil of bromeliad leaves near a water-filled funnel. Stroking, nudging, and sometimes dancing in small circles occur before the female lays her clutch of two to four eggs, which then are fertilized by the male. The male tends the eggs for at least the first two or three days and returns when they hatch in about 14 days (though there are reports of some clutches hatching in as little as eight days, probably because of higher temperatures). The tadpoles are transported to individual bromeliad funnels or similar containers for raising, where they feed on detritus, algae, mosquito larvae, and whatever else they can catch. There are persistent rumors in the German literature that the tads are given food eggs by the female, but if this occurs at all it does not seem to be necessary for the growth of the tadpoles. Fungus is more of a problem to both the eggs and tadpoles than any other single pest. Transformation takes at least 60 days, often longer if food is marginal. Froglets take a week or more to develop the adult orange back and often show a pair of dorsolateral back stripes made from several large black spots, remnants of the pattern more typical of *D. ventrimaculatus* complex species.

Unfortunately, the Red-backed Poison Frog is too small to appeal to most hobbyists and is not a good display animal. Additionally, like many other related species, adults may be quite aggressive, and the tadpoles have a reputation as cannibals. These are among the many little poison jewels that would be best viewed in nature, but few tourists or even ecotourists are likely to be able to find these shy frogs.

OTHER *DENDROBATES*

Dendrobates reticulatus is closely related to *D. fantasticus* and *D. imitator*, as well as to the average run of *D. ventrimaculatus*-like poison frogs. Notice that the black and pale (usually blue or blue-green) reticulation of the legs extends all along the sides and even onto the lower back. The skin is quite coarse for a small poison frog. Photo by A. v. d. Nieuwenhuizen.

OTHER *DENDROBATES*

This specimen of *Dendrobates reticulatus*, the Red-backed Poison Frog, retains traces of the juvenile markings in the form of large black spots within the red area of the back. In froglets two bands of black spots extend forward to the eyes. Photo by A. v. d. Nieuwenhuizen.

OTHER *DENDROBATES*

The large orange spot on the chin of *Dendrobates reticulatus* is a distinctive character of the species that seemingly is shared only with the rare and poorly known *Dendrobates sirensis*. Photo by A. v. d. Nieuwenhuizen.

OTHER DENDROBATES

Though it is small, the Red-backed Poison Frog is an agile animal that likes to climb and if given a preference seldom will be found on the floor of the terrarium. Photo by A. v. d. Nieuwenhuizen.

OTHER *DENDROBATES*

Dendrobates reticulatus takes the black limb spotting of the *Quinquevittatus*-Group to new highs, the reticulation even including the lips. It seems possible that *Dendrobates sirensis* might be a closely related species differing mostly in having lost all the black spotting of the reticulation, perhaps just a one-gene character. Photo by R. Bechter.

OTHER *DENDROBATES*

Though it seems likely that the Red-backed Poison Frog is common in the appropriate habitats of its Peruvian range, it seldom is collected or even seen even by scientists looking for it. Because it frequents bromeliads and other epiphytes high in the tangled rainforest, it becomes the invisible frog. Photo by A. v. d. Nieuwenhuizen.

OTHER *DENDROBATES*

Dendrobates sirensis, the Sira Poison Frog.

SIRA POISON FROG
Dendrobates sirensis

Found as far as known only in the isolated Serrania de Sira in eastern central Peru, *D. sirensis* is one of the more stunningly colored recently discovered poison frogs. Only 15 to 17 mm in adult length, the slightly granular back is completely dark red, contrasting with bright blue-green arms, legs, and belly. The belly has a small but apparently constant bright red 5 by 3 mm patch, which should help distinguish it from some of the more aberrant phases of *D. pumilio* (which should always have some type of dark dorsal markings and is larger). *D. granuliferus* has much more coarsely granular skin and is larger. The skin toxins have not been analyzed and the tadpoles are unknown, so assignment of this species to *Dendrobates* is something of a guess, as there are no external characters to separate it from species of *Minyobates*, all of which differ in color pattern from *D. sirensis*. The first finger is short and lacks a disc, while the first toe is very short and also lacks a disc, typical of species related to *D. quinquevittatus*. Assigned to the *Quinquevittatus*-Group in the original description, the Sira Poison Frog does bear a certain resemblance to *D. reticulatus*, if you can imagine a *reticulatus* in which the black spots on the legs, arms, and belly have all disappeared and the red of the back has expanded to cover the entire dorsal surface. This possible relationship might also be indicated by the presence of a dark red chin in *D. sirensis*, a typical character of *D. reticulatus*. However, the omosternum was described as absent in *D. sirensis* (checked by dissection), a condition otherwise typical of the *Histrionicus*-Group and *D. leucomelas*, but not typical of species related to *D. quinquevittatus*.

Known only from near the type-locality at 750 to 1560 meters, this is an active little species that is out and about during the daytime. Apparently very uncommon, it has been found on the ground and on low trees over a meter from the ground near streams. There probably are only two eggs in a clutch, but virtually nothing really is known of its biology. Only five specimens were taken during a year of research in the area by a herpetological party.

SPLENDID POISON FROG
Dendrobates speciosus

A species with a restricted distribution in the highlands of western Panama, the Splendid Poison Frog has been kept in the terrarium on occasion but has not proved easy to maintain. Closely related to *D. pumilio*, it is distinguished by its larger size (27.5 to 30 mm versus 19 to 24 mm in *pumilio*) and uniformly bright red coloration on the back, belly, and legs (the legs are almost always some color other than red in *pumilio*). Some living specimens seem to have a faint brownish network under the red of the back, but it never seems to quite "come through" the red color to form distinct spots or marbling. Structurally, *D. speciosus* lacks the tarsal fold found in *pumilio* and

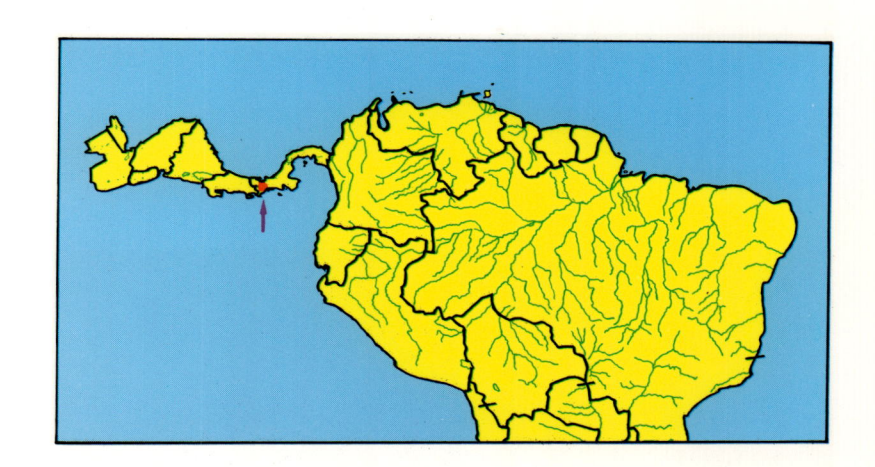

General distribution of the Splendid Poison Frog, Dendrobates speciosus.

has the tarsal tubercle absent or weakly developed. *Dendrobates granuliferus* has a strongly granulated back and usually has dark legs and arms, while *D. histrionicus* generally has a spotted pattern and often has dark mottling on the belly as well as being somewhat larger in most populations. The red species of *Minyobates* average only half the length of the Splendid Poison Frog and should not cause an identification problem.

Like its close relative the Strawberry Poison Frog, the Splendid Poison Frog needs food eggs to complete its development. Give specimens a roomy terrarium with lots of hiding places on the floor. A high humidity is necessary, so spray each day, but watch

General distribution of the Sira Poison Frog, Dendrobates sirensis.

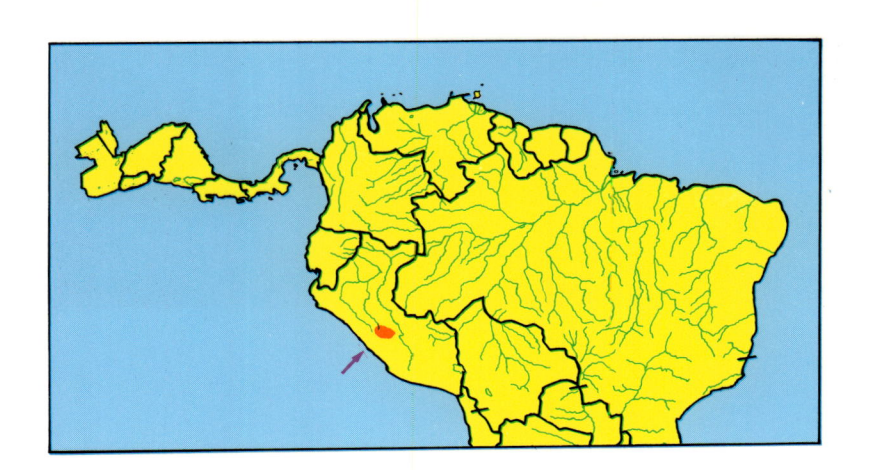

OTHER DENDROBATES

out for the development of fungus—forced ventilation or moving water may be best. The tadpoles are carried by the female to bromeliads or other water bodies for raising, and the female visits each funnel in turn to feed the tads on food eggs throughout their development. This makes the species hard to breed in captivity, though various substitutes from egg yolk to cottage cheese have been used with varying (mostly poor) success. The tadpole is much like that of *D. granuliferus*, having a pointed tail, but has the row of teeth above the beaks (anterior) absent. In captivity, metamorphosis occurred over five months after laying, which seems exceptionally long and probably is not typical of natural situations. It is doubtful if captive-bred specimens ever will be common in the hobby.

The Splendid Poison Frog, *Dendrobates speciosus*, is seldom collected and remains poorly known. Its great similarity to some color patterns of *Dendrobates pumilio* is confusing in photographs (where size cannot be determined), when the two species become almost impossible to identify with certainty. The illustrated specimens are from Concepcion, Panama, and the pair at bottom appear to be attempting to mate. All photos by A. v. d. Nieuwenhuizen.

OTHER *DENDROBATES*

Though the literature repeatedly described *Dendrobates speciosus*, the Splendid Poison Frog, as bright red with no pattern, every photo I have seen of captive animals indicates some type of nebulous brown streaking and reticulation. Notice the severe case of "bumblefoot" on the more heavily marked frog, probably a response to damage during shipping. Photo by A. v. d. Nieuwenhuizen.

OTHER *DENDROBATES*

This frog also is from Concepcion, Panama, and has been identified as *Dendrobates speciosus*. Notice the dull orange coloration, distinct dark speckling on the back and belly, and rather coarse skin texture. To me it appears to be either a variation of *Dendrobates pumilio* or *D. speciosus* carrying genes from the closest *D. pumilio* population. Concepcion is on the Pacific versant (slope) of Panama and thus supposedly out of the range of *D. pumilio*. Photo by A. v. d. Nieuwenhuizen.

OTHER *DENDROBATES*

There is little terrarium experience with the Splendid Poison Frog, *Dendrobates speciosus*, but it seems to be an exceptionally delicate species that is hard to maintain. Its habitat in the highland rainforest of Panama could be quite different from that of the Strawberry Poison Frog. Photo by A. v. d. Nieuwenhuizen.

OTHER *DENDROBATES*

Dendrobates truncatus, the Yellow-striped Poison Frog.

The Yellow-striped Poison Frog, *Dendrobates truncatus*, may closely resemble several species of *Dendrobates* and also of *Epipedobates*. Notice the expanded toe discs, however. Photo by J. P. Bogart.

YELLOW-STRIPED POISON FROG
Dendrobates truncatus

Here we have a very attractive poison frog that seldom is available to hobbyists. A close relative of *D. auratus* and *D. tinctorius*, it is smaller than typical specimens of either species (only 23.5 to 31 mm body length in adults) and has a distinctive pattern of complete yellow dorsolateral stripes, a usually incomplete yellow lateral stripe on each side, and a black back. The black legs and arms are variably striped or mottled with yellow, while the belly is black with little to much irregular blue mottling and curved lines. Often there is a distinct pale blue curved line

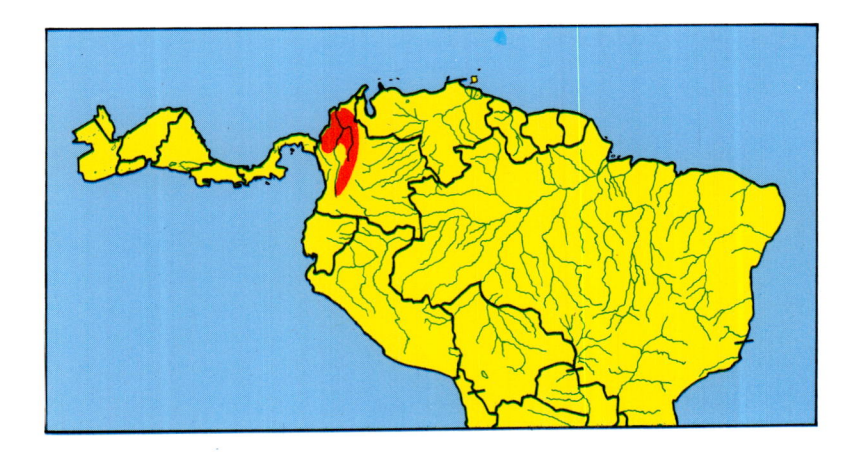

General distribution of the Yellow-striped Poison Frog, *Dendrobates truncatus*.

under the chin. The skin of the back is weakly granular (smooth in *D. auratus*) and there is no distinct tarsal tubercle; the first finger is only a bit shorter than the second finger, unusual in the genus. The Yellow-striped Poison Frog often has a distinctly "dumpy" look compared to many other species. It occasionally has been confused with the *Phyllobates* species having yellow dorsolateral stripes, but those species have finely dotted hind legs as well as differences in structure (smaller finger discs, longer first finger, teeth present). A superficial similarity also exists to *Epipedobates andinus*, which differs in many details of pattern and structure.

Though it is widely distributed in much of western Colombia, including relatively dry lowland forests, little seems to be known about the natural history of this species. A ground-litter species, it would appear to be very similar to *D. auratus* in keepability, and the two species are said to have been hybridized in captivity. It needs high humidity, as might be expected. Clutches of about six eggs are laid.

BRAZILIAN POISON FROG
Dendrobates vanzolinii

One of the more distinctive species related to *D. ventrimaculatus*, the Brazilian Poison Frog is found in humid rainforests of eastern central Peru and adjacent Brazil, where it apparently is not commonly collected. Structurally it is similar to its relatives, with short first finger and toe lacking discs and nearly smooth skin. The finger discs are greatly expanded, indicating the species is arboreal and probably associated with bromeliads like its relatives. Adults are about 17 to 19 mm long. The arms and legs are covered with small black spots on a bluish white to greenish white background, producing the usual fine metallic reticulation of species related to *D. ventrimaculatus*. The back is glossy black and covered with three regular rows of large bright yellow round spots that run from the snout to the rump. Occasional spots are connected with a neighbor through either horizontal or vertical yellow bars, but this always is a spotted frog, never a striped one. The belly pattern is of irregular black spots and marbling on white to bluish white, while the black-marked throat is bright yellow. The dorsal pattern resembles

General distribution of the Brazilian Poison Frog, *Dendrobates vanzolinii*.

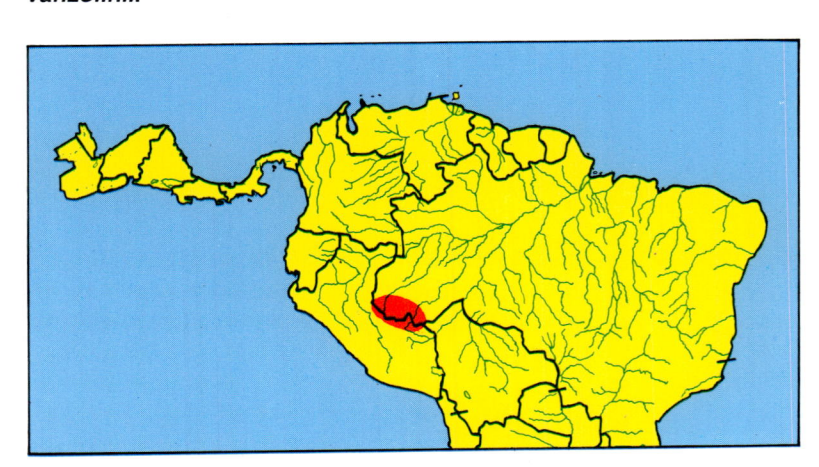

202

OTHER DENDROBATES

Dendrobates vanzolinii, the Brazilian Poison Frog.

somewhat that of *D. castaneoticus* and perhaps *D. captivus*, but both those species lack the reticulated arms and legs of *D. vanzolinii* and have "flash marks" on the arms and thighs. If you ever run across one in a pet shop, it should be easy to recognize *D. vanzolinii*.

The Brazilian Poison Frog is native to a vast tract of lowland rainforest on the Peru-Brazil border, especially in the Rios Ucayali and Jurua drainages. The Ucayali is a favorite fishing river for tropical fish hobbyists, and numerous species of cichlids and tetras have been brought back from there in recent years by ecotourists, so perhaps *D. vanzolinii* eventually will make it to the terrarium hobby. Expect it to breed and behave much like *D. ventrimaculatus*, so it should do well is a high terrarium with lots of plants and other cover (expect it to hide in the plants), a temperature around 26°C during the day, and 80 to 100% humidity. The clutches probably will be of about four eggs that hatch in two weeks, the tadpoles being put in individual water bodies for raising on detritus and insect larvae. Of course, it might prove to be very different from *D. ventrimaculatus*, but so far I've seen no published literature on the natural history of the Brazilian Poison Frog. If it has been kept in the terrarium, it has not made headlines.

General distribution of Zimmermann's Poison Frog, Dendrobates variabilis.

ZIMMERMANN'S POISON FROG
Dendrobates variabilis

Zimmermann's Poison Frog has been considered a synonym of *D. ventrimaculatus* in the past, mostly because it has never been fully defined in relation to variation in *ventrimaculatus*, but on that basis all the other similar species (*D. biolat, vanzolinii, lamasi, imitator, fantasticus,* and *reticulatus*) with reticulated arms and legs would have to be considered synonyms

A fairly typical specimen of Dendrobates variabilis, Zimmermann's Poison Frog. Photo by A. v. d. Nieuwenhuizen.

of *ventrimaculatus* as well, which certainly is not the case. In its own way, *D. variabilis* is just as distinct and recognizable as these other species, and the name serves a purpose in recognizing a specific color pattern type that *may* represent a biological species. Remember that the frogs called *D. ventrimaculatus* display several types of patterns and certainly represent several species, so I see no confusion in recognizing one more that is readily recognizable.

Basically, *D. variabilis* is just like *D. imitator* in pattern, with two rows of large black spots on the back separated by a golden to greenish middorsal stripe. The sides have large rounded black spots on a yellow background, so this frog is simply black-spotted on yellow. The middorsal stripe forks in front of the eyes and isolates a large, round, black spot covering most of the snout, the distinctive character of the species. In *D. imitator* the snout has a pair of squarish black spots, while *D. biolat* has the spots of the back either unbroken or fused into continuous black bands. In the typical terrarium pattern of *D. ventrimaculatus* the black pattern of the back forms a Y from the eyes over the center of the back; other *D. ventrimaculatus* have variant patterns but are not so regularly spotted as *D. variabilis*. There is no doubt that intermediate patterns connect *D. variabilis* to other described species of the *D. ventrimaculatus* complex, and not all specimens can be identified with certainty (something that can be said of the other described species as well). The belly of *D. variabilis*

OTHER *DENDROBATES*

has the usual black spots and marbling, and the throat is yellow. Structurally this species does not seem to differ from the usual run of *D. ventrimaculatus* complex species. Adults are about 15.5 to 18 mm in body length.

Keep and breed this species just as you would *D. ventrimaculatus* and you will not have any trouble.

Like most other frogs related to *Dendrobates ventrimaculatus*, Zimmermann's Poison Frog is quite variable both in color and details of color pattern. The frog above is distinctly on the yellow side, while the frog below is a much colder greenish yellow. Note also the difference in background color on the limbs, from pale greenish above to distinctly bluish below. The large central dark spot on the snout is constant, however, the major species character. Photos by A. v. d. Nieuwenhuizen.

Although *Dendrobates variabilis* has not been recognized as valid by most American workers, it seems as well or better defined than most other species related to *Dendrobates ventrimaculatus* and I see no harm in using the name for frogs bearing the distinctive snout spot. Photo by A. v. d. Nieuwenhuizen.

This color pattern is fairly common in the terrarium hobby and is one of the species often called *D. quinquevittatus* in the older literature. It is fairly common in the rainforest of Dept. San Martin, Peru, where it can be found with at least three other related species and various odder pattern types of the same basic frogs. It is arboreal and prefers bromeliads. There are numerous suggestions in the literature that each pattern type ("species") of the *D. quinquevittatus*-Group may have a distinctive territorial (advertisement) call when the sounds are analyzed scientifically as spectrograms. Calls are useful in identifying many other amphibians (think of the North American treefrogs, for instance) and of course are essential to bird identification. If these little poison frogs really do recognize themselves by their calls as well as by details of color patterns, it may be decades before scientists have sufficient information to sort them out correctly.

204

OTHER *DENDROBATES*

Like the other species similar to the Amazonian Poison Frog, Zimmermann's Poison Frog, *Dendrobates variabilis*, is an arboreal species living in bromeliads and other epiphytes. It is collected fairly often and even has been bred with some regularity, especially in Europe. This specimen is carrying at least three tadpoles, which could represent an entire egg clutch. Photo by R. Bechter.

OTHER *DENDROBATES*

Though it has been suggested that the various spotted poison frogs of Peru, including *Dendrobates variabilis*, could recognize their species by behavior and calls rather than details of spotting and color, there really is little experimental evidence to back this up. Additionally, there is some evidence that calls may change in the terrarium, reducing the value of tapes of captive animals. Photo by R. Bechter.

Epipedobates tricolor, the Phantasmal Poison Frog

Few species of *Epipedobates* are kept in the terrarium, which is a pity. Though not as flamboyant as many *Dendrobates*, they are hardy little frogs, often have bright colors, and deserve more attention. The most common species in the hobby now is the Phantasmal Poison Frog, a small (16.5 to 26.5 mm long in adults), brightly colored species from southwestern Ecuador and adjacent Peru. Common in many types of wet and dry forests from only 150 meters to over 1700 meters, it is an adaptable little beast that adjusts well to the terrarium and responds to the most minimal care.

Smooth-skinned both above and below and with the typical *Epipedobates* characters of tiny teeth and the first finger longer than the second, the finger discs not especially widened, it varies tremendously in color from nearly black to bright orange-brown or even a cinnamon red. There are wide yellow to white stripes along the sides (the oblique lateral stripes) and a broad and often complete stripe down the middle of the back and over the snout. In some specimens the middorsal stripe becomes broad enough to cover most of the back, producing a light frog with two narrow dark stripes at the sides of the back. The arms and legs are variously spotted and striped with yellow or white, while the belly is tan to dark brown or red with white to yellow or even reddish spots and marbling. There may be distinct yellow "flash marks" in the armpits and groin, or the spots may be incorporated into the lateral stripe. The toes are webbed basally. Sometimes the frog appears to be bright red with bright yellow stripes, but other specimens are brown with whitish or cream stripes. Most specimens on the market now appear to be reddish with yellowish stripes, but a decade ago the common form was black with gold stripes.

Of the *Epipedobates* with basal toe webbing, this is the only species that has smooth skin and a broad middorsal stripe. Additionally, the complete oblique lateral stripe is unusual in the genus. However, this combination of simple characters may be hiding a group of several similar species. Certainly the colors are varied enough.

General distribution of the Phantasmal Poison Frog, *Epipedobates tricolor.*

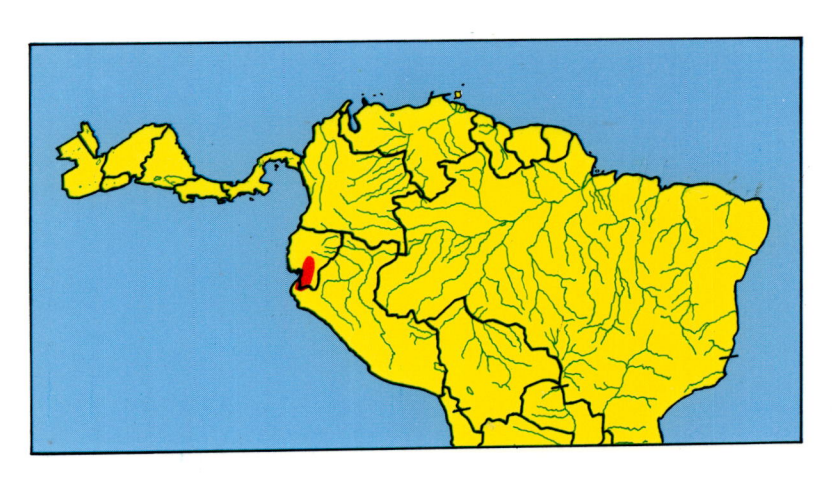

Epipedobates tricolor, the Phantasmal Poison Frog, in a natural pattern carried by the synonym *E. anthonyi*.

After only a couple of generations in the terrarium, the captive-bred frogs begin to lose their colors and pattern. The middorsal stripe seems to be the first to go, becoming shorter and thinner. The lateral stripes also become thinner and more diffuse, losing their strong contrast to the background color. After a few more generations the frogs begin to become dull red with only traces of pale stripes. This loss of pattern can be assumed to be due to the lack of some essential nutrient in the terrarium diet. Carefully planned feeding experiments might lead to some interesting results.

This species has a fairly broad range for a poison frog and, as mentioned, is found in both wet and drier habitats. This has led to taxonomic complications, because the frog is quite variable. Until recently, *E. anthonyi* was recognized as a distinct species from the same areas. It was thought to differ from the Phantasmal Poison Frog by being smaller (16.5 to 21 mm in *anthonyi*, 19 to 26.5 mm in *tricolor*) and having white bones while the bones of *tricolor* supposedly were green. It has since been shown that there is no real break in the sizes and that any differences in color and pattern are lost in a maze of differences from population to population and within populations, so the two names have been synonymized—which is not to say *anthonyi* won't be resurrected at a later date. Additionally, a preserved specimen of *E. tricolor* from Ecuador was described as *Colostethus paradoxus* by Rivero and later placed as a synonym by its author. This specimen was compared to several species of *Colostethus* at the time of description without a hint that it might belong to a different genus, which just serves to show how difficult it is to identify frogs in this family. The holotype of *C. paradoxus*, by the way, lacked a

EPIPEDOBATES TRICOLOR

This colorful Phantasmal Poison Frog, *Epipedobates tricolor*, represents captive-bred stock that has lost most of the dark natural colors. Notice the bright red "flash mark" behind the thigh, a feature often found in poison frogs of this genus. Photo by R. D. Bartlett.

middorsal stripe and was solid light brown above in preservative.

In the terrarium this is a mostly ground-living frog, but if the terrarium is heavily planted with bromeliads and similar plants, kept warm and sprayed daily, males may establish territories well above the ground. They call constantly during the day and often wrestle with neighbors that enter their territory. The call is a loud trill, repeated ad nauseum, but it is attractive to the females, who respond by approaching the calling male of their choice. When the male sees a plump female he increases the intensity of his calling and keeps his eyes on the female. They eventually begin to move toward the first bower on the male's list, the female following hesitantly as usual and being spurred on by the male's calls. Several possible laying sites may be inspected before the female approves one. In the bower the frogs do a bit of mutual back stroking and head nudging before laying. In some specimens, perhaps differing from population to population, there is a type of true amplexus, the male climbing onto the female's back and grasping her under the throat. This cephalic amplexus seems to be the last remnant of more typical frog clasping behavior. Not all *E. tricolor* clasp, however, and in some cases the female simply lays her eggs and then the male fertilizes them. Instances even have been seen when the male actually left the bower while the female laid her eggs, returning to fertilize them after the female had left. These behavioral differences may prove to be correlated with differences in structure and perhaps skin chemistry, and it is quite probable that *E. tricolor*, as are so many poison frogs, is a complex of several virtually indistinguishable species still to be defined.

The clutches are gigantic for a poison frog, often numbering 15 eggs and occasionally approaching 40. Phantasmal Poison Frogs are happy breeders in the proper surroundings, and females will produce a clutch of eggs every 15 to 20 days month after month for a year or more before burning out. It might be best to move these overproductive frogs to a terrarium that is a bit drier and cooler (perhaps 60% relative humidity and 22°C) for a month every four or five months. You don't want them to waste too much energy with clutches you can't take care of anyway.

The bower is guarded avidly by the male, who keeps other males and females away, drives off predators, and apparently eats fungused eggs. The eggs hatch after about 14 days (10 to 16 is the range given in the literature for terrarium clutches), and the male manages to take all or most of the tads onto his back and sides at one time. The male may appear to be literally covered with tadpoles! He transports them for as many as four days at a time before depositing all in one or more water bodies. The tadpoles are

This much darker Phantasmal Poison Frog has the stripes distinctly blue, with a bright blue mark at the base of the arm. Captive-bred specimens produce unpredictable colors and patterns in this species. Photo by R. D. Bartlett.

EPIPEDOBATES TRICOLOR

feeders on detritus and small prey and are said to not be cannibalistic. Like most other tads of the genus, they are somewhat elongated and speckled with brown and gray. The oral disc is deeply indented at the corners and there is a single row of papillae around the edges of the entire disc except the center front margin. There are three rows of teeth below the relatively weak beaks and two rows (the bottom one split) above the beaks. Though they may feed well, mortalities are high and many tadpoles develop "spindly leg" syndrome, a common poison frog tadpole affliction in which the front legs either fail to break through the skin or come out dwarfed and with few muscles. Spindly leg is thought to be the result of a deficient diet of either the tadpoles themselves or perhaps the mother, but little really is known about the condition, which is noncurable.

Metamorphosis occurs after some 50 days in the terrarium, producing froglets about 1 cm long and easily drowned in a shallow layer of water. Caution in advised. Tiny foods are needed, as expected. Maturity comes quickly, and males may start calling only six months after metamorphosis. Because these little frogs breed so avidly and mature relatively quickly, they might make excellent laboratory animals. Certainly their varied colors and sizes and the tendency to lose pattern in captive-bred generations pose several interesting genetic questions.

Not all *Epipedobates tricolor* are stunning examples of natural art, though all are attractive little frogs. Notice the great variation in striping pattern in these yellowish cream and tan to reddish tan specimens. The specimen at the upper left is carrying a large clutch of tadpoles. Photos by R. Bechter (top left), and A. v. d. Nieuwenhuizen.

209

EPIPEDOBATES TRICOLOR

More specimens of *Epipedobates tricolor*, the Phantasmal Poison Frog. The pair of photos at the left represent a wild-collected specimen, contrasted to captive-breds on the right. The specimen at upper right has lost virtually all of the pattern to become a cream poison frog with reddish touches. Notice also the differences in belly patterns visible in the two lower specimens. All photos by A. v. d. Nieuwenhuizen.

EPIPEDOBATES TRICOLOR

In this wild-collected specimen of *Epipedobates tricolor* the stripe down the center of the back is broad and has very uneven edges. This is a highly variable frog even in nature, and it is not impossible that more than one species may be included under the name, though the great variability in captive-bred specimens makes one doubt that the variation is strictly under genetic control. Photo by A. v. d. Nieuwenhuizen.

211

Epipedobates trivittatus, the Three-striped Poison Frog

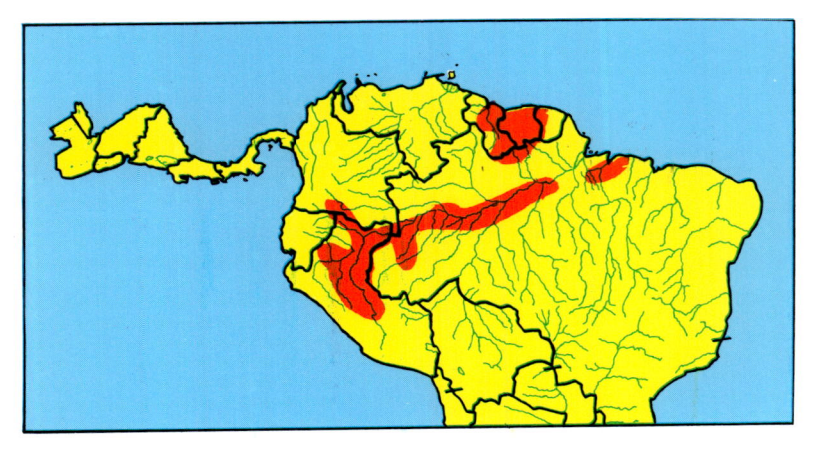

A fairly typical specimen (a bit toward the greenish side) of the Three-striped Poison Frog, *Epipedobates trivittatus*. Yes, I know there are only two stripes, but the three-striped form is seldom seen in the terrarium. Photo by D. Green.

This large poison frog (31.5 to 49.5 mm in adults, males 31.5 to 42 mm long and thus smaller than females from the same locality) is generally green and black. The back is relatively smooth though covered with fine granules, and the belly is smooth. The teeth are absent (present in the similar *E. bassleri*), basal webs are not present between the toes, and the first finger is longer than the second. Though there is much variation in pattern and colors, generally the back, sides, and most of the belly are deep black, the belly covered with large irregular green or blue-green spots. The top of the hind leg usually is some shade of green, sometimes with brownish bars. In almost all specimens a sharply defined, rather broad oblique lateral stripe runs from the groin to the eye and meets with its partner across the snout. This stripe usually is green or yellow-green but may be pure yellow. A middorsal stripe that usually is green may be present or absent, complete or broken into spots, or even expanded to cover most of the middle of the back. Such green-backed specimens are rare. A creamy yellow stripe runs from the upper lip back to the arm and then along the top of the arm.

The large adult size limits the number of species that could be confused with the Three-striped Poison Frog. The striped species of *Phyllobates* may appear similar at first glance, but in their case the stripes are dorsal in position rather than lateral, ending above the thigh rather than in the groin. *Phyllobates* species

Above and below: This Three-striped Poison Frog, *Epipedobates trivittatus*, comes from Surinam and represents the usual dark-backed, yellow-green lateral stripe form. The skin in not as rough as it seems. Like other *Epipedobates*, males may carry many tadpoles at once. Photos by A. v. d. Nieuwenhuizen.

General distribution of *Epipedobates trivittatus*, the Three-striped Poison Frog.

EPIPEDOBATES TRIVITTATUS

A male Three-striped Poison Frog carrying a large clutch of tadpoles may almost disappear under the wriggling mass. Photo by J. P. Bogart.

also tend to have the thighs covered with tiny dots of color producing a metallic peppery effect, and the dorsal stripes also appear to be metallic or glossy in tone. *E. bassleri* may be very similar to *E. trivittatus*. It has teeth, which may be a useless character to hobbyists, and tends to be lemon-yellow with a yellow suffusion over most of the back, the back tending to appear more irregularly spotted duller yellow on dull black than in typical *E. trivittatus*. The belly may be more heavily mottled than in *E. trivittatus* and appear less spotted than striped. *E. trivittatus, bassleri,* and *silverstonei* have been placed in the genus *Phobobates*, which following Myers is not recognized here. However, they all are large, distinctively patterned frogs that bear little superficial resemblance to the other *Epipedobates* while being very similar to each other in almost all features of structure and pattern.

The Three-striped Poison Frog is one of the more widely distributed poison frogs, being found in the Guianas, Brazil through the Amazon, and much of Peru, with populations in Colombia and Ecuador. It is not found south of the Amazon except at the mouth and in the upper drainages, and seems to be absent from Venezuela and most of Colombia. An inhabitant of lowland humid rainforests, it is found from near sea level to almost 700 meters; it does not penetrate into the Andes. Typically a shy, difficult to collect ground-dweller, it likes thick cover and tangles of vines, branches, and fallen trees. It is not a conspicuous member of the forest fauna, even though often locally very common, but its long-repeated call ("tutututututututu") can be heard through the wet season.

In the terrarium these are not difficult frogs to care for, and their large size makes them easy to feed. Provide a large, humid, warm terrarium as usual, preferably heavily planted. Males seem to be a bit territorial and are large enough to inflict some damage, so be sure every frog in the terrarium can establish a territory if desired. They have a reputation as jumpers when disturbed suddenly, and they never seem to overcome their shyness. Their breeding biology is much like that of the Phantasmal Poison Frog. Females are attracted to calling males, following them to selected bowers (usually a dead leaf hidden on the ground). Cephalic amplexus is reported, but again may not occur in all pairs. The clutches are large, 15 to 30 eggs. Hatching occurs in about 14 to 18 days. Males transport large numbers of tadpoles to a water body where they feed on the usual mix of detritus and what small invertebrates and plants they can catch. The mouthparts are typical of the genus, strongly indented at the corners and with a single row of papillae broken only at the front rim of the disc. The tail sometimes ends in a rather sharp point and is flecked with brown and gray. Metamorphosis is rapid, at least under terrarium conditions, taking only two months.

Though far from common in the hobby, this frog deserves more attention. Some captive-bred stock is available, but the general shyness of the frogs and their relatively common color pattern have not aided their popularity.

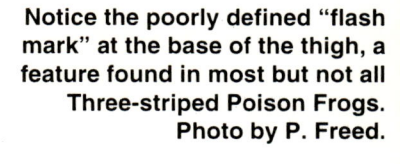

Notice the poorly defined "flash mark" at the base of the thigh, a feature found in most but not all Three-striped Poison Frogs. Photo by P. Freed.

EPIPEDOBATES TRIVITTATUS

This colorful variant of *Epipedobates trivittatus* has the back suffused with bronzy pigment. Notice that the lateral stripe is almost white instead of greenish. This specimen probably is a juvenile and will change the pattern somewhat as it grows, but there is no doubt that the Three-striped Poison Frog is one of the most variable poison frogs and deserves a complete review. The similarity to *Epipedobates bassleri* also should not be ignored. Photo by M. Panzella.

EPIPEDOBATES TRIVITTATUS

This view of a Three-stripe not only shows skin texture very well, but it shows that the lateral stripes are continuous across the snout. This male (at least it probably is a male) is carrying at least eight tadpoles. He may move about with them on his back for several days before putting them into the water. Photo by P. Freed.

EPIPEDOBATES TRIVITTATUS

At last, a real three-striped Three-striped Poison Frog, *Epipedobates trivittatus*. This specimen, said to be from Surinam, has much more yellow-green in the pattern than the forms usually seen and may be hard to identify with the other specimens pictured here. Compare it to the specimen pictured on the facing page, however, to see how few real differences there are from two-striped specimens. Photo by A. v. d. Nieuwenhuizen.

EPIPEDOBATES TRIVITTATUS

This specimen of *Epipedobates trivittatus* also is from Surinam, yet it differs considerably from the specimen on the facing page. The apparent difference in skin texture may be an artifact of photography or may be real—there is nothing that keeps a gene for skin texture from being associated with a gene for midback striping. Photo by A. v. d. Nieuwenhuizen.

EPIPEDOBATES TRIVITTATUS

Another view of the yellow two-striped Surinam form of *Epipedobates trivittatus*. It is not unlikely that the species called *E. trivittatus* actually represents several very similar species, perhaps with two or more occurring in the same range. Photo by A. v. d. Nieuwenhuizen.

Other *Epipedobates*

Though *Epipedobates* is a large genus with 25 described species, some very widely distributed, only two are at all common in the terrarium hobby. Many of the remaining 23 species are relatively dull in coloration or very rarely collected, but some are spectacular frogs that have been bred on occasion and deserve an effort to make them more common. We'll keep this look at the other species brief, but remember that there is a lot of ground to cover in this one chapter. So here goes....

Epipedobates species structurally can be recognized by the only moderately expanded finger discs and the first finger as long as or longer than the second (but both these characters are quite variable). Teeth usually are present, but this can vary among populations of a single species. Many species have dorsolateral bright stripes and complete or incomplete lateral stripes, while the belly usually is blue or yellow with black marbling. Most of the species exceed 20 mm in adult length, but there are plenty of exceptions. From the species of *Phyllobates* they are most readily distinguished by looking at the hind legs—variously banded, spotted, or marbled in *Epipedobates*, finely dotted in *Phyllobates*.

LA PLANADA POISON FROG
Epipedobates andinus

E. andinus is a paradoxical frog. First, it is arboreal, living in water-filled bromeliads in the trees; second, the finger discs would be called fairly well expanded by most observers and the first finger is a bit shorter than the second, both characters atypical for the genus; and third, the color pattern consists mostly of a pair of bright yellow dorsolateral stripes ending above the thighs, not in the groin as usual in *Epipedobates*. The La Planada Poison Frog is overall dark brown or nearly black, with bright yellow stripes on the back connected over the snout. There is no pattern on the dark sides. The upper arm has a bright yellow "flash mark," the belly is brown mottled with bluish green to yellow (the throat is black), and there is bright greenish or bluish speckling on the arms and legs, especially the hands. A bright yellow spot or short stripe covers the underside of the upper shank. Adults are 19.5 to 21 mm long. Teeth are

Epipedobates andinus, the La Planada Poison Frog.

present, the skin is smooth, and there are no basal webs on the toes. Though probably related to *E. erythromos*, which lacks dorsolateral stripes and has a bright reddish orange mark on the upper arm, among many other differences, superficially it resembles *Phyllobates aurotaenia* and *Dendrobates truncatus*, which occur in the same general area of southwestern Colombia. *P. aurotaenia* has much wider, more metallic stripes as well as quite different feet and finely speckled thighs, while *D. truncatus* has a much more complicated color pattern as well as numerous other differences in structure and pattern; both species lack a bright yellow spot under the shank. *E. pulchripectis* is similar at first glance, but the bright yellow stripes end in the groin rather than above the thigh, while *E. azureiventris* has the dorsal stripes correctly placed but bright golden orange in color and matched with an incomplete but very obvious oblique lateral stripe.

E. andinus is known only from high altitude (1700 to over 2000 meters) very dense wet rainforest in the La Planada Nature Reserve of Colombia in the Rio Mira drainage. The trees are covered with bromeliads and numerous other epiphytic plants, providing dense cover for a small frog. The call of *E. andinus* is unusual, a series of distinct "crreek" notes given during the day. The frogs are shy and retreat to the shelter of their bromeliads when approached, though their color pattern makes them almost impossible to see anyway. Males seem to have definite territories and attract females with their calls. Cephalic amplexus was observed once, but a type of cephalic holding also was noted between two males, assumedly a type of aggressive behavior. Clutches of three or four eggs are laid just above the water level in a bromeliad funnel. Tadpoles were not found.

The discovery of *E. andinus* and quite a few other poison frogs apparently restricted to (or at least collected only in) various nature preserves developed recently in several South American countries is interesting, pointing out that a great diversity of frogs already may have been lost from unprotected rainforest areas. It is a shame to think of the American rainforest as a series of small, isolated preserves surrounded by pastures and fields, but this

General distribution of the La Planada Poison Frog, *Epipedobates andinus*.

OTHER *EPIPEDOBATES*

may be the future. After all, that's what has happened already in both the United States and most of Europe.

SKY-BLUE POISON FROG
Epipedobates azureiventris

A truly stunning little poison frog, the Sky-blue is of moderate size (females about 27.5, males about 25 mm) and has a distinctive color pattern. On each side of the back is a rather narrow but well-defined golden orange to yellow-orange stripe that starts over the thigh (not in the groin) and runs forward over the eye to meet its partner on the snout. The back is bright black to dark brown and moderately granular. There is a broad, sometimes broken, bright yellow stripe

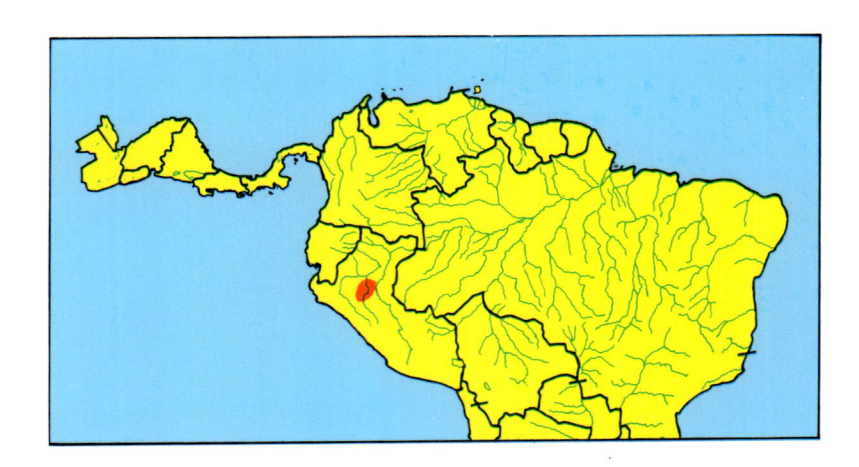

General distribution of the Sky-blue Poison Frog, *Epipedobates azureiventris*.

Epipedobates azureiventris, the Sky-blue Poison Frog.

along the lip that runs back to cover the upper part of the arm. Most distinctively, a bright golden yellow or orangish stripe runs from the groin toward the arm, usually stopping before reaching the arm. The throat and belly are bright blue with scattered black spots and marbling, while the legs are metallic greenish blue with scattered black spots and mottling, very much like the leg pattern of *D. ventrimaculatus* and allies. A similar pattern marks the lower arm. The undersides of the arms and legs are mostly blue with small black spots. A true beauty! The first finger is a bit longer than the second and small teeth are present. The finger discs are small.

A careful look at the color pattern will not allow this species to be confused with any other, as the combination of bright stripes from the snout to above the thighs and a bright oblique lateral stripe on each side in combination with a blue belly and throat is unique. Because of the position of the dorsolateral stripes the Sky-blue Poison Frog could be confused with *Phyllobates* species and *E. andinus*, but the differences are too numerous to even try to mention.

Apparently uncommon, *E. azureiventris* is known from the vicinity of its type-locality in San Martin Department, Peru, an area that is heavily collected by poison frog enthusiasts. It is a ground-litter species, seldom found far above the ground. Active during the day, the males call (a trill) to attract females, and both sexes have gained a reputation as being very aggressive frogs that should not be kept in colonies in order to avoid fights. A receptive female is led to a bower chosen by the male and lays 12 to 16 eggs in a clutch. The eggs hatch in about two weeks, and the tadpoles are transported to a water body by the male. Tadpoles eat almost anything, including flake fish food, algae, bloodworms, and detritus. They probably will eat each other as well. The species is not commonly raised in the terrarium, though it certainly is large enough (comparatively speaking, of course) and bright enough to draw interest. The fights between adults are a problem, however, that must be considered when designing a terrarium for the Sky-blue Poison Frog. Be sure that each frog has plenty of hiding places and the males don't have to fight for territory. Expect egg clutches to be eaten by competing females if they are left for the male to tend. Though this may prove to be a difficult species, it is colorful enough to be worth the extra effort. The occasional specimens available in pet shops and from dealers's lists tend to be quite expensive.

PLEASING POISON FROG
Epipedobates bassleri

The Pleasing Poison Frog is not only large (32.5 to 40 mm in adults, perhaps to 45 mm in some females), it is variable. Usually it is orangish on the back with few to many scattered black spots and two broad dull orangish lateral stripes setting off the black sides. The upper lip has a whitish stripe that continues to the base of the arm, and the belly is black with blue mottling (the throat and chest often almost all black). Some specimens may be more greenish than orange, many others more yellowish. Occasional specimens are virtually black above except for the stripes and a few small bright spots down the middle of the back, while others are bright orange to lemon yellow from side to side with black restricted to the area around the vent. The legs usually are dark, with paler, sometimes greenish, dotting and mottling. A close relative of *E. trivittatus*, it differs in lacking a distinct middorsal stripe and having teeth. *E. silverstonei* also is similar but tends

OTHER *EPIPEDOBATES*

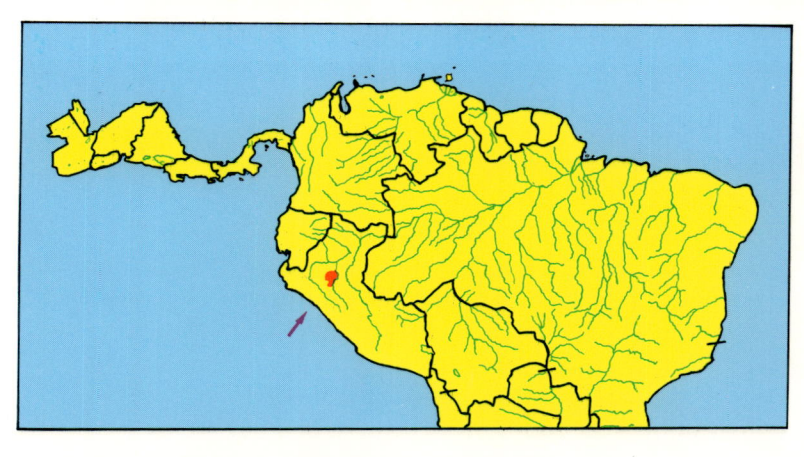

General distribution of the Pleasing Poison Frog, *Epipedobates bassleri*.

Pleasing Poison Frogs, *Epipedobates bassleri*, are big, pretty frogs that are not common in the hobby but deserve more attention. This specimen is exceptionally yellow—many others are much more orange. Photo by R. Bechter.

more toward the reddish side in coloration and has the belly variously mottled with black and red instead of blue. Though large and attractive, *E. bassleri* has proved hard to maintain and breed in captivity. It needs a large terrarium with lots of cover. Specimens from higher altitudes (it occurs from under 300 meters to over 1100 meters) may need relatively cooler temperatures, so wild-caught specimens have a better chance of survival if their point of origin is known. Eggs are laid in large clutches of a dozen or more. The tadpoles have proved difficult to raise. Juveniles are black with little yellow or orange, the bright colors increasing with growth. If captive-bred specimens were to become more common and the tadpoles hardier in later generations, this would make a poison frog attractive to even the beginning hobbyist. Unfortunately, at the moment it is a difficult species. Notice that the combination of large size and teeth allows this frog to eat crickets even in nature.

OTHER *EPIPEDOBATES*

More typical of *Epipedobates bassleri* is this specimen showing two broad lateral stripes and having many small black spots over the back. The Pleasing Poison Frog is closely related to both *Epipedobates trivittatus* and *E. silverstonei*, and the three species can be confusingly similar. Photo by A. v. d. Nieuwenhuizen.

OTHER *EPIPEDOBATES*

Young Pleasing Poison Frogs, *Epipedobates bassleri*, have much more black on the back than do most adults. Notice the position of the yellow lateral stripes, which extend into the groin rather than continuing over the back to end over the vent as in *Phyllobates*. Photo by A. v. d. Nieuwenhuizen.

OTHER *EPIPEDOBATES*

Epipedobates bilinguis, the Ecuadorean Poison Frog.

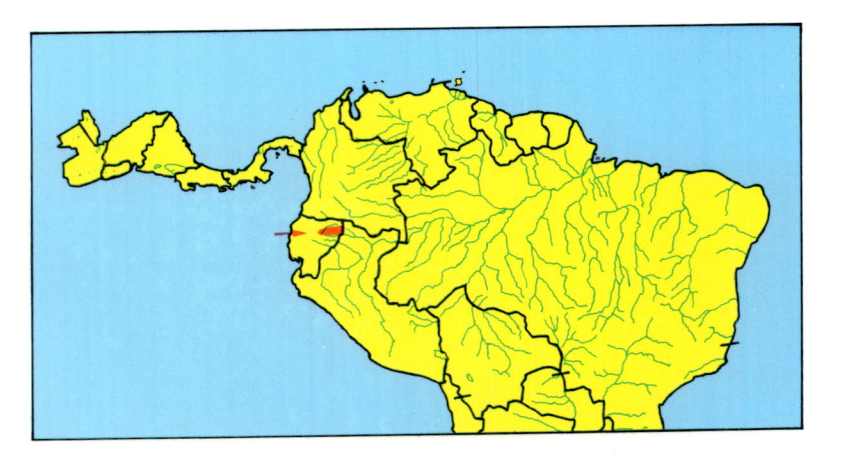

General distribution of the Ecuadorean Poison Frog, *Epipedobates bilinguis*.

An exceptionally nice specimen of *Epipedobates bilinguis* displaying bright red back granules and the conspicuous "flash marks" at the bases of the limbs. Photo by P. Freed.

ECUADOREAN POISON FROG
Epipedobates bilinguis

This species represents a splitting of *E. parvulus* into a northern (*bilinguis*, Rio Napo drainage) and southern (*parvulus* in the strict sense, Rio Pastaza drainage plus Loreto, Peru) species. Most of the range of both species is restricted to Ecuador, and the natural history of the two species seems to be virtually identical as far as known. *E. bilinguis* differs from the Ruby Poison Frog mainly in having bright

Ecuadorean Poison Frogs, *Epipedobates bilinguis*, seem to be available occasionally in the hobby though usually misidentified as the Ruby Poison Frog, *E. parvulus*. Though small, it certainly is one of the more attractive poison frogs. Photo by P. Freed.

yellow "flash marks" both on the upper arm and the upper thigh, the thigh spot round and very well-defined. In the Ruby these areas are bluish to pale yellow and never well marked, especially on the thigh. The red granules of the back are the same in both species, the size may be a bit smaller (19 to 21 mm) in *E. bilinguis*, and the belly and short oblique lateral stripe both are bright blue, the belly variously mottled with black. The Ecuadorean Poison Frog is not commonly seen in the hobby, but it is present (usually misidentified as *E. parvulus*). Males defend a calling territory from other males, staying on or near the ground. Cephalic amplexus seems to be the rule in this species. Females may lay clutches of six to nine eggs every two weeks to a month for almost six months in a row before needing a break. The eggs hatch in about 20 days (an awfully long incubation if correct), and the tadpoles are transported (often the whole clutch at once) to a water body for raising. The tiny froglets are difficult to feed. Though very attractive, the small size of *E. bilinguis* and its tendency to hide in the ground litter will not endear it to terrarium hobbyists. Additionally, the red granules of the back that look so attractive in photos and paintings often are just bronzy brown. An interesting though difficult species, it presently is for the specialist.

OTHER *EPIPEDOBATES*

In *Epipedobates bilinguis* the "flash marks" at the upper base of the arm and on the thigh are bright yellow and rounded. The thigh mark is especially well-defined and often outlined with black. Back color and details of the rest of the pattern may vary much as in the Ruby Poison Frog. Photo by R. Bechter.

225

OTHER *EPIPEDOBATES*

Though the back color of this specimen of the Ecuadorean Poison Frog, *Epipedobates bilinguis*, is relatively brownish, the "flash marks" still are distinct and several smaller yellow spots can be seen on the legs and feet. Photo by R. Bechter.

OTHER *EPIPEDOBATES*

The Bolivian Poison Frog, *Epipedobates bolivianus*. Colors have been based on related species as this species apparently is not known alive.

BOLIVIAN POISON FROG
Epipedobates bolivianus

This poorly known poison frog has a brownish or perhaps reddish brown granulated back with narrow, complete, yellowish oblique lateral stripes running from the groin to the eye. The thighs are mottled dark and light, rather than being mostly dark as in *E.*

General distribution of the Bolivian Poison Frog, *Epipedobates bolivianus*.

macero and *E. cainarachi*. The most obvious difference from similar species is that the belly is pale, probably yellowish, in life. Adults are 22 to 26 mm in length. Teeth are absent, though they are present in similar species. So far the Bolivian Poison Frog apparently is known only from the types from Bolivia, taken at elevations between 800 and 1200 meters in the Amazon drainage.

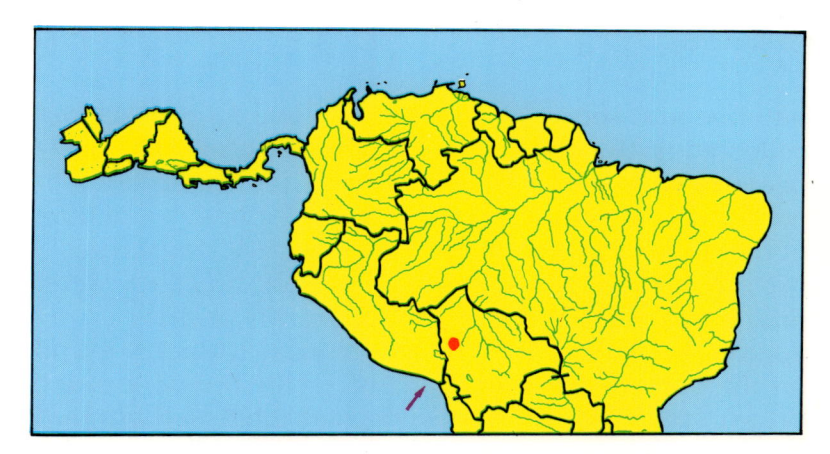

General distribution of the Marbled Poison Frog, *Epipedobates boulengeri*.

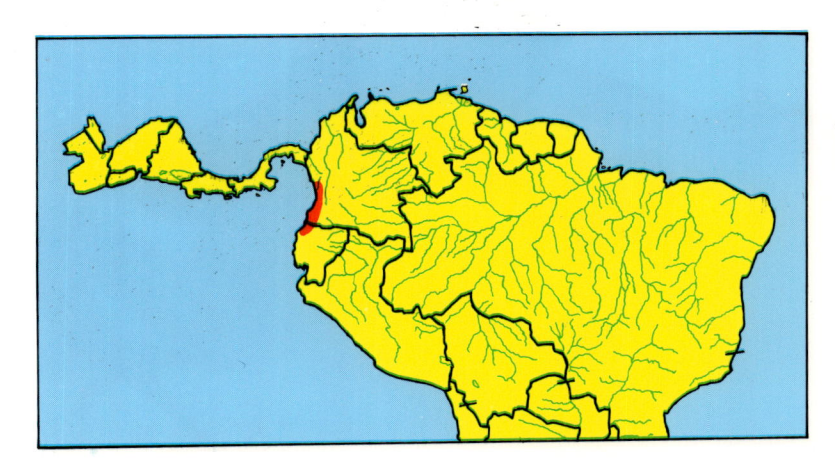

Nondescript is the best description for *Epipedobates boulengeri*, a variable species of uncertain distinctness. It can be confused with *E. femoralis*, but that species has the lateral stripe continued beyond the eye, usually has a half stripe on the side, and has "flash marks." Photo by W. P. Mara.

MARBLED POISON FROG
Epipedobates boulengeri

An active little (15 to 21 mm in adults) ground-living frog of wet rainforests, *E. boulengeri* has been poorly studied though it appears to be common in coastal southwestern Colombia and adjacent Ecuador at 10 to almost 1200 meters elevation. Its exact relationship to the red-backed *E. espinosai* is uncertain, but most specimens can be distinguished by the brown back. The skin is more or less smooth, the back brown often with darker or paler spots and marbling, and there is a complete yellow to red oblique lateral stripe running from the groin to behind the eye. The belly is black with white marbling or vice versa (the white occasionally greenish), and the throat never is solid black as in *E. femoralis*. A white to yellowish stripe runs from the upper lip to the top of the arm, while the thigh is black with yellow spots or stripes. Little is reported on the biology of this species and it seldom is kept in captivity, though its great range of elevations should indicate considerable adaptability. Keep it humid.

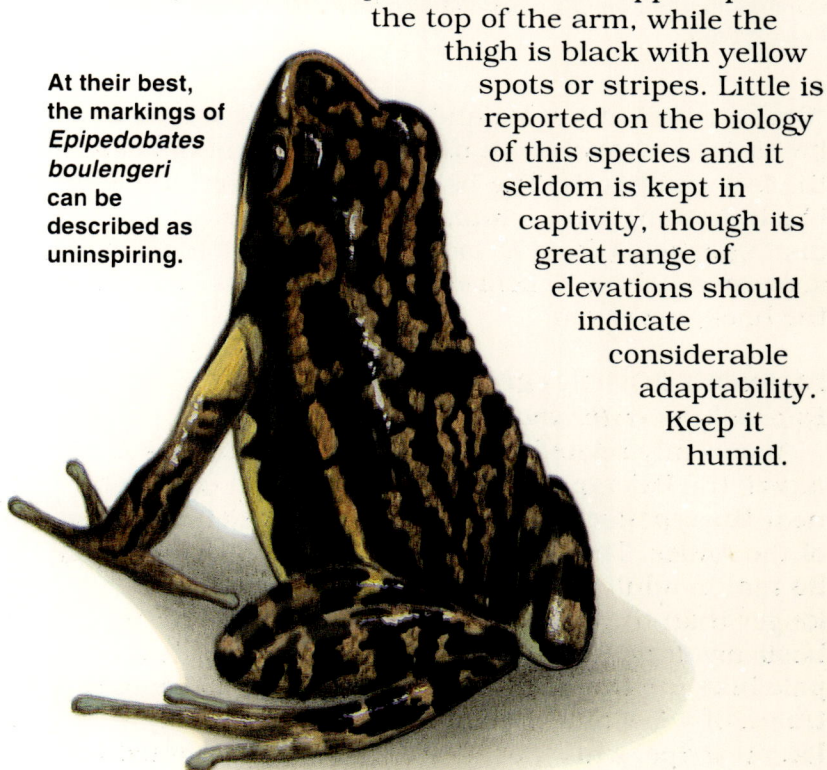

At their best, the markings of *Epipedobates boulengeri* can be described as uninspiring.

227

OTHER *EPIPEDOBATES*

Epipedobates cainarachi, the Cainarachi Poison Frog.

CAINARACHI POISON FROG
Epipedobates cainarachi

This *E. petersi* relative is known from the Rio Cainarachi valley in Peru, along the classic Tarapoto to Yurimaguas road collecting locality for so many poison frogs. The back is strongly granulated and deep dark red to brick red in color. There is a pale yellow to whitish stripe, the oblique lateral stripe, running from the eye (vaguely indicated to the nostrils) back to the groin and contrasted to black sides. A somewhat paler stripe runs from the upper lip to the base of the arm. There are brighter yellow

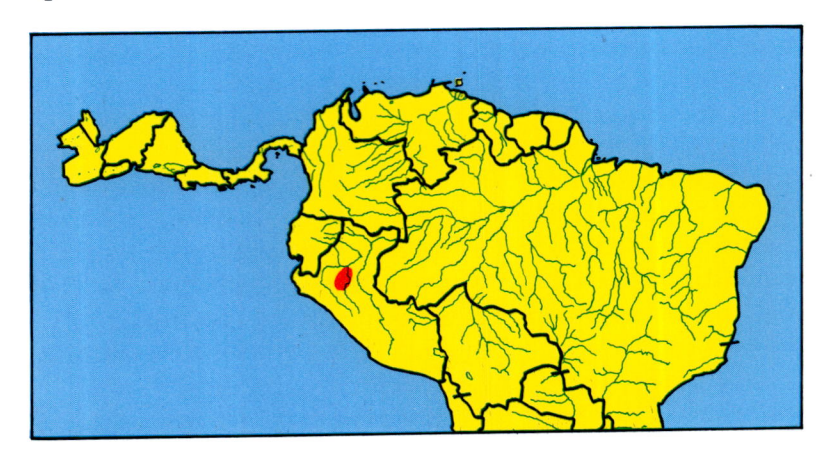

General distribution of *Epipedobates cainarachi*, the Cainarachi Poison Frog.

"flash marks" at the leg and arm insertions, and the limbs are brownish with paler mottling and blue on the feet and hands. The belly is dark bright blue with black mottling. The complete yellow stripe distinguishes it from *E. macero*, while the blue belly separates it from *E. bolivianus*. *E. petersi* is brown on the back, never red.

PALENQUE POISON FROG
Epipedobates erythromos

Apparently related to *E. andinus* and perhaps *E. ingeri*, the Palenque Poison Frog is known only from near the type-locality in the lowlands of Ecuador west of the Andes. This ground-litter dweller is about 20 to 24 mm in adult length, the females a few millimeters longer than the males. Not a colorful species, it is basically dark brown above, darker on the sides, with pale blue mottling on the black belly. There are only traces of a few blue spots to represent the oblique lateral stripe, while dorsal stripes are represented by vague bronzy stripes. The thighs are banded in dark brown and tan or greenish tan, while the arms are brownish. The major distinguishing feature of the species is a bright reddish orange "flash mark" covering the upper base of the arm. Teeth are present, the first finger is longer than the second, the back skin is smooth, and there is no webbing at the base of the toes. The underside of the upper shank lacks a bright spot (probably present in *E. ingeri* and certainly present and bright yellow in *E. andinus*). The type locality near the Centro Cientifico Rio Palenque is wet rainforest that is relatively steep terrain with much

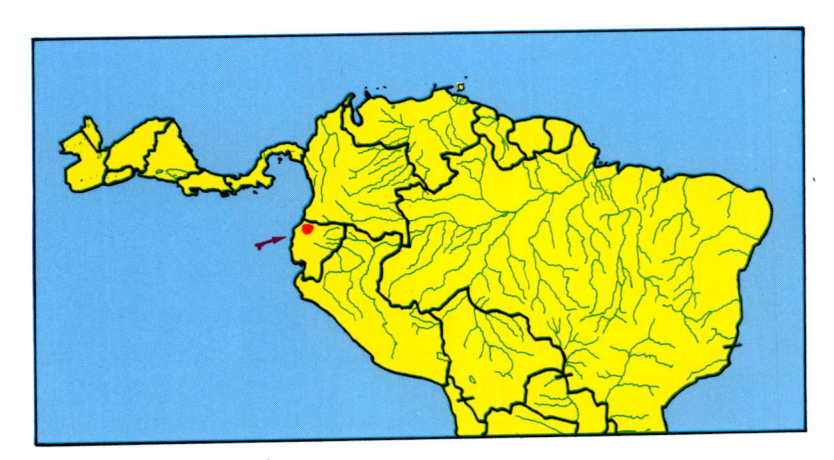

General distribution of *Epipedobates erythromos*, the Palenque Poison Frog.

bamboo and second-growth areas. The frogs all were collected in the nearly dry streambed, probably because they were simply easier to find there, but certainly had wandered there from the heavy leaf litter of the adjacent thick forest. They were active during the day and did not seem to climb, but still they were difficult to collect. The calls (apparently of this species) were described as soft chirps. Tadpoles found on the back of an adult male were pale tan with much brown speckling, the speckling restricted to the top of the tail and leaving the fins colorless. The oral disc is indented at the corners and has a single row of papillae around the disc except at the upper (anterior) center. Apparently there is only one row of teeth anterior to (above) the beaks.

The Palenque Poison Frog, *Epipedobates erythromos*.

OTHER EPIPEDOBATES

Though they are not found near each other, *E. rufulus* bears some resemblance to *E. erythromos* in its nearly plain back colors lacking stripes and nearly unpatterned sides. Probably both species simply have independently lost the striping pattern found in their ancestors. The discovery of other obscurely colored little *Epipedobates* should be expected.

ESPINOSA POISON FROG
Epipedobates espinosai

A quick-moving, nervous little (16 to 17.5 mm adult length) poison frog, *E. espinosai* is known from only a few localities in northwestern Ecuador. The back is uniformly dark red, distinct from the black sides and with lightly granulated skin. The oblique lateral stripe is indicated by only a few pale blue spots or at best a very broken line of blue. The belly is brownish with blue spots and marbling, while the thigh is blackish with blue spotting; the shank has a reddish tint. There is narrow webbing at the bases of the toes. *E. zaparo* may be quite similar but has a continuous white stripe from the upper lip to the thigh (present as only a few spots on the lip in *E. espinosai*). *E. parvulus* is a bit larger and lacks small webs at the bases of the toes, besides being more granular. From what little is known of the Espinosa Poison Frog, it seems to be a species of wet lowland (300 to 500 meters) rainforests, where it is active by day and prefers shaded areas on the jungle floor. Juveniles were found on the banks of a small river, so perhaps they are raised in small streams draining into the river. Though bred in the laboratory of a few zoos, this species has never been well-represented in the hobby.

Epipedobates espinosai, the Espinosa Poison Frog. Most specimens are more brownish than this painting.

General distribution of the Espinosa Poison Frog, *Epipedobates espinosai*.

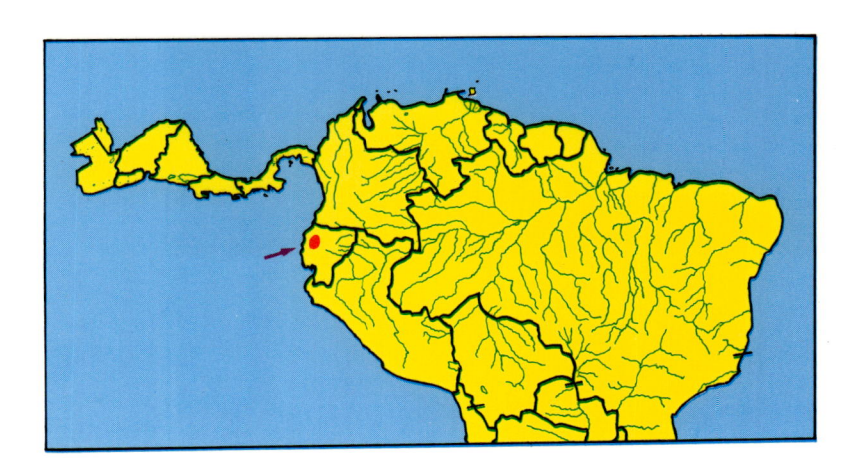

BRILLIANT-THIGHED POISON FROG
Epipedobates femoralis

This colorful little frog is one of the mostly widely distributed poison frogs, being found from the Guianas through the Amazon to Colombia, Ecuador, and Peru (it seems to be scarce or absent south of the Amazon). Though variable, it generally is black above, the skin quite granular. On each side there are two narrow white to golden stripes, one running from the groin to the tip of the snout (to meet its fellow from the other side), the other running from the tip of the snout (where it touches the oblique lateral stripe) back toward the thigh (sometimes incomplete). The top of the arm has yellow and white stripes. The thigh is black, setting off a strongly contrasting comma-shaped pale spot that usually is bright yellow or even bright red. The lower leg is brownish, without a bright spot under the shank. The black belly is variously mottled with white, and the throat usually is solid black. Structurally, the toes have narrow basal webs, teeth are present, and the first finger is distinctly longer than the second. Adults range from 20 to 33.5 mm in length.

Various details of the pattern will distinguish *E. femoralis* from similar species such as *E. boulengeri* and *E. myersi*, but the real problem is telling it from the almost identical (at least in color pattern) *E. pictus*, a notoriously variable species that belongs to a different species group. The two species occur in the same areas and have been found in the same patch of ground litter. Both display contrasting thigh patterns ("flash marks") that would seem to warn predators

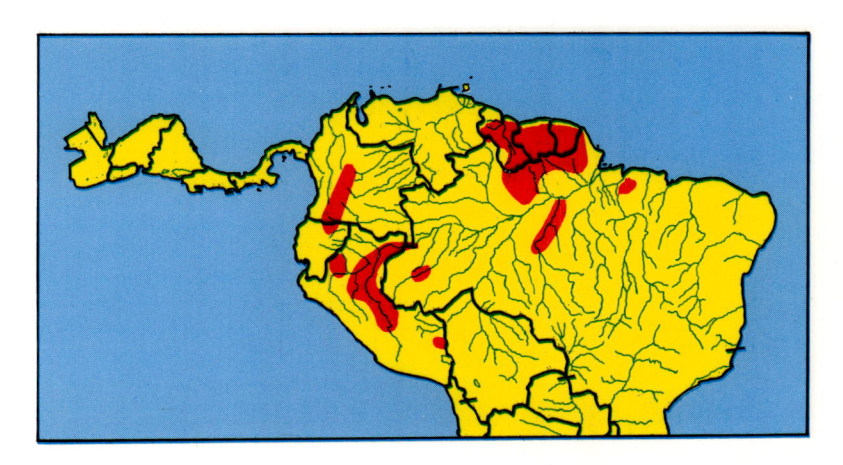

General distribution of *Epipedobates femoralis*, the Brilliant-thighed Poison Frog.

they are noxious. Although *E. femoralis* from any one locality should be a few millimeters longer than *E. pictus* from the same locality, this character does a hobbyist little good. Structurally, *E. pictus* lacks basal toe webbing and has the first finger about equal in length to the second. The top of the underside of the shank of *E. pictus* has a bright spot (absent in *E. femoralis*), and the two bright stripes do not meet on the side of the snout (not always easy to see). Because of the great range of this species, it should

OTHER EPIPEDOBATES

be expected that specimens from different areas will show variations in life history and behavior. Typically breeding seems to correspond to the start of the rainy season, but in some localities the species breeds through the entire year. Males are loud and persistent callers, often with a doubled note ("peep-peep"). This is a frog of the ground litter, and males call from the floor or from low shrubs and logs. Tadpoles are raised in bromeliad funnels, holes in logs, and similar small water bodies. They are carnivorous and feed on a variety of foods both in nature and in captivity. A roomy terrarium with lots of hiding places, high humidity and good ventilation (preferably with moving water), and high temperatures should lead to success.

Though *Epipedobates femoralis* is fairly variable in color, size, and details of pattern, most specimens can be recognized by the bright "flash marks" on the thigh and in the groin combined with other pattern elements. The Surinam juvenile at the top actually is more typically marked than the specimen below, which seems to be lacking the lower white stripe from the lip back toward the groin. In fact, if the bottom specimen really has a red shank spot (which might be barely visible here), it actually could be *pictus*. Photo at top by A. v. d. Nieuwenhuizen; photo below by P. Freed.

OTHER *EPIPEDOBATES*

A fairly typical Brilliant-thighed Poison Frog, *Epipedobates femoralis*, showing a subdued pattern. Notice the bright yellow spot at the base of the arm. Photo by R. Bechter.

OTHER *EPIPEDOBATES*

Epipedobates femoralis is virtually identical to *E. pictus*, which is found alongside it over much of the range. Both species have the bright thigh marking, displayed especially well in this Peruvian Brilliant-thighed Poison Frog, but *E. pictus* also has a bright spot on the upper shank that is absent in *E. femoralis*. Photo by A. v. d. Nieuwenhuizen.

OTHER EPIPEDOBATES

Epipedobates flavopictus, Lutz's Poison Frog.

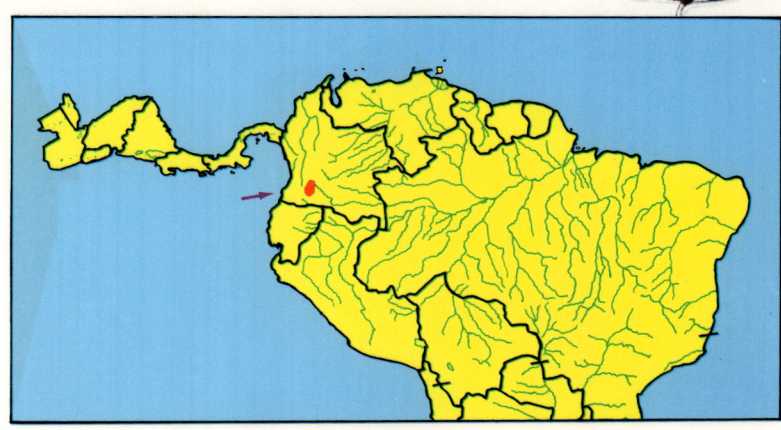

LUTZ'S POISON FROG
Epipedobates flavopictus

Recently distinguished (although tentatively) from *E. pictus*, this *pictus*-lookalike from the southeastern states of Brazil ranges from about 22 to 31 mm in body length in adults, a bit longer than most *pictus*-type frogs. Basically, it is distinguished from more typical *pictus* by having two rows of small yellow spots on the back between the bright stripes. The thigh colors and shank spot are similar to *E. pictus*, and the belly remains white with brownish to blackish mottling, though the mottling may be almost absent in some populations. *Epipedobates pictus* is a wide-ranging and variable species, and no doubt it is composed of several distinguishable species. Full studies on this group have not yet been published, and Lutz's Poison Frog is merely the first of several "names" to be removed from *pictus*.

General distribution of Lutz's Poison Frog, *Epipedobates flavopictus*.

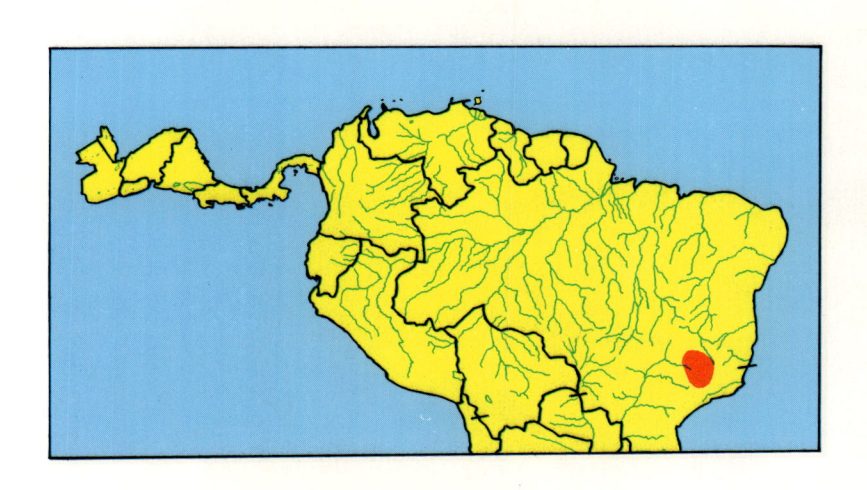

General distribution of Niceforo's Poison Frog, *Epipedobates ingeri*.

NICEFORO'S POISON FROG
Epipedobates ingeri

This species, described from a few specimens from southwestern Colombia, apparently remains unknown in life—at least I've run across no records of living colors. The skin is strongly granular on the back, smooth on the belly. No stripes are present, the preserved frogs appearing to be almost uniformly dark with small white spots at the bases of the arms and legs and a white spot at the upper undersurface of the shank. The belly may be marbled with a lighter color. The frog is closely related to *E. pictus*, so the back in life may be dark brown to black and the white spots may be yellow or even reddish. Adult size reaches at least 27 mm. Teeth are present, there are no webs at the bases of the toes, and the first finger is longer than the second.

The types were taken at 400 meters elevation near Aserrio, near the Rio Pescado, Caqueta, Colombia...perhaps a hobbyist with time on his hands might rediscover the species.

Niceforo's Poison Frog, *Epipedobates ingeri*. Life colors of this species appear to be unreported.

OTHER EPIPEDOBATES

The Manu Poison Frog, *Epipedobates macero*.

MANU POISON FROG
Epipedobates macero

This poison frog is of moderate size (24 to 30 mm adult length) and closely related to the group of species clustered around *E. petersi*. The back is strongly granular and bright red, while the sides are black. Separating the back from the upper side is a broad yellow stripe that runs from the groin to behind the eye, where it tapers and disappears before reaching the head. Another yellow stripe runs from the nostrils to the insertion of the arm. The entire undersurface, including the legs, is bright blue with black marbling. The upper sides of the limbs are covered with small blue spots on a dark brown or nearly black background. Truly a beautiful little animal! The color scheme closely resembles that of *E. cainarachi*, but that species has a complete yellow dorsolateral stripe and bright yellow "flash marks" in the arm and leg insertions. Other similar species differ in belly color, duller back color, or entire lack of the dorsolateral stripes.

Known so far only from Manu National Park in southeastern Peru, the Manu Poison Frog calls most actively near dawn and dusk. In the dry season the frogs normally are found near shallow, slow streams, but during the wet season they apparently move into the forest. The adults are ground-litter frogs feeding mostly on ants and tiny beetles. Mating and egg-laying have not been observed, but two males carrying tadpoles had two and four tads on their backs. The tadpoles are raised in the stream where the adults were found (at least in the dry season), not in plant funnels or standing water bodies, an unusual occurrence in the genus. A metallic gold stripe on the upper edge of the tail of the tadpole also is unusual.

CONFUSING POISON FROG
Epipedobates maculatus

About 130 years ago, Moritz Wagner, a European traveler and collector, passed through western Panama, a region then known as Chiriqui. He picked up and preserved a single 19-mm female poison frog that remains the only known specimen of a unique and confusing little species that has not yet been rediscovered. The brown back and belly (much paler on the belly) are smooth, teeth are present, the first finger is longer than the second, the finger discs are small, and there is narrow webbing at the bases of some of the toes. These all are fairly normal characters of *Epipedobates*, but the color pattern is unique in the genus: large rounded bright spots (said to be golden yellow, but perhaps red in life) edged with slightly darker brown to distinguish them from the background. There is a trace of a yellow spot on the belly, and otherwise the frog is unmarked. Large yellow spots are more typical of *Dendrobates* species

***Epipedobates maculatus*, the Confusing Poison Frog. This species is unknown in life and the colors are guesses.**

General distribution of *Epipedobates macero*, the Manu Poison Frog.

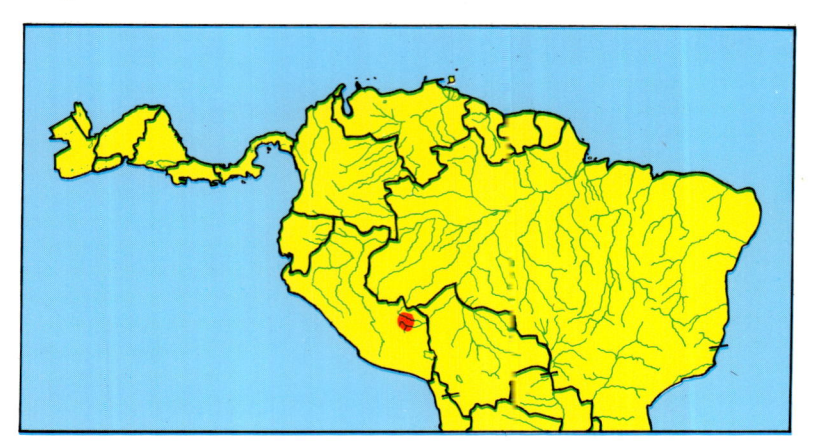

General distribution of *Epipedobates maculatus*, the Confusing Poison Frog. There is a possibility this species actually is from Ecuador.

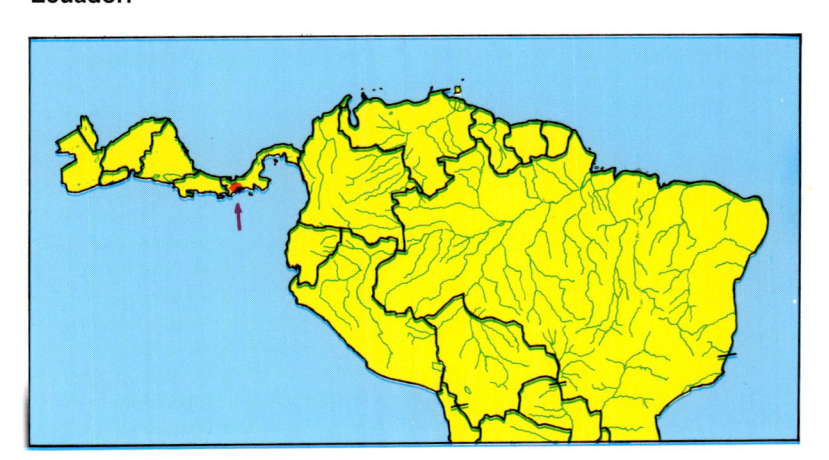

234

OTHER *EPIPEDOBATES*

than *Epipedobates* species, but the foot structure will distinguish the Confusing Poison Frog from any *Dendrobates* species. The type-locality is rather indefinite, covering a huge territory of rainforest that is either largely unexplored by herpetologists (and very difficult to collect in) or turned into pastures and plantations. If *E. maculatus* really comes from western Panama it may be extinct if its range has been converted to human use. However, it could simply have been overlooked. Additionally, there is a possibility (and a strong one at that) that the frog actually came from Ecuador, where Wagner also collected and where many species of *Epipedobates* are found in often very small ranges. It's not time to give up hope of ever seeing the Confusing Poison Frog alive—there are lots of isolated mountain ranges and rainforest islands in Ecuador (and even in western Panama) that have not been touched by herpetologists looking for poison frogs.

Epipedobates myersi, Myers's Poison Frog.

MYERS'S POISON FROG
Epipedobates myersi

This close relative of *E. femoralis* was described from the Vaupes area of southeastern Colombia, where it was found calling from the forest floor and low perches before sunset. The loud double-noted whistle ("peep-peep") lasted for a minute at a time and first drew the attention of the discoverer to the frogs. This is a relatively large species of the genus (28 mm body length) that is closely related to *E. femoralis* but has the dorsolateral stripes indistinct or absent and the red of the thigh present only as a diffuse blotch or wash over the back of the thigh, not a strongly defined "flash mark." The skin is granular and the toes have small webs at the base. In life Myers's Poison Frog (named after Dr. C. W. Myers of the American Museum, the most prolific worker on the group) is dark brown on the back with somewhat darker granules and the sides are black. The colors of the back and sides are separated by an indistinct brighter area, not a real stripe. There is a well-defined white ventrolateral stripe from below the nostrils to the groin, the white becoming bright yellow in the groin. The throat and chest are blackish brown, grading through dark marbling into a nearly white lower belly. The front surface of the thigh is bright yellow, the posterior surface red. Virtually nothing is known of the natural history of this species, though males are aggressive to other poison frogs and the loud call is assumed to be a territorial "advertisement" call. It has been maintained in captivity but apparently not bred.

RUBY POISON FROG
Epipedobates parvulus

The Ruby Poison Frog is one of the half-dozen or so species in which the black back is covered with red (sometimes bronzy) granules. In this fairly small species (adults 17.5 to 24 mm adult length) the black sides are marked with only a short blue stripe that runs from the groin about half way to the arm. A whitish line along the jaw runs back to the arm insertion and ends in a bluish "flash mark"; a yellow spot is absent from the base of the thigh. There is no light spot under the shank, though a weakly defined bright area rarely may be present. The belly is marbled with blue and black, either color dominating. The legs and arms are virtually black above. The Ruby Poison Frog has teeth and lack webs at the bases of the toes. *E. pictus* has a distinct bright spot

The Ruby Poison Frog, *Epipedobates parvulus*.

General distribution of Myers's Poison Frog, *Epipedobates myersi*.

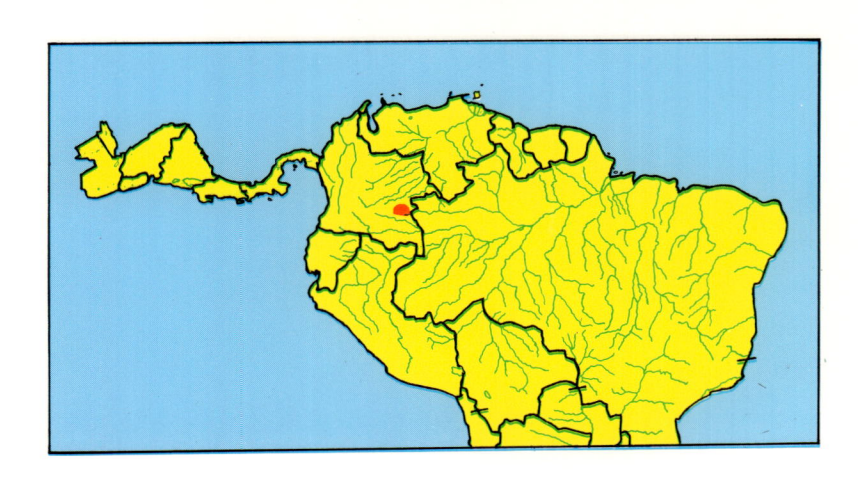

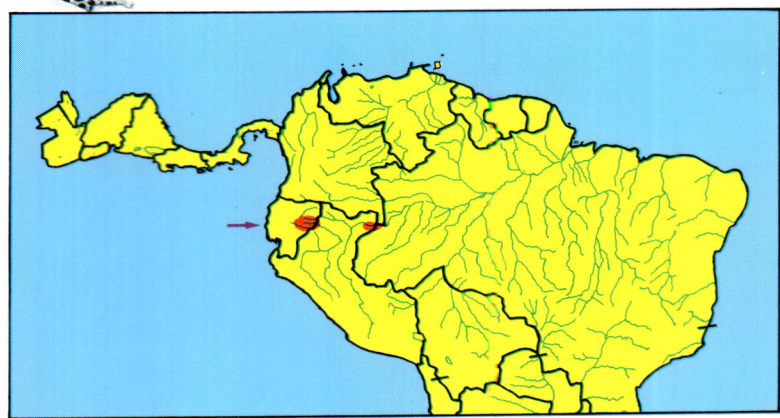

OTHER EPIPEDOBATES

General distribution of the Ruby Poison Frog, *Epipedobates parvulus*.

under the base of the calf and lacks the red granules on the back. The virtually identical E. bilinguis has yellow "flash marks" at the base of the arm and, especially prominent and circular, on the upper thigh; the ranges do not overlap. The Ruby lives along with E. zaparo, a similar species that has a nearly complete narrow line low on the side, is somewhat smaller, and has webs at the bases of the toes. E. espinosai is smoother, smaller, and has small webs at the bases of the toes. The species related to E. petersi have a bright stripe between the back and the side.

Epipedobates parvulus is a fairly common ground-litter species of the Rio Pastaza system of northeastern Ecuador east of the Andes Mountains; there is a record from near Loreto, Peru, as well. There is a record of a specimen taken at night, but this must be exceptional; other records refer to the species as active and calling during the day, as would be expected.

Not often available, the Ruby is a beautiful little frog that can be kept in relatively small terraria. The tadpoles feed on powdered flake food and similar items, but the problem is the small size of the froglets—it is very hard to feed frogs that are 10 mm long. For the first two months they have to be kept in small cages with a multitude of springtails and other truly tiny insects, then they can be switched over to vitamin-dusted fruitflies. Good luck—this is a tough species but worth the effort.

PERUVIAN POISON FROG
Epipedobates petersi

The granular back skin of the Peruvian Poison Frog is brown, with at most a faint reddish tinge, and sharply set off from the sides by a fairly wide yellow or whitish stripe that runs from the tip of the snout to the groin. A second, usually paler, stripe runs

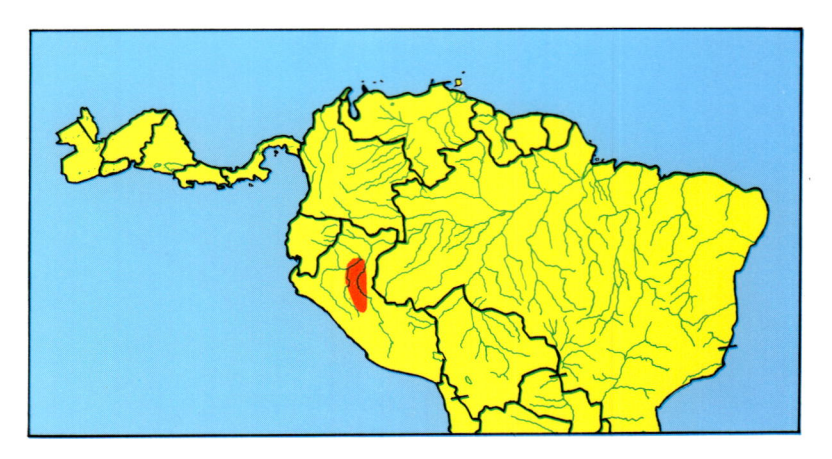

General distribution of *Epipedobates petersi*, the Peruvian Poison Frog.

This is an especially dull example of the Ruby Poison Frog, *Epipedobates parvulus*. Notice the poorly marked "flash marks" compared to *Epipedobates bilinguis*. Photo by R. D. Bartlett.

236

OTHER *EPIPEDOBATES*

Epipedobates petersi, the Peruvian Poison Frog.

Though it is far from common in the terrarium, *Epipedobates petersi* can be common in nature and deserves more attention. The colors are not spectacular but sometimes can be very attractive. The granules on the back never are red in this species. Photo by R. Bechter.

along the lip to the base of the arm, which bears a golden spot or short stripe. The legs are brown with a few scattered dark spots and a greenish wash on the thigh. The belly is boldly marbled with blue and black. Adults are 21 to 31 mm long. *E. cainarachi* has a distinctly reddish back and brighter dorsal stripes, as well as large yellow "flash marks" in the armpit and groin, while *E. macero* has an incomplete oblique lateral stripe and a red back. *E. bolivianus* has a yellow and black belly. The lack of webs at the bases of the toes in combination with the presence of teeth should separate it from other similar species, including *E. pulchripectus*, which has a black back, paler blue belly marbling, and more conspicuous yellow spot in the groin.

E. petersi occurs rather widely in the Rios Ucayali and Huallaga systems of central Peru, an area noted for many early collections of tropical fishes and still today drawing amateur fish collectors. Unfortunately, this ground-living species seldom in collected for the hobby, and admittedly its colors are not bright enough to appeal to many other than specialists. It may raise its tadpoles in tiny streams like *E. macero*.

OTHER *EPIPEDOBATES*

Like most related *Epipedobates*, the Peruvian Poison Frog, *E. petersi*, is terrestrial and secretive, calling from in hiding for only a few hours each day. Photo by R. Bechter.

OTHER *EPIPEDOBATES*

SPOT-LEGGED POISON FROG
Epipedobates pictus

I've already said almost everything you need to know about this species under the discussion of *E. femoralis*. It is a wide-ranging, very variable species (or almost certainly a group of several species) with a dark brown granular back, two complete whitish or yellowish stripes on the sides that do not meet on the snout, bright spots in the armpits and on top of the thigh, and a black/blue/white marbled belly. There is a bright spot, usually yellow to red, under the base of the shank (the "proximoventral calf spot" of the technical literature) that is absent in *E. femoralis* and almost all other similar species (see *E. flavopictus*, which has a double row of small yellow spots down the middle of the back). Like *E. femoralis*, with which it often is collected, the Spot-legged Poison Frog ranges widely over the Guianas and the Amazon basin and can be quite common. It is easy to keep in humid, ventilated terraria and has been bred on occasion. The tadpoles feed on powdered fish flakes, algae, yeast, boiled lettuce, and similar foods. Like other small poison frogs, the tiny froglets are difficult to feed and have a low rearing success rate.

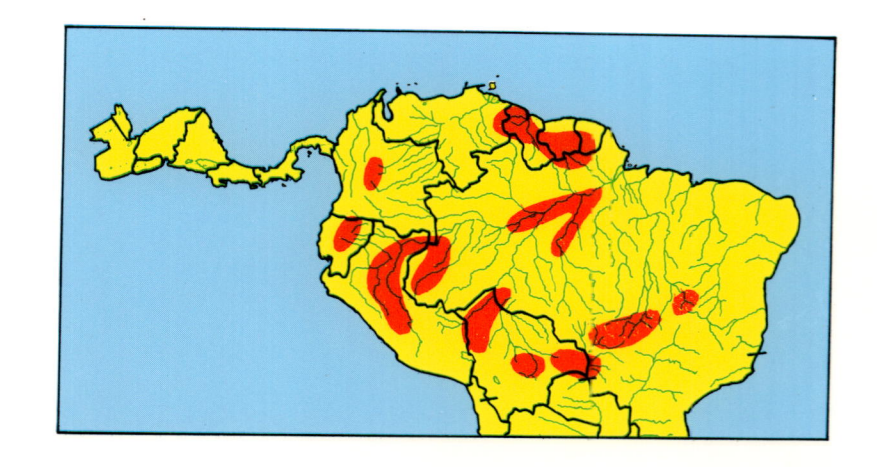

General distribution of the Spot-legged Poison Frog, *Epipedobates pictus*.

Epipedobates pictus is perhaps the only poison frog common in the inundated Amazon basin, but it survives poorly in captivity and is too small to attract much attention. Compared to *Epipedobates femoralis*, the "flash mark" on the thigh usually is smaller and there is an additional bright area (barely visible on the upper leg in this photo) on the shank. Photo of a specimen from the Ucayali area, Peru, by P. Freed.

OTHER *EPIPEDOBATES*

I have no idea how you would separate this Amazon basin specimen of *Epipedobates pictus* from the southern Brazilian *E. flavopictus*. Obviously the dorsal pattern of paired spots and broken lines won't work. Notice the extensive yellow area over the entire thigh in this specimen and notice also the bright yellow just visible on the back of the shank. Photo by A. v. d. Nieuwenhuizen.

OTHER EPIPEDOBATES

Epipedobates pulchripectus, the Blue-breasted Poison Frog.

BLUE-BREASTED POISON FROG
Epipedobates pulchripectus

This beautiful poison frog is black above and on the sides; bright blue with black spots and marbling below and under the legs; and has two bright yellow stripes, one running from the groin to the tip of the snout and the other along the lip to the base of the arm. The oblique lateral stripe ends in a large bright yellow spot on the thigh, while the lip stripe ends in a smaller spot at the base of the arm. The thighs are dark, washed with blue. The back skin is granular, and there are no teeth and no webs at the bases of the toes. Adults are 22.5 to 27 mm long. Though this pattern resembles other species related to *E. femoralis* and *E. pictus*, it is likely to be confused at first glance only with *E. azureiventris*, which has a golden dorsolateral stripe ending over the legs, not in the groin, an incomplete golden oblique lateral stripe, and paler yellow lip stripe. (Also, *E. azureiventris* is from the Andes on the opposite side of the continent from the Blue-breasted Poison Frog.)

The Blue-breasted Poison Frog is known only from near Serra do Navio, a manganese mining town in northeastern Brazil near the Atlantic Ocean and the Guianas. It is day-active, nervous, and hides in the litter when disturbed. The tadpoles probably are raised in holes in palm logs and other small water bodies. Ants were found in the stomachs of the type specimens. The type-locality is wet rainforest with an average temperature of 25 to 26°C.

General distribution of the Blue-breasted Poison Frog, *Epipedobates pulchripectus*.

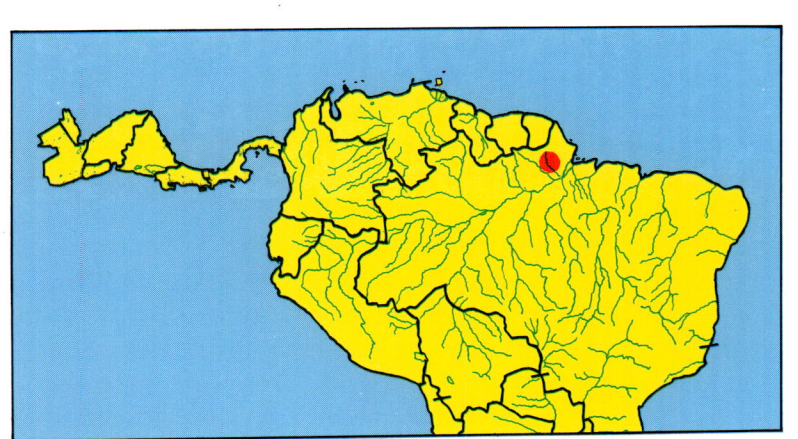

TEPUI POISON FROG
Epipedobates rufulus

This confusing and poorly understood species was described from two specimens taken at 2100 and 2600 meters on the Chimanta Massif of southeastern Venezuela at Amuri and Murey tepuis. Though described as a *Dendrobates* species, teeth are present, the finger discs are not greatly expanded, and the first finger seems to be about equal to or slightly longer than the second (variable in the two type-specimens), so it appears to be an *Epipedobates*. The holotype is a female about 23 mm long and with simple reddish brown back and sides without obvious pattern. The

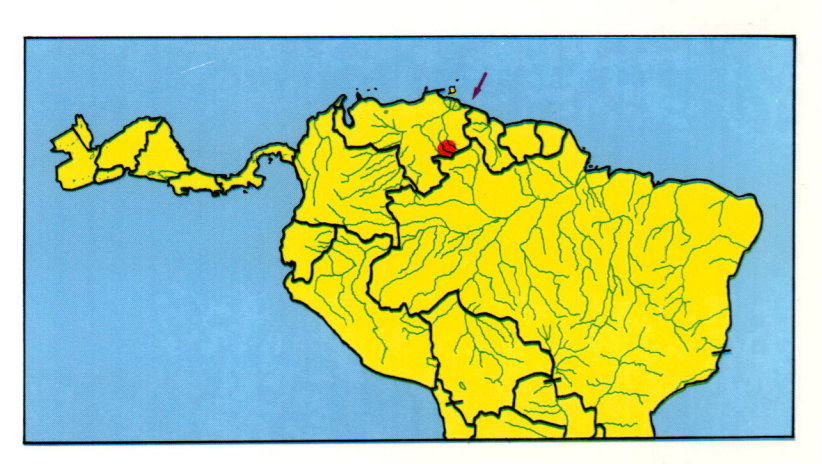

General distribution of the Tepui Poison Frog, *Epipedobates rufulus*.

belly is strongly mottled with black and bright yellow, the throat almost black. The skin is fairly smooth but there are traces of two roughened lines on the sides that may correspond to the dorsal stripes of other *Epipedobates*. The first finger is described as shorter than the second in this specimen and appears that way in the published photograph. The male paratype is about 20 mm long and very similar in general appearance but is almost black above, the yellow of the belly almost white, and has tinges of orange on the feet. The first finger is equal in length to the second.

It seems as though this species might be compared to *E. erythromos* but with an even more reduced dorsal pattern and yellow instead of blue mottling on the belly (and of course no red on the upper arm), but the limited size of the type series and small amount of information presented in the original description make

Epipedobates rufulus, the Tepui Poison Frog.

OTHER EPIPEDOBATES

SILVERSTONE'S POISON FROG
Epipedobates silverstonei

Silverstone's Poison Frog is one of the most beautiful of all the poison frogs—quite a statement when you consider the many wonderful patterns in species of the group. Restricted (apparently) to the Cordillera Azul, a small mountain range to the east of the Andes in Peru, it was not discovered until a road was cut from the highlands down to Tingo Maria, opening the area to patient and hardy collectors. (The first specimen was taken in 1946 by a curious entomologist—the insect people always seem to be in the oddest places first.) The bright reddish orange frog immediately drew interest, and it was figured as an undescribed species in Silverstone's *Phyllobates* revision. A few years later Myers and Daly described it as *Dendrobates silverstonei* in honor of Silverstone's contributions to the understanding of the poison frogs. Because the species has teeth, the first finger is a bit longer than the second, and the finger discs are not greatly expanded, Silverstone's Poison Frog is today placed in *Epipedobates*, where it is thought to be closely related to *E. bassleri* and *E. trivittatus*. *Phobobates* is an available generic name for these species if future workers decide they need their own genus.

E. silverstonei is large, 36 to 42.5 mm in adults, and, as mentioned, bright orange or reddish orange above. The legs are black, as is the body over the vent, the black continuing forward as black spots or a black network over the back, though the head is always unmarked (except sometimes a black spot between the eyes). The black network may be relatively weak or may be extensive, isolating bright orange spots against a black background. The arms are orange, sometimes with black spots, and a black "mask" may cover the jaws and eardrum. Belly color varies considerably, from almost solid black to almost solid pale orange, but usually almost black under the head and vent and under the legs. There may be a bright orange spot under the upper shank. Sometimes the hind legs are heavily marked with orange spots or an orange network.

Though the color pattern may resemble that of *Phyllobates bicolor*, the granular skin of the back (smooth in *bicolor*) will separate the two species at a glance. *E. bassleri* may be similar in general appearance, but it usually gives the appearance of having yellow, greenish, or dull orange dorsal stripes with an irregular dark suffusion between the stripes, rather than being bright orange with a black network. Actually, it should be almost impossible to confuse *E. silverstonei* with any other described poison frog, at least once the full coloration is developed. Silverstone's Poison Frog appears to be restricted to the Cordillera Azul, where it is found from about 1300 to 1800 meters elevation. The humid rainforest here is relatively cool because of the altitude (22 to 25°C would be best in the terrarium). It was easiest to collect in areas that had just been cut for pastures or roads, probably simply because it was easier to find the frogs there than in the heavier undergrowth of the undisturbed forest. Almost strictly a ground-dweller, it is active during the day, calling from late morning on. In the terrarium the species is very territorial and

Silverstone's Poison Frog, *Epipedobates silverstonei*, is a large and brilliantly colored frog that is popular with advanced hobbyists. The bright orange or reddish coloration is constant, but the black net on the back varies greatly. The group of frogs in the bottom photo present a sight few hobbyists will ever have the pleasure of seeing. Photos by R. Bechter.

comparisons difficult. Although the two type-specimens were collected only 45 km apart, they differ significantly in color and structure and possibly could represent two species.

The species called by day from among groves of shrubby *Bonnetia* trees. Though several poison frogs were heard calling, they proved impossible to locate and collect. The Venezuelan tepuis are cool isolated mountains with an average temperature of only 14°C and occasionally seeing low temperatures of just 1 to 4°C. These are extreme conditions for poison frogs, few of which can tolerate temperatures much below 20°C on average.

OTHER *EPIPEDOBATES*

Views of Silverstone's Poison Frog, *Epipedobates silverstonei*. Even dull specimens of this species are an incredible sight. Photos by A. v. d. Nieuwenhuizen.

often fights. Males probably have defended territories in the wild and attract females with their distinctive trill call. Females lay gigantic clutches for a poison frog, 30 eggs being common. Hatching seems to take about two weeks on average. The male tends the clutch and takes the mass of tadpoles to standing water in a ditch, ruts, or a depression in the ground for raising—a very strange tadpole habitat for a poison frog. It seems that the male makes only two trips for an entire clutch, his large body size making this possible. The tadpoles are omnivores, feeding on what they can get, and probably are cannibalistic. Metamorphosis takes about 80 days, the froglets beginning to feed on tiny insects (fruitflies in captivity) after about four days. The brown-speckled tadpoles have an oral disc of the usual sort for an *Epipedobates*, with strong corner indentations and a single row of papillae around the entire disc except the center anterior (front) edge. There are two rows of teeth (one split) above the beaks and three rows below. After the front legs break out the tadpoles begin to change colors, becoming dull golden yellow on the front of the head in contrast to the dark brown body. Froglets have a distinctive coppery snout and are orangish yellow, the color intensifying with growth over the first year. As they grow the black of the back is "overrun" by an increasing amount of orange. By the age of seven months, frogs are orange on the snout and display orange stripes on the upper lip to the upper arm and along each side of the back, with round orange spots between the stripes. Over the next six to eight months the orange spots increase in size and fuse, reducing the black background to a network and also causing the dorsolateral stripes to lose their distinctness, merging into the orange back pattern. In the same way, the black side of the head and body gradually turns orange, sometimes leaving a black mask. The few known populations show distinct differences in

General distribution of Silverstone's Poison Frog, *Epipedobates silverstonei*.

243

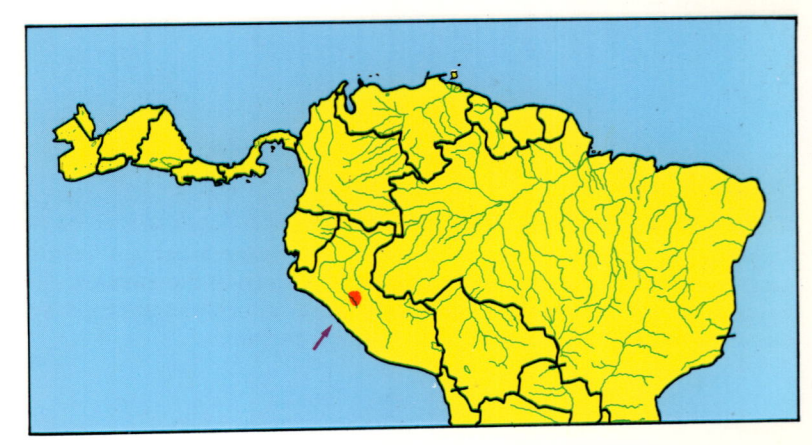

OTHER *EPIPEDOBATES*

Contrasting the Silverstone's Poison Frogs, *Epipedobates silverstonei*, on this and the facing page will give you some idea of both the constancy of coloration and variability of pattern of the species. This frog is large enough and conspicuous enough to appeal to any frog keeper, but unfortunately it has a very small natural range (apparently only one or two valleys) and is not bred often enough to supply a constant market. Photo by A. v. d. Nieuwenhuizen.

OTHER *EPIPEDOBATES*

Silverstone's Poison Frog, *Epipedobates silverstonei*. Photo by A. v. d. Nieuwenhuizen.

OTHER EPIPEDOBATES

development of the orange pattern. It may take as much as 18 months to reach maturity in this species, which may be expected to have a very long life under terrarium conditions. When this frog turns up on the market it is snapped up by appreciative specialists, so it is not easy to acquire a breeding pair. Remember that, like some other *Epipedobates*, they may be very aggressive, and they have large enough bodies to cause some damage to each other. Be sure the terrarium has sufficient hiding places. Egg clutches probably should be removed from the male's care to prevent their being eaten by non-parental females if you use a colonial breeding setup. According to some sources, the tadpoles must be fed on egg yolk at first, but this is not confirmed by some other observations. There are no indications from the oral disc that they are egg-feeders. Specialists want this frog, and beginners would love to have it a reasonable price. Perhaps as more captive-bred specimens enter the market the price will drop for quality specimens. Until then, this is the poison frog that many keepers dream of.

Epipedobates smaragdinus, the Emerald Poison Frog.

EMERALD POISON FROG
Epipedobates smaragdinus

This strange little Peruvian frog (about 26 to 27 mm in the type specimens) has a relatively simple but unique color pattern: It is black above (the skin strongly granular), has a bright green stripe from the snout to the groin, has a green stripe from the lip to the arm, is green under the head and on the front of the belly, and is blue at the back of the belly and under the legs. The throat of the single known male had two large black spots under the chin. Though stunning, the Emerald Poison Frog remains known from only its type-locality in Peru east of the Andes at 360 to 380 meters. It would make a great addition to the terrarium hobby.

The Sanguine Poison Frog, *Epipedobates zaparo*.

SANGUINE POISON FROG
Epipedobates zaparo

Think of *E. parvulus* with a white stripe low on the sides and you've got *E. zaparo*. Actually, the Sanguine Poison Frog is one of the several blue-and-black-bellied species with red granules on the back. At 26.5 to 30.5 mm in adult length it is one of the larger species of the genus. The black back is covered with bright red granules. The sides are black, as is the throat, and a narrow greenish white stripe runs from the snout along the lip over the arm insertion, where it joins a similar white stripe that continues to the groin. The base of the arm may be orangish. The limbs are brownish black and there may be a bluish wash on the thighs. Most of the belly and the undersides of the hind legs are black with pale blue or whitish mottling. Teeth are present, as are small webs at the bases of the toes. The low position of the stripe on the side and the absence of any stripes along the back, combined with the presence of both teeth and webs, make this species relatively distinctive.

E. zaparo is, like its relatives, active during the day on the ground in dense forests. It seems to be fairly common in the Rios Pastaza and Napo drainages of Ecuador at elevations of over 200 to 1000 meters; it also is recorded from Loreto, Peru.

General distribution of the Emerald Poison Frog, *Epipedobates smaragdinus*.

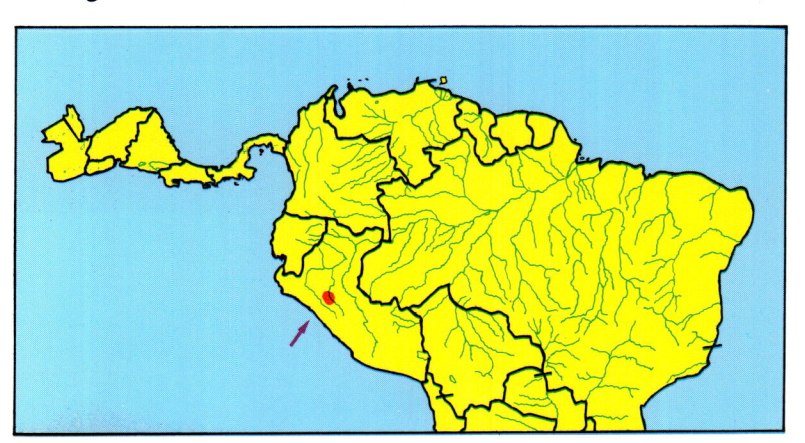

General distribution of the Sanguine Poison Frog, *Epipedobates zaparo*.

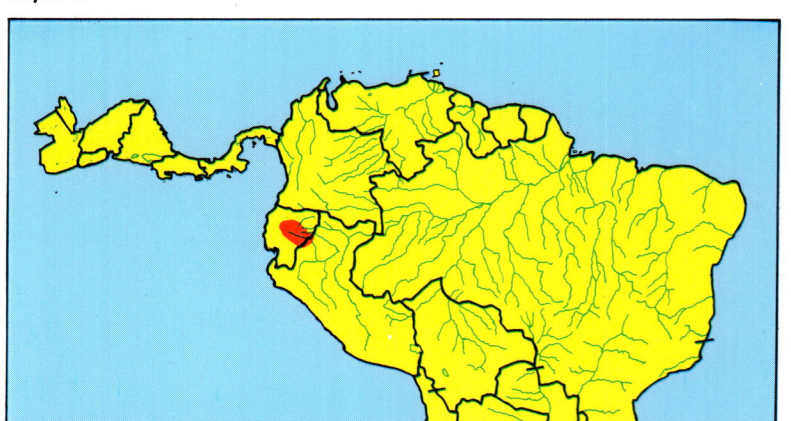

The Genus *Minyobates*

The tiny frogs of this genus are poorly known in captivity and apparently not often collected, though *M. minutus* is common and widely distributed. Their small size (all are under 20 mm in length) and sometimes plain colors make them hard to see in the ground litter or bromeliads where most are found. Several of the species are known only from the vicinity of their type-localities, and at least three species are restricted to isolated mountains. Additional species are known and await scientific description. One species, the Blue-bellied Poison Frog, appears occasionally in the terrarium, but it has a poor reputation and is not especially colorful. This genus contains some of the smallest known species of frogs, most of the species having maximum adult lengths of only 16 to 18 mm, about three-quarters of an inch. The difficulties in feeding such tiny animals should be obvious, and taking care of newly transformed froglets has proved virtually impossible for most keepers.

All this is not to say that some of the species are not striking. Three of the species (*M. steyermarki*, *M. virolinensis*, and *M. opisthomelas*) are bright red in life, while one (*M. altobueyensis*) is golden yellow with small black spots and another (*M. viridis*) is solid metallic green. Like many other species of the family, they would best be viewed in nature rather than in the terrarium, but their often restricted ranges make even this difficult.

Externally *Minyobates* is very similar to *Dendrobates*, with the widened toes discs of that genus and the first finger shorter than the second. Teeth are absent. A tarsal tubercle may be present at the proximal (closest to body) end of the tarsal fold. The oral disc of the tadpole is indented at the corners. The species are relatively easy to distinguish by color pattern and origin, though up to three species have been found at one locality.

COLLINS'S POISON FROG
Minyobates abditus

In October of 1971, Joe Collins and William Duellman of the University of Kansas literally stumbled upon this distinctive little frog on a trail along the eastern base of Volcan Reventador in Ecuador. Occurring in a remnant segment of cloud forest far to the south of the other species of the genus, the species occurs at great elevation for a poison frog, over 1700 meters (about a mile). Adults are only 16 to 18 mm long and are uniformly brown above and below (sometimes closer to black above and chocolate below) except for bright metallic golden orange spots ("flash marks") at the bases of the arms and legs. *M. abditus* appears to be strictly terrestrial, a species of the ground litter that raises its tadpoles in the cups of ground-living bromeliads. The closest relative may be the Andean Poison Frog. The oral disc of the tadpole lacks papillae at the center of the back edge.

Volcan Reventador is an active volcano that has erupted at least as recently as 1960. Additionally, there is some development in the area, so the future of *M. abditus* appears bleak at best.

ALTO DEL BUEY POISON FROG
Minyobates altobueyensis

Apparently restricted to the summit of Alto del Buey, Dept. Choco, Colombia, this bright greenish yellow poison frog is only 15.5 to 17 mm long in adults. The belly is brighter yellow than the back, and scattered black spots may pepper the back. The

Minyobates abditus, Collins's Poison Frog.

General distribution of Collins's Poison Frog, *Minyobates abditus*.

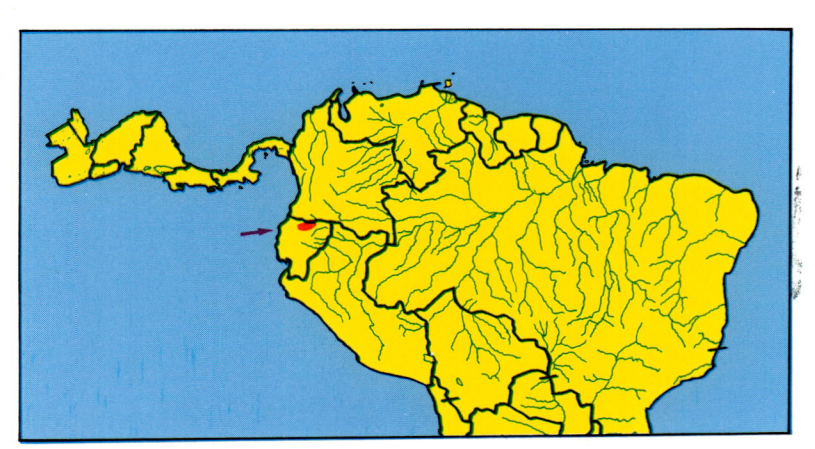

General distribution of the Alto del Buey Poison Frog, *Minyobates altobueyensis*.

THE GENUS MINYOBATES

The Alto del Buey Poison Frog, Minyobates altobueyensis.

belly skin is slightly granular, and there is no tarsal tubercle (distinctions from the bright red *M. steyermarki*). The summit of Alto del Buey, at 1070 meters, is a cool, misty environment with secondary growth of grasses and ferns resulting from clearing of native forest for erection of an aluminum summit marker. Most of the frogs were found on or near the marker, which was warmer than the surrounding area. Surprisingly, the frogs were not found in the forested natural areas. The Alto del Buey Poison Frog was found along with *M. minutus* and *M. fulguritus*.

CAUCA POISON FROG
Minyobates bombetes

Black or dark brown with a thin bright red stripe on each side of the back, the Cauca Poison Frog is one of more interestingly patterned species of the genus. The stripes tend to converge posteriorly and usually stop somewhere beyond midbody, though they can stop over the arms or extend nearly to the vent. The snout also is red, as is a large spot behind the eyes; the snout spot is connected to the side stripes, but the other spot may be free on all sides. The belly is black and very pale blue-green to yellowish, almost white. The skin is granular on both the back and belly, and the tarsal tubercle is weak. Adults are 16 to 20 mm long. The red stripes are unique (so far) in the genus, and among poison frogs in general, for that matter.

Minyobates bombetes is a frog of the ground litter, active during the day and feeding of various small insects. The call is a quite loud buzz. Tadpoles have the oral disc indented at the corners and lack papillae along both the anterior and posterior central edges (a feature shared with *M. abditus*, *opisthomelas*, and *virolinensis*). Virtually nothing is known of their breeding biology, though it is assumed that the tadpoles are raised in bromeliad funnels near the ground and that the egg clutches are of only one or two eggs. This presently is not a species of rainforest, instead being known from relatively dry areas with grasses and cactus as well as bromeliads. The type locality is a couple of small

The Cauca Poison Frog, Minyobates bombetes.

islands of low forest in the middle of a region cleared for pastures. The known sites are at 670 to 780 meters and 1580 to 1600 meters. It is possible that this species has not yet been discovered in more natural habitats and currently is known only from secondary, disturbed habitats to which it has adapted quite well.

YELLOW-BELLIED POISON FROG
Minyobates fulguritus

This tiny frog (only 13.5 to 20 mm long in adults) of western Colombia and central Panama has a distinctive pattern of golden or yellow dorsolateral stripes and incomplete lateral stripes on a black background. There is an incomplete golden stripe (often forked on the snout) down the middle of the back from the snout to about midbody. Most

General distribution of the Cauca Poison Frog, Minyobates bombetes.

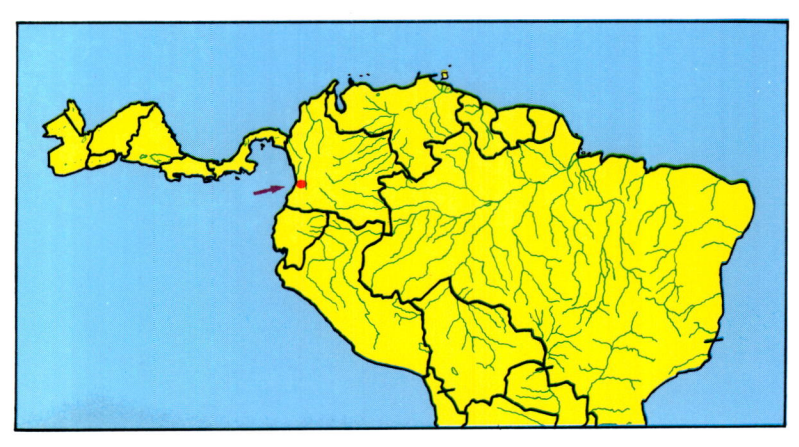

General distribution of the Yellow-bellied Poison Frog, Minyobates fulguritus.

THE GENUS *MINYOBATES*

The Yellow-bellied Poison Frog, *Minyobates fulguritus*.

distinctive is the bright yellow or golden belly with some black marbling or spots. There is no red or blue present in the pattern. The skin of the belly is a bit granular, and there is no tarsal tubercle or only a trace of one.

M. fulguritus and *M. minutus* are very similar, but *M. minutus* usually lacks the middorsal stripe and has a dark belly with small white and blue spots and marbling. The two species have been taken together, so they would appear to be full species.

The Yellow-bellied Poison Frog occurs in humid forests from about 160 to 800 meters elevation. It is largely terrestrial, taking cover among tree roots, but has been seen at least a meter above the ground. The tadpoles presumably are raised in bromeliads.

BLUE-BELLIED POISON FROG
Minyobates minutus

The common name of this species is somewhat misleading, as the blue on the belly usually is present as inconspicuous small spots or marbling on a black background. At only 12 to 15.5 mm in adult length, this is the smallest described poison frog. The back is dark brown, outlined by complete yellow to orange dorsolateral stripes, and there usually is a complete or incomplete yellowish to bluish lateral stripe lower on the side. The limbs may have scattered bluish spots, and the entire back may be covered with an orangish tint. The skin of the back and belly is somewhat granular, and there is no tarsal tubercle. The absence of yellow on the belly distinguishes *M. minutus* from the very similar *M. fulguritus*. Most specimens are dully colored and not too interesting in appearance.

General distribution of the Blue-bellied Poison Frog, *Minyobates minutus*.

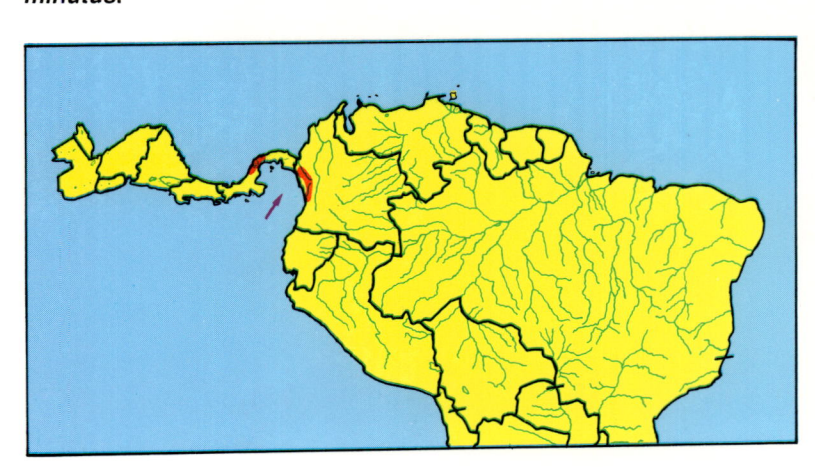

Like the other species of the genus, the Blue-bellied Poison Frog is a species of the ground litter in humid tropical forests from about 25 to over 1000 meters elevation. Relatively common in Panama and along the Pacific coast of Colombia, it has been taken from the leaf axils of bromeliads a few meters above the ground, but it basically is terrestrial. The tadpoles are raised in bromeliad funnels and similar water-holding structures, where supposedly they feed on (very small) mosquito larvae. The eggs are laid in clutches of only one to three, and it is thought that development from egg to metamorphosis takes about 60 days. Unlike the tadpoles of some other species in the genus, the posterior (lower or back) edge of the oral disc has a row of large papillae that continue to above the indented corners (many other species have the papillae absent from the posterior center of the disc).

Above and Below: Though it often is abundant in proper habitats in Panama, the Blue-bellied Poison Frog, *Minyobates minutus*, is too small and dull to appeal to many keepers. Additionally, it is very difficult to feed and maintain. Photos by A. v. d. Nieuwenhuizen.

THE GENUS *MINYOBATES*

These are very active little frogs, so they need a rather large terrarium with a lot of cover. Though it is not hard to keep the adults (feeding them on the usual tiny insects) at about 24°C, there has been limited success breeding them in captivity. The few tadpoles that have hatched have not fed well, and the metamorphosed froglets are virtually impossible to feed. A report that adults and larvae both feed on mosquitos in nature indicates a possible different approach to raising this species, as mosquitos are rather easy to raise in captivity.

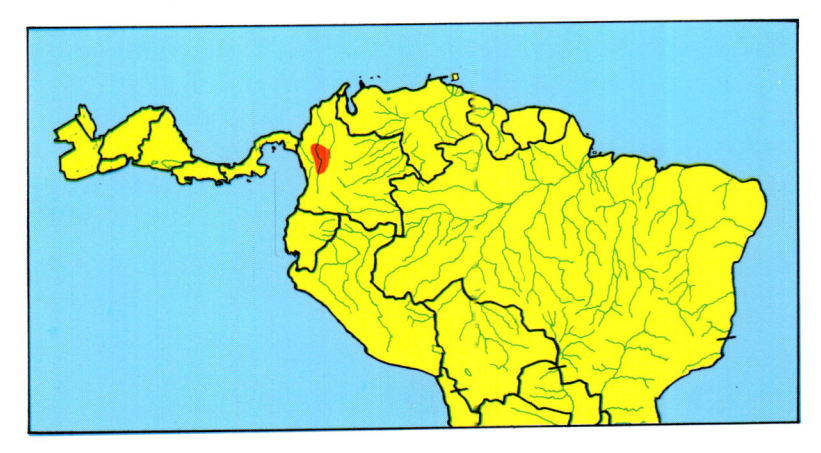

General distribution of the Andean Poison Frog, *Minyobates opisthomelas*.

ANDEAN POISON FROG
Minyobates opisthomelas

This little (14.5 to 19.5 mm adult length) red poison frog is found at high elevations (1000 to over 2000 meters, well over a mile) in relatively undisturbed wet forests of western Colombia. Uniformly reddish above, it is chocolate brown below, with or without red spots. The lower limbs are brownish, and there may be brownish suffusions over the back as well. The belly skin is somewhat granular, and there is a distinct tarsal tubercle. It is likely to be confused only with the Demonic Poison Frog, which is brighter red on both the back and belly and has smooth skin, and the Santander Poison Frog, which is scarlet anteriorly and brown posteriorly with the belly brown but spotted with blue-gray. Specimens may be superficially similar to *Dendrobates pumilio*, *granuliferus*, and *speciosus*, but those species are somewhat larger and lack a well-developed tarsal tubercle.

Mostly a ground-dwelling species, it may occur a few meters above the ground in bromeliads. The tadpoles are raised in bromeliad funnels. This species seems to be absent from disturbed forests and may be disappearing from much of its range. It has been suggested that it needs ground-living bromeliads for its tadpoles and disappears when bromeliads are destroyed in an area.

DEMONIC POISON FROG
Minyobates steyermarki

One of the most poorly known poison frogs, *M. steyermarki* is brilliant red, almost scarlet, in life, with tiny indistinct brownish spots scattered over the back, limbs, and belly. The back and belly skin are smooth, and there is a distinct tarsal tubercle. (The smooth skin, unusual in the genus, could be the result of preservation in strong formalin—the frog needs to be redescribed from fresh material.) Adults are about 14 to 16 mm in length. It occurs, as far as known, only at the summit of Cerro Yapacana in southern Venezuela, well to the east of the other species of the genus. Cerro Yapacana is a relatively low (1200 meters), isolated, flat-topped mountain of the type known as tepuis. Tepuis are eroded portions

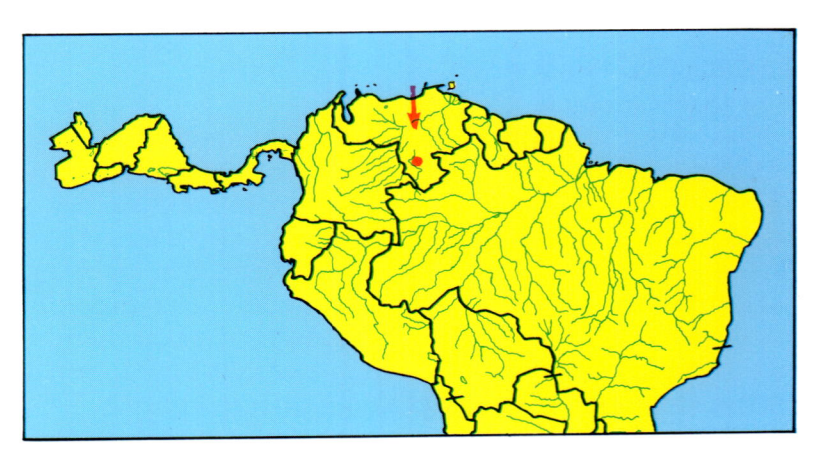

General distribution of the Demonic Poison Frog, *Minyobates steyermarki*.

The Demonic Poison Frog, *Minyobates steyermarki*.

Minyobates opisthomelas, the Andean Poison Frog.

THE GENUS *MINYOBATES*

of sandstone plateaus that rise directly from the surrounding forest and usually have limited vegetation at the summit. The Demonic Poison Frog was taken from mossy areas on sandstone crags where the surrounding trees usually were less than 10 meters high. Expeditions to tepuis are expensive and often necessitate helicopters to allow reasonable access, thus their faunas are poorly known and likely to remain so for some time. Gold miners started extensive forest fires on the slopes and base of the tepui in the 1980's that may have hurt this unusual poison frog (Gorzula, pers. comm.).

GREEN POISON FROG
Minyobates viridis

Like the Cauca Poison Frog, this striking little unicolored green poison frog is known from two localities, in this case 120 km apart; the elevations for the localities are 850 to 1200 meters and just 100 to 200 meters. Only 14 to 15.2 mm long in adults, this species is recognizable by its uniform metallic green color above and below (a bit darker and less metallic above), weakly granular skin (almost smooth on the back), and no tarsal tubercle. *M. viridis* was collected from relatively scrubby forest with few bromeliads and much moss on some of the trees. Much of the area was under development for pastures, reducing the forests to patchy islands. The frogs were most common in the ground litter and were active at midday, coming out in force after a rain. The call seems to be a low buzz. The species probably is widely distributed along the Cordillera Occidental of Colombia, but increasing loss of forest in this area may be leading to destruction of the species.

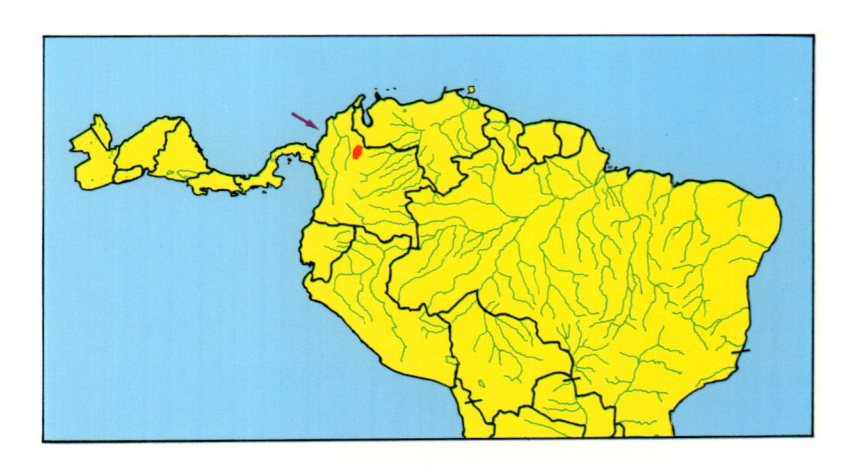

General distribution of the Santander Poison Frog, *Minyobates virolinensis*.

SANTANDER POISON FROG
Minyobates virolinensis

This most recently described *Minyobates* is from the Cordillera Oriental of Colombia at elevations between 1700 and 1850 meters. Like most of its relatives, it is small (about 14.5 to 19 mm in adults), has fairly granular skin, and has a tadpole with indented oral disc corners and a large gap in the row of papillae at the posterior edge of the disc. The colors are stunning—the head and front two-thirds of the back are scarlet, the posterior third brown with red granules. The belly is chocolate brown with blue-gray spots. The tarsal tubercle is well-developed. It seems to fall into a sequence of species including *M. abditus*

General distribution of the Green Poison Frog, *Minyobates viridis*.

Minyobates viridis, the Green Poison Frog.

The Santander Poison Frog, *Minyobates virolinensis*.

THE GENUS *MINYOBATES*

(brown above and below, with golden "flash marks"), *M. bombetes* (red dorsal stripes), *M. opisthomelas* (belly with red spots, back more suffused with brown), and *M. steyermarki* (red above and below, the skin smooth). The habitat of *M. virolinensis* is Andean selva forest, relatively scrubby and dry, with both oaks and abundant bromeliads. Stomach contents were mostly mites, with small insects, including ants, definitely in the minority. The frogs are found during the day in the crowns of trees and arboreal bromeliads at heights from 0.5 to 2 meters. Egg clutches would appear to be small (one to three eggs). Males carry the tadpoles to funnels in bromeliads up to 2 meters above the ground. One to two dozen tadpoles in various stages of growth and deposited by several different males could be found in a single bromeliad. The tads could be cannibalistic and probably are generalized feeders.

Color and pattern changes with growth in the Golden Poison Frog, *Phyllobates terribilis*. The tadpole develops golden stripes before the front legs emerge. At about 14 mm in length (bottom left) the frog is largely black with two broad but rather well-defined golden stripes. Soon (bottom center) the golden pigment begins to overlie the black, with the hind legs being the last area to change to gold in the adult (bottom right).

Phyllobates terribilis, the Golden Poison Frog

This frog was undoubtedly the herpetological sensation of 1978. Although it long had been known that various Amerindian tribes of northwestern South America used the secretions of poison frogs to treat the darts they used in hunting and warfare, there was positive evidence of only two species, *Phyllobates bicolor* and *P. aurotaenia*, actually being used. Rumors of other species being toxic enough to be considered deadly, including *Dendrobates auratus*, proved to be unfounded. In 1978, Myers, Daly, and Malkin published the description of *Phyllobates terribilis*, basing the name on specimens collected mostly during 1971 and 1973. They discovered the frog by following up on reports by the anthropologist Wassen originally published in 1935 on a poison frog in the Rio Saija drainage of the Colombian Choco.

Phyllobates terribilis is a stunning poison frog from several perspectives. It is large, almost 50 mm long, entirely bright golden yellow in color, and one frog produces enough batrachotoxins to kill 20,000 mice (and perhaps eight humans). It apparently is restricted to the vicinity of the Rio Patia, a tributary of the Rio Saija, Dept. Cauca, southwestern Colombia. Common to abundant in its small range, it is active during the day and not at all shy, apparently with some "knowledge" that its potent toxins give it protection from virtually all predators. Even the local Amerindians collect it carefully, using leaves to prevent contact with the hands.

Females mature at 40 to 41 mm in length and reach at least 47 mm, while males mature at 37 mm and reach 45 mm (based on specimens raised in the laboratory). The skin is smooth and the overall shape is "husky"; the first finger is at least as long as the second; teeth are present; and the discs of the fingers are not especially expanded. In other words, it is a typical *Phyllobates* in structure. It differs from all other species by being uniformly bright golden yellow (occasionally golden orange and rarely pale metallic green), including the belly and the hind legs, in mature adults. Juveniles 25 mm long are entirely golden above and heavily suffused with bright yellow on the belly. Its closest relative certainly is *P. bicolor*, which is about 4 or 5 mm shorter in adult maximum length and even when fully mature still has mostly black thighs with golden to greenish tints and a belly that is at least partially black though it may be washed with yellow. The ranges of the two species are separated by territory seemingly lacking similar frogs (with only one specimen collected in an intermediate locality, and it possibly represents a different species yet). *P. aurotaenia* is smaller and has two broad yellow dorsolateral stripes (ending above the thighs) separated by a blackish back (which may be suffused with golden yellow in some specimens, but never enough to obscure the stripes). Both *P. bicolor* and *P. aurotaenia* are toxic with high levels of batrachotoxins, but neither approaches the toxicity of *P. terribilis*.

The Rio Saija area is lowland humid rainforest. Much of it is relatively rocky and steep, and it has not (yet) been greatly developed. The Golden Poison Frog seems to be a strictly ground-living species never found more than a few centimeters above the ground. It feeds on ants, which may provide part of the chemical basis for its toxins, because captive specimens gradually lose much of their toxicity and captive-bred specimens tend to be less toxic than their parents. All Golden Poison Frogs should be considered at least potentially toxic, even captive-bred specimens, and never handled with bare hands. Wild-caught specimens, if they should be encountered, should be considered as deadly as any

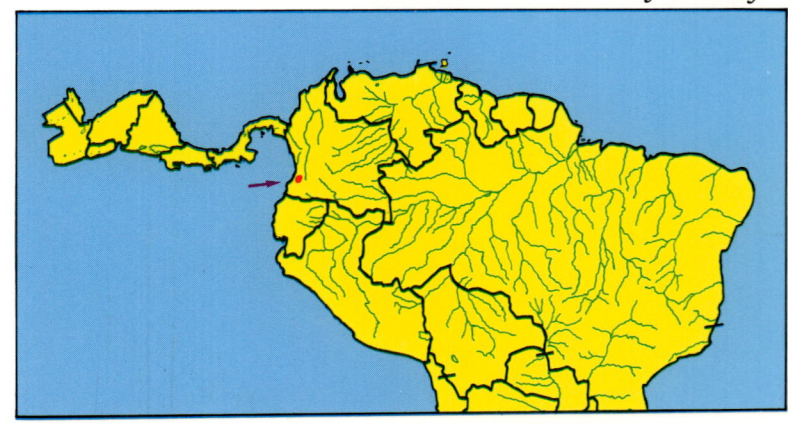

General distribution of the Golden Poison Frog, *Phyllobates terribilis*.

venomous snake because the toxins are secreted when the frog is even minimally disturbed. Batrachotoxins in the level found in the Golden Poison Frog could (at least in theory) cause human death just from a bit passing through the skin even without a cut.

Golden Poison Frogs have proved rather easy to maintain and breed in captivity. They can be kept as pairs or as colonies. Males call to attract females, increasing their calling when an obviously gravid female comes into view. The female follows the male to a bower, where limited activity in the form of the female stroking the male's back and sides takes place. Both sexes need not be present at the same time in the bower when egg-laying takes place, so presumably the male fertilizes the eggs after they are laid. Clutches are large (15 to 30 eggs), as in other *Phyllobates*, and are guarded for only the first two or three days by the male.

Hatching takes about 14 to 18 days, at which time the male returns to take the tadpoles onto his back. Nine tads have been recorded on a single male, but it seems likely he often carries fewer. Several trips are necessary to transport all the tads to water bodies for their growth. The tadpoles feed on a variety of detritus and plant and animal foods and will take almost anything from boiled lettuce to bloodworms in captivity. Their oral disc has three rows of teeth behind the relatively weak beaks and two rows (one split) above; one or two rows of papillae surround the disc except for the anterior (top) edge; the disc is

PHYLLOBATES TERRIBILIS

indented in the corners. After the hind legs come out, two bronzy gray stripes become visible on the body, the stripes becoming brighter later. Metamorphosis takes about two months, and the froglets begin to feed by ten days after transforming.

The froglets have gained a reputation as difficult to raise. They must be kept very clean, so some keepers use small containers with damp foam rubber on the bottom and a few hiding places. The terrarium must be kept spotlessly clean and sanitized with hot water every week at longest. The usual diet of tiny crickets and fruitflies, supplemented with vitamins and calcium, will suffice. Maturity takes about 18 months. Presumably the frogs live at least ten years in nature, longer in captivity if properly maintained. Though colorful and available, the keeper must never forget that this is a deadly animal and risky to have around the house. It cannot be kept safely with other frogs, and the risk of one escaping to be mouthed by a cat, dog, or even a child is very real. Wild-caught juveniles are at least as toxic as adults, and there is no real guarantee that all captive-bred specimens are harmless or nearly so because the mechanism that leads to a decrease in batrachotoxins in captivity is unknown. Caution is the watchword with this beautiful species.

This subadult Golden Poison Frog, *Phyllobates terribilis*, still shows large amounts of black on the limbs, belly, and even lips. Within a few weeks most of this should be covered by golden yellow. Photo by A. v. d. Nieuwenhuizen.

PHYLLOBATES TERRIBILIS

It is no exaggeration to say that, at least under certain circumstances, a wild-collected Golden Poison Frog, *Phyllobates terribilis*, could cause a human death on contact. The toxin is one of the most virulent of any known animal toxin, is produced in large amounts, and is released quickly as the result of little annoyance of the frog. The toxin kills monkeys at very low dosages and also has killed dogs and chickens that chewed paper towels dirtied by the skin mucus. Fortunately, captive-bred later generation Golden Poison Frogs seem (!) to lose most or all their toxicity. Photo by A. v. d. Nieuwenhuizen.

PHYLLOBATES TERRIBILIS

A gorgeous half-grown Golden Poison Frog in which the two golden stripes are still distinct. Notice, however, the golden spots starting to develop over the black midback. Photo by R. Bechter.

PHYLLOBATES TERRIBILIS

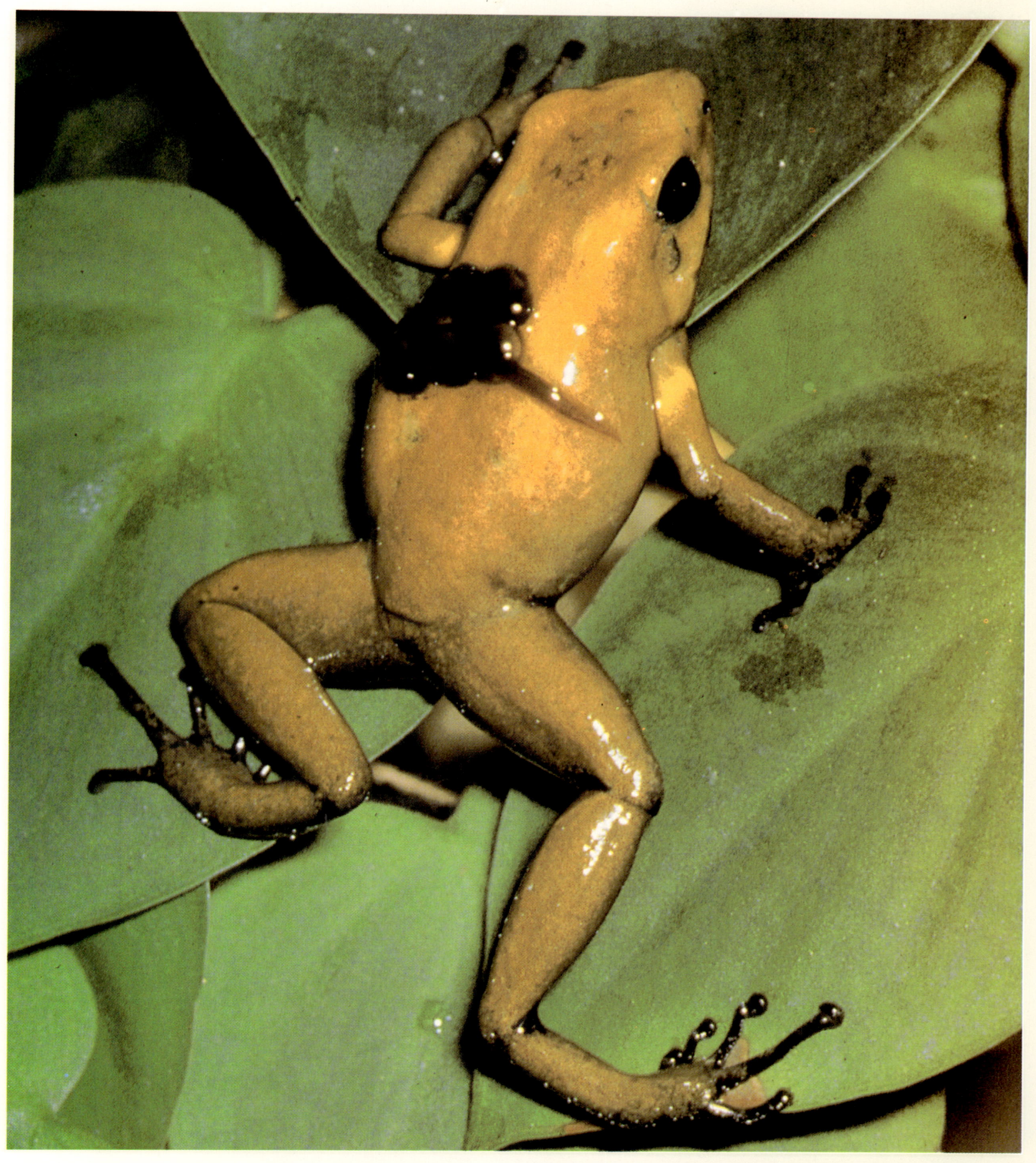

Fully adult Golden Poison Frogs, *Phyllobates terribilis*, are virtually golden frogs except for blackish toes. They lay large egg clutches and carry large numbers of tadpoles at one time. Whether this species is safe for any but the specialist poison frog keeper still is a matter of debate. Photo by R. Bechter.

Aspects of the life history of the Golden Poison Frog, *Phyllobates terribilis*. The mating pair is at the top left (female visible in side view). Even in the tadpole the golden stripes run straight back from the eyes over the rump toward the vent rather than being deflected downward into the groin as in *Epipedobates* species. All photos by R. Bechter.

Phyllobates vittatus, the Golfodulcean Poison Frog

This is another popular small poison frog from Costa Rica. Restricted to the Pacific coast of Costa Rica in Puntarenas Province, it is so closely related to the Caribbean *P. lugubris* that they once were considered to be a single species. The Pacific species is a bit larger (males 22.5 to 26 mm, females 26 to 31

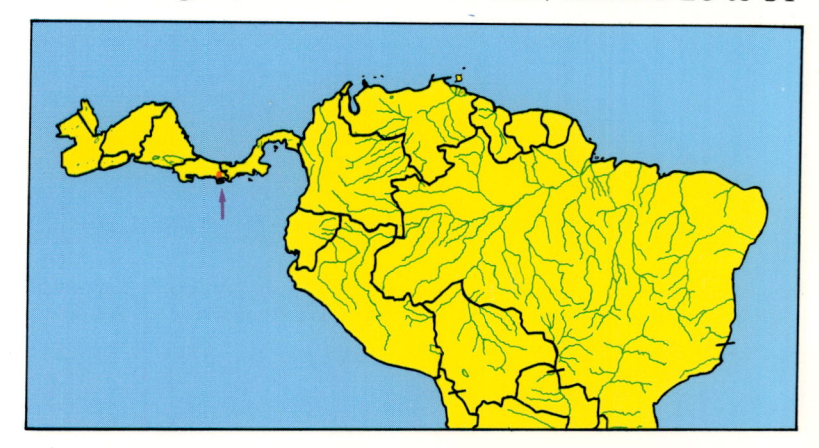

General distribution of *Phyllobates vittatus*, the Golfodulcean Poison Frog.

mm) than the Atlantic species (males 18.5 to 21 mm, females 21 to 23.5 mm in length) and is most easily distinguished by the wide, bright metallic orange dorsal stripes on a black back (narrow and yellower in *lugubris*) combined with finely dotted bright green hind legs (yellowish in *lugubris*). The belly is black with greenish or white mottling and there is a white stripe from the lower lip back to the arm. There may be traces of a broken middorsal stripe, and the snout usually is bright orange like the dorsal stripes. All the colors are metallic and the skin is smooth and glossy, producing a beautiful lacquered effect. In the Colombian *P. aurotaenia*, the belly is black with only small green spots, never green mottling or marbling.

A species of lowland rainforests, *P. vittatus* probably breeds all year except during limited dry seasons. The males are territorial and call from the ground or low plants, preferring bromeliad leaves. There may be wrestling and pushing between males if one intrudes on the territory of the other. Females are attracted to calling males and eventually (the entire courtship may extend over several days) follow the selected male to a bower. There may be much touching between the frogs, including stroking and grasping. The male may sit on the female's back, but their cloacas are never in contact. The female first lays her clutch of 10 to 20 eggs and then the male fertilizes them. The parents need not be together for successful laying and fertilization. After the first day or two the male does not tend the nest, though he returns to "check up" on things every week or so.

Hatching takes place after about 14 to 18 days, at which time the male has returned to gather the tadpoles. Several trips are necessary to get all the tads from a large litter to their water body, but they may stay on the back of the male for several days, still feeding on yolk stored in their guts. Once in the water they will eat almost anything but are not known to be cannibalistic. Metamorphosis takes place after about 40 days both in nature and in the terrarium. If food of the proper size is given along with vitamin and calcium supplements, the froglets are not difficult to raise. Sexual maturity is reached in about a year.

Other than its small size, *P. vittatus* makes an excellent terrarium animal even for the beginner. It is both colorful and easy to keep, and it is available at moderate prices for captive-bred specimens. What more could one ask?

Top: Male *Phyllobates vittatus* in combat. The heavy mottling on the belly and the green hind legs are characteristics of this species that should separate it from relatives. Photo by R. Bechter. *Bottom:* The large egg clutch of *Phyllobates vittatus* is laid in the moist axil of a bromeliad just above the funnel. Photo by R. Bechter.

Aspects of the life history of the Golfodulcean Poison Frog, *Phyllobates vittatus*. The tadpoles show various signs of spindly leg syndrome and probably will not survive for long after metamorphosis. The tadpole-carrying male at upper left is an amputee. Photos by R. Bechter (top left) and A. v. d. Nieuwenhuizen.

PHYLLOBATES VITTATUS

Phyllobates vittatus has proved to be a popular and hardy terrarium frog, though its small size is a negative factor. This tadpole-carrying male has only the palest of blue tints to the legs, but still enough to distinguish it from the yellow-legged *Phyllobates lugubris*. Photo by A. v. d. Nieuwenhuizen.

PHYLLOBATES VITTATUS

Tadpoles of the Golfodulcean Poison Frog develop most of the adult pattern before metamorphosis is completed. Unfortunately, these two tadpoles have spindly leg syndrome, an all-to-common malady of *Phyllobates* and *Epipedobates* in captivity. Photo by A. v. d. Nieuwenhuizen.

PHYLLOBATES VITTATUS

Phyllobates vittatus often has broad, deep golden orange stripes on the back. In frogs of this genus the pattern often appears extremely glossy, almost lacquered, and the hind legs appear to be peppered with fine bronzy glands just below the surface. The irregular golden spots down the midback, if present, help distinguish the Golfodulcean Poison Frog from the extremely similar Lovely Poison Frog. Photo by A. v. d. Nieuwenhuizen.

PHYLLOBATES VITTATUS

If stripes are visible on the back, they usually can be used to distinguish *Phyllobates* species from somewhat similar *Epipedobates* species. In most (but not all) *Epipedobates* the stripes begin to diverge at the sacral hump (the break in the back) and each ends low on the side at the base of the hind leg (the groin). In all *Phyllobates*, the stripes stay straight or actually converge behind the sacral hump to end still on the back in a line with the vent. Photo of *Phyllobates vittatus* by A. v. d. Nieuwenhuizen.

PHYLLOBATES VITTATUS

Three color shades of the Golfodulcean Poison Frog, *Phyllobates vittatus*. This species comes from a very small area of Costa Rica and, though still common, probably should be protected from over-collection. Captive-bred specimens are rather easy to obtain with a little looking around and make better terrarium inhabitants than stressed adults flown in directly from Costa Rica. Photos by: K. Lucas (top); D. Green (center); R. S. Simmons (bottom).

OTHE *PHYLLOBATES*

The Kokoe Poison Frog, *Phyllobates aurotaenia*, is dangerously toxic and should be considered risky to keep. Few Kokoes appear on the market, perhaps because of their similarity to the more common *Phyllobates vittatus*. In the Kokoe, the belly is patterned much as are the limbs with fine blue to green spots or speckles rather than the broad, coarse vermiculations of the Central American species. Photo by A. v. d. Nieuwenhuizen.

Other *Phyllobates*

Though *Phyllobates* is a small genus with only five recognized and very similar species, it is perhaps the most fascinating one because it contains the most toxic types. We've already discussed two species in some detail, and here we will go over the other three. Hobbyists and naturalists should remember that these frogs should all be considered very dangerous, at least when first caught and for the first year or so in captivity, and they should never be treated casually.

The genus *Phyllobates* can be recognized by the relatively narrow finger discs, the first finger as long as or longer than the second, and the presence of teeth. The species are at least 19 mm long in adults, reaching 47 mm. All have bright (usually golden or reddish) dorsolateral stripes (ending on the back over the thighs, not on the sides in the groin), black bellies, and finely dotted hind legs—at least in juveniles, as you learned in the discussion of *P. terribilis*. The species are found from Costa Rica to Colombia and replace each other geographically without apparent overlap. These are whistling frogs, often with relatively loud trills that last for several seconds.

KOKOE POISON FROG
Phyllobates aurotaenia

The Kokoe (pronounced something like *co-coin*) is one of the three definitely dangerous to humans poison frogs and is known to be used by Amerindians to treat darts. Adults are 23.5 to 34 mm in body length (females averaging 3 mm longer than males). These are black frogs with brilliant golden yellow, golden orange, or greenish yellow dorsolateral stripes that may be narrow or relatively broad. The status of the two stripe-width forms is uncertain, though they seem to represent ecotypes (the broad-striped form is somewhat larger than the narrow-striped); they interbreed in captivity and produce viable offspring. The type of *P. aurotaenia* is of the narrow-striped form. The belly and limbs are black, finely dotted with blue and green points. The two Central American species, which also are striped in adults, have the belly brightly mottled with bluish, greenish, or white on black and tend to have fairly well defined bright stripes on the sides. This is the common and widely distributed dangerous poison frog of the Colombian Choco, occurring in lowland rainforest of northwestern Colombia between the Atrato and San Juan drainages. Though it has been kept and bred in captivity, there are few published reports. Give it plenty of room and hiding places, keep it warm and humid, and expect behavior much like that of the closely related *P. vittatus*.

BLACK-LEGGED POISON FROG
Phyllobates bicolor

A gorgeous but very dangerous frog, *P. bicolor* is closely related to *P. terribilis* and they probably share a common ancestor. Adults have the entire back and sides golden yellow or orange (almost red), but the legs and belly are black. The legs often are covered with small blue and green spots, and it is not uncommon for the legs and belly to have a bright wash of pale yellow or orange tint. Assumedly the juveniles have bright dorsolateral stripes on a black background (as in *P. terribilis*), but this is poorly documented. There is a faint possibility that the Black-legged and Golden Poison Frogs intergrade, but it is more likely that their ranges currently are widely separated. The Golden Poison Frog is a bit larger and is uniformly golden yellow above and largely golden below by a size of 25 mm, so adults would never have even faintly black legs and belly.

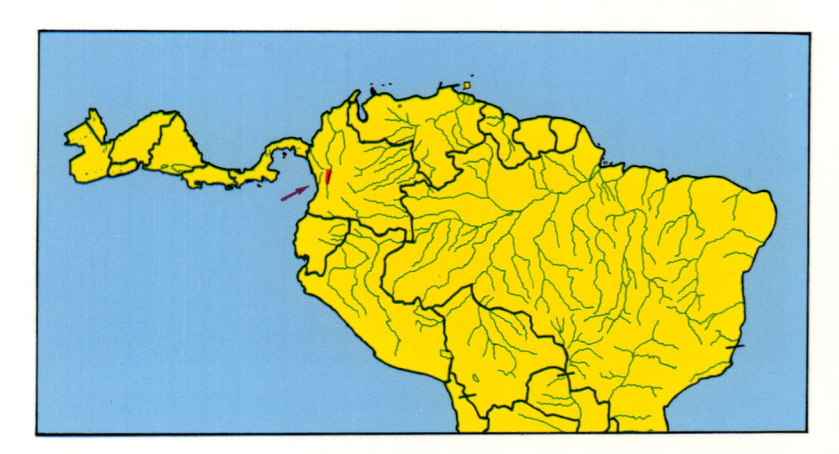

General distribution of the Black-legged Poison Frog, *Phyllobates bicolor*.

Phyllobates bicolor is a fairly large frog, ranging in adult length from 32.5 to 42 mm, with females about 3 mm larger than males. Its range appears to be small, centered about Santa Cecilia and the Rio Sipi of Colombia as well as the upper drainages of the Rios Atrato and San Juan. There is a gap of about 300 km (180 miles) between the ranges of *P. bicolor* and *P. terribilis*, with only one rather odd specimen known in the intervening area. It is a ground-dwelling frog like the others of the genus. Though highly toxic, the skin of a single frog contains only one-fiftieth as much batrachotoxins as the skin of a single *P. terribilis*. Remember, this frog can cause extreme discomfort if the toxin should enter a cut or get in the mouth or eyes, so it should be handled

General distribution of the Kokoe Poison Frog, *Phyllobates aurotaenia*.

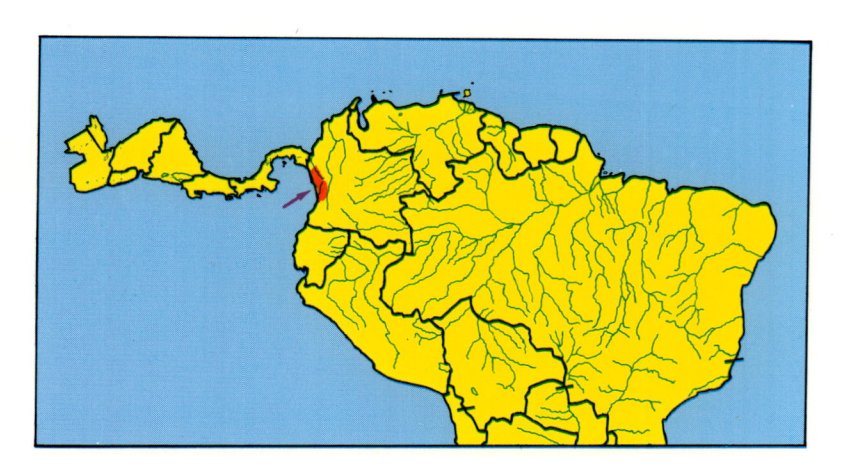

Distinguishing the Black-legged Poison Frog, *Phyllobates bicolor*, from the Golden Poison Frog can be difficult unless you are sure you are dealing with adults. Even full adult *Phyllobates bicolor* have much black on the legs and the golden pigment is present as distinct small spots.

The juvenile in the photo at bottom left is three weeks younger than in the photo at bottom right. Photos by A. Kerstitch (top pair); A. v. d. Nieuwenhuizen (others).

OTHER *PHYLLOBATES*

Although the back of this *Phyllobates bicolor* is distinctly reddish, there still is much black visible on the sides between the irregular golden yellow blotches. Photo by A. v. d. Nieuwenhuizen.

OTHER PHYLLOBATES

with gloves...or not at all.

Limited reports of reproduction in captivity indicate that the Black-legged Poison Frog is fairly easy to maintain in captivity and does well in small colonies of two or three males and four to six females. Males and females both fight and go through fairly typical courtship behavior, including chasing, female dancing in place, and wrestling. Eggs should be removed after laying or they might be eaten by competitive females. This is a rather large poison frog, and the clutches are equally large, up to a dozen eggs per mating.

LOVELY POISON FROG
Phyllobates lugubris

The Lovely Poison Frog and the Golfodulcean Poison Frog are closely related striped species (siblings) from Central America. *P. lugubris* occurs on the Atlantic slope of Costa Rica and Panama, while *P. vittatus* is restricted to the Pacific slope of Costa Rica. As a pair, the species can be distinguished from the similar *P. aurotaenia* in having the belly mottled with bluish or whitish and usually having an indistinct lateral bluish stripe. The Lovely is smaller (18.5 to 23.5 mm) than the Golfodulcean (22.5 to 31 mm), but females are larger than males in both species so there is considerable overlap. Usually *P. lugubris* has relatively narrow dorsolateral stripes and golden to yellow-green toned legs, while the stripes of *P. vittatus* are a bit broader (and a middorsal stripe or at least row of spots may be present) and the legs are blue-green. The two species have been considered synonyms in the past, and they certainly are very closely related, but no intermediates are known. The Lovely Poison Frog inhabits the lowland rainforests of Atlantic coastal Costa Rica and Panama, where it is a ground-litter species. A mountain range separates it from *P. vittatus*, and it only ranges south to about the Panama Canal Zone, so its range is widely separated from that of *P. aurotaenia*.

Like *P. vittatus*, the Lovely Poison Frog is easy to keep and fairly easy to breed. It will tolerate a fairly small terrarium with lots of cover and hiding places and a temperature of about 25 to 28°C, cooler at night. Eggs are laid in rather large clutches, often a dozen to as many as 20 at a time, and hatch in about two weeks. As usual, they are tended by the (male) parent, who carries them in small groups to bromeliads or other suitable water bodies. The

A fairly typical Lovely Poison Frog, *Phyllobates lugubris*, from Bastimentos Island, Panama. If you do not know the origin of the specimen, the Lovely and the Golfodulcean Poison Frogs may be very hard to distinguish. If the stripes are narrow, the specimen probably is a Lovely. Leg color may help, as the Lovely usually has yellowish legs, but in photographs and certain lights bronzy yellow may appear greenish or bluish. Photo by A. v. d. Nieuwenhuizen.

tadpoles feed readily on powdered high-protein flake food, freeze-dried bloodworms, and similar food (probably including mosquito larvae in nature). They commonly are carnivorous in captivity. Development takes about two months, the young frogs then taking almost a year to reach maturity. Recently metamorphosed froglets can be delicate, but if the temperature, humidity, and food supply are maintained at suitable levels they rapidly will grow to a hardier size. When captive-bred stock becomes more available, this should be a relatively simple frog to maintain, even for the beginner.

General distribution of the Lovely Poison Frog, *Phyllobates lugubris*.

OTHER *PHYLLOBATES*

This odd poison frog is said to be from Bastimentos Island, Panama. The large blue lines and blotches on the belly eliminate *Phyllobates aurotaenia* from consideration, and geographically it must be *Phyllobates lugubris*, the Lovely Poison Frog. Though the limbs all appear to be at least somewhat yellowish, notice that the dorsal stripe is broad (and actually appears to bend ventrally in this photo) and there appears to be a large midback area of broken yellow pigment. I guess this is indeed a *Phyllobates lugubris*, but it certainly is a strange one. Photo by A. v. d. Nieuwenhuizen.

Of Rockets and Skunks

Throughout this book we've talked almost exclusively about the poison frogs, the four genera of dendrobatids that have distasteful or toxic chemical secretions in the skin. This group of 65 species is quite diverse in colors, patterns, and natural history, and at least a dozen are regularly found in the terrarium hobby if you look hard enough. However, the poison frogs represent less than half the number of species in the family Dendrobatidae. Here we'll briefly discuss the 106 or more species of *Colostethus*, the rocket frogs, and the single species of *Aromobates*, the Skunk Frog.

SKUNK FROGS

First let's get the easy one out of the way. The Skunk Frog, *Aromobates nocturnus*, is a strange and probably primitive dendrobatid so far known only from streams in the Venezuelan Andes of Trujillo State. This area is cloud forest at an elevation of over

The Skunk Frog, *Aromobates nocturnus*, is the most unusual dendrobatid discovered so far, though there may be other surprises awaiting discovery in a stream somewhere in South America.

2200 meters and is remote and difficult to access. Unlike any other dendrobatids, the Skunk Frog appears to be nocturnal, sitting and feeding in shallow (0.1 to 0.5 meter), narrow (less than 0.5 meter), cold (12.4°C) streamlets in the dense undergrowth of the cloud forest. The streams are edged with grasses and ferns in the areas that could be collected near trails and with more dense tangled vegetation deeper into the forest, where collecting was virtually impossible. The tadpoles are almost black and up to 6 cm long, with deeply indented corners of the oral disc, two rows of teeth above the beaks, and three rows below. The tooth rows closest to the beaks are barely broken in the center. Two rows of small papillae edge the disc except for most of the top (anterior) edge, which is naked.

Adults of the Skunk Frog are large for dendrobatids, males 45 to 52 mm, females 53 to 62 mm in body length, with fully webbed hind feet and the first finger about equal in length to the second. The skin is coarsely granular in life, the head appears short and blunt, teeth are present, and scutes can be seen on the finger discs. Living specimens are dark olive or olive green, usually with scattered bronzy specks over the back and legs. Often traces of a broken bronzy stripe can be seen extending from the groin toward the base of the arm. Some specimens have the back covered with a network of bronzy lines, producing an indistinctly olive-spotted pattern. The undersurfaces are pale gray, sometimes faintly mottled with darker gray. Males have a dark collar across the base of the throat that sometimes is quite blackish but more commonly is just somewhat darker gray than the rest of the undersurface.

When handled, *Aromobates* exudes a chemical, perhaps a mercaptan, that is "defensively malodorous"—in other words, it stinks to high heavens. The smell is strong enough that the collector may become sick to the stomach. Presumably this still unidentified chemical serves to discourage predators, and it certainly discourages collectors. Probably it will prevent this frog from ever becoming a popular terrarium subject even if it were to become available. Of course, like a skunk it might stop producing the smell once it got to know its keeper. So far I have seen nothing published on the reproduction or calls of the Skunk Frog, and no one seems to have speculated on its breeding habits. The frogs may escape onto land and hide in the leaf litter when disturbed, and they apparently hide on land along streams during the day, so possibly eggs are laid on land like other dendrobatids. Other species of *Aromobates* may be found in similar habitats on isolated Andean peaks in the same general area in the future now that collectors know what to look for. *Aromobates* seems to be related to *Colostethus*, but admittedly both these genera have few distinctive characters at the familial level to distinguish them

The tadpole of the Skunk Frog is dark grayish black and over 50 mm long, with a primitive configuration of oral disc teeth.

from the rainfrogs of the family Leptodactylidae. The serious hobbyist interested in seeing the complexities of just what makes a frog a dendrobatid should read the papers by Myers, Paolillo, and Daly, 1991, describing *Aromobates*, and by Myers and Ford, 1986, concerning the placement of the genus *Atopophrynus*, described as a dendrobatid, in the family Leptodactylidae.

ROCKET FROGS

How do you cover a group of over 100 species in just a couple of pages and do them justice? You can't, and I won't even try. Just listing the species would take pages, and most hobbyists will have no chance of ever seeing more than two or three species. Additionally, the taxonomy of the group is chaotic, with uncertainty as to generic limits and species limits. Because the genus *Colostethus* is defined by an absence of specialized characters, it almost certainly is not a "real" genus in the modern sense. In fact, currently some authorities recognize a second genus, *Mannophryne* LaMarca, 1992, for eight species clustered around an obscure species called *M. yustizi*, including two species that have been studied extensively in the wild and sometimes in the terrarium: *collaris* and *trinitatis*. These species have dark collars at the edge of the throat in one or both sexes (usually the female). The old name *Hyloxalus* was in the running at one time for use as a generic name for at least some of these collared species, but difficulties with determining the characters of the type-species seem to have led to the erection of the new genus *Mannophryne* instead. For the moment we'll just use *Colostethus* for all 106 or so species and ignore the taxonomic technicalities. *Prostherapis* is an old synonym you occasionally will still see used in some of the literature, by the way.

Almost all the rocket frogs are small (20 to 35 mm adult length) species found near streams, often conspicuously perched on the tops of boulders actually in the stream, though some species are found in relatively dry forests in the leaf litter.

Mating behavior in *Colostethus inguinalis*. In some species of this genus the female has more color than the male, but in this species what little color is present is found in the male. Males are territorial, defending selected areas and boulders in and along streams, while females have looser territories on the edges of the streams. All rocket frogs fight, however. Photo by R. Heselhaus.

Egg-laying by *Colostethus inguinalis*, one of the best-known rocket frogs. This Central American and Colombian species frequents the edges of rocky streams and has been studied by several behaviorists. Photo by R. Heselhaus.

Though not aquatic, often the hind feet are partially webbed, and it is not uncommon for these frogs to seek safety in the water when approached. They are fast movers ("like a rocket," thus the common name) and can hide in small crevices in either rocks or under logs, as well as hiding in the silt at the bottom of the stream for minutes at a time. The tadpoles of most species are fairly normal looking, with five rows of teeth, but in some species (such as *C. nubicola* of Costa Rica and Panama) the oral disc is turned upward and looks vaguely like an inverted umbrella covered with irregular rows of papillae and lacking the usual tadpole teeth. Such strangely modified tadpoles feed at the surface of the water on detritus and small organisms swept into the mouth by a current created by the flexible edges of the oral disc; the disc also helps them hold on to rocks in fast-moving streams. Most rocket frog tadpoles have more normal feeding methods, using the beaks and disc teeth to rasp algae and detritus from the bottom or rip open small prey.

Rocket frogs are found throughout southern Central America and the northwestern corner of South America, extending down the western side of the Andes and across northern South America to the Guianas. One species has been found in small coastal ponds near the Pacific Ocean in Peru, while a few inhabit relatively dry scrub forests. More typically they are species of the rainforests and even the high cloud forests. As a rule, rocket frogs are brown above,

OF ROCKETS AND SKUNKS

Rocket frogs lay large egg clutches. This (probably) female *Colostethus inguinalis* appears to be carrying at least ten tadpoles, which may be half of a clutch. In this species males aggressively defend territories and females guard the bower and carry the tadpoles. Photo by A. Kerstitch.

The taxonomy of *Colostethus* is even more unsettled than that of poison frogs, and certainly many new species await description. This specimen from Cerro Gaital, Panama, has been suggested to be an undescribed species. There is an orange "flash mark" in the groin as in *C. inguinalis*. Photo by A. Kerstitch.

often with reddish brown or tan dorsolateral stripes. Females of some species (*C. collaris* and *C. trinitatis*, for example) have bright yellow throats that they display while defending their territories. Undersurfaces tend to be whitish or grayish (but sometimes black), often with faint blue speckling. The males of some rocket frogs can change colors rapidly, going from brown to almost solid black in a matter of minutes when defending territory.

Few rocket frogs are found more than a few meters from streams or puddles, though none actually is

Colostethus marchesianus, a common—and quite dully colored—little rocket frog from the Ucayali area of Peru. Most rocket frogs look much like this and even if they were easy to keep (which they are not) they would not be popular with hobbyists. Photo by P. Freed.

aquatic. As a general rule (that horrible expression again), one sex assumes and defends a territory on a rock or log in or near the water, wrestling with any other rocket frogs that pass through their territory. Wrestling between the same and different sexes is common, and these definitely are aggressive little frogs. Of the three species that have been studied most closely in nature, two (*C. collaris* and *C. trinitatis* from Venezuela and Trinidad) have large, yellow-throated females that defend conspicuous territories and one (*C. inguinalis* of Central America and Colombia) has males with bright orange "flash marks" that defend territories. Which sex defends the territory seems to have a lot to do with breeding biology, including transport of tadpoles. Males of female-territorial species have no fixed territories and often cover several meters during their daily foraging for ants and other small insect foods. Females leave their territories on rocks in the stream to go to a calling male and follow him to a bower chosen in advance (apparently) by the male. The eggs, often two dozen or more, are laid in a dead leaf often several meters from the stream and are tended (at least in some species) by the male. When the tadpoles hatch in eight to ten days, he takes them, often an entire clutch at a time, to a shallow backwater of the stream. Here they feed on whatever food they can find and metamorphose in about six to eight weeks. *Colostethus inguinalis* is the opposite in behavior, the males having conspicuous perches on boulders in or near water and aggressively defending their territory from any other rocket frog that comes near. Mating is the same as in female-territorial species, but here it is reported that the female tends the bower and transports the tadpoles to water. Terrarium observations of *C. inguinalis*, however, report that the male tends the bower and transports the tadpoles—perhaps a warning that behavior in the

OF ROCKETS AND SKUNKS

terrarium cannot be trusted to truly display natural behavior patterns.

In the terrarium, rocket frogs make fairly good pets, especially if you can give them a large terrarium with a small stream of running water (remember the drain!) and perhaps a waterfall. Yellow-throated females of *C. trinitatis* and *C. collaris* are quite attractive and easy to observe as they always choose a conspicuous perch from which to survey their domain. The cricket-like calls of the males may carry for quite a distance, often being much louder than the calls of typical poison frogs.

The major problem in captivity may be food, because several keepers have reported that their rocket frogs were not interested in fruitflies, the old standby, preferring instead tiny mealworm and waxmoth larvae, moths, and "meadow plankton," the small insects taken by sweeping with an insect net along the edges of fields and woodlands. Rocket frogs are virtually never seen in pet shops or on dealers's lists, however, so you probably won't get a chance to keep one unless you can get a few specimens from the excess stock of a friend who travels down to Panama to collect a few.

In *Colostethus trinitatus* the female aggressively defends a territory, often in plain sight on a boulder in a stream, while the male is non-territorial or nearly so. A female can be an extremely aggressive frog, defending her spot against all comers and displaying a bright yellow throat as part of the intimidation behavior. Photo by A. v. d. Nieuwenhuizen.

Colostethus trinitatus is an abundant little frog on the island of Trinidad as well as the mainland of Venezuela. At the right is an adult female (with a yellow throat as she is territorial), on the left a metamorphosing froglet. Photos by A. v. d. Nieuwenhuizen.

Most *Colostethus*, like these unidentified Surinam species, are small, very nondescript frogs that cannot be identified by the average hobbyist even with access to the literature. Even herpetologists specializing in this group have many problems identifying specimens. Photos by A. v. d. Nieuwenhuizen.

The Social Poison Frog

Okay, so now we've reviewed, perhaps in too much detail, the species of poison frogs and touched on their non-toxic relatives. I hope that all you terrarium keepers out there have enjoyed this coverage and gotten enough information from it to want to try your hand with a captive-bred pair of one of the larger, cheaper, more common species. I hope that the shorter writeups and the paintings of the rare or uncommonly collected species will help broaden your viewpoint to include the wonder of the virtually unknown segments of the Neotropical fauna that depend on the rainforests for life. Without the rainforests these living jewels would not exist, and neither would perhaps millions (well, at least hundreds of thousands) of species of life that also depend on the rainforests. Perhaps some day there will be a market for a book on the tiny beetles and true bugs of the rainforest, many of which have bizarre forms and fantastic color patterns that put even the poison frogs to shame.

But I don't want to end this book on just a taxonomic note, as the poison frogs now have entered society as more than just brightly colored unusual frogs. They now are almost as familiar to children as are the dinosaurs, and their toxins may hold some interesting medical prospects. Of all the frogs, at the end of the twentieth century perhaps the poison frogs are the most truly a part of society, and the most deserving of that position.

THE PERFECT PAINKILLER?

Earlier we very briefly touched on the great variety of different toxic chemicals secreted by poison frogs. Their chemistry is highly complex and I for one, with just my basic organic chemistry courses over 20 years ago, really cannot follow the chemical consequences of the various toxins. I know that most *Dendrobates* have a group of chemicals called histrionicotoxins, most poison frogs have pumiliotoxins of two or three major types, and *Phyllobates* produce the truly dangerous group of chemicals known as batrachotoxins. However, well over 100 different chemicals have been found in poison frog toxic secretions, many poorly understood chemically yet alone biologically.

One of these minor chemicals is epibatidine, originally isolated (according to the short summary by Bradley, 1993) from *Epipedobates tricolor*, which is one of the more common terrarium species. Epibatidine has a strange structure involving both a carbon ring with six members and a nitrogen bridge plus a pyridine ring containing chlorine. This type of structure is rare in animals, and it appears that the strange structure is able to "fit into" and block the complex molecular structure of specific pain receptors in the mammalian body. Epibatidine, in other words, can function as a painkiller. In studies on mice, it proved to be 200 times more effective in stopping pain than morphine, the common but sedative (i.e., it puts you to sleep) and addictive painkiller of choice in many extreme situations. As an extra bonus, epibatidine is not a sedative, so it has

Does the Phantasmal Poison Frog hold the secret to a truly effective painkiller without side-effects? Photo by R. D. Bartlett.

no side-effects. At the moment epibatidine also is non-addictive, because it kills any mouse into which it is injected. Yeah, great...just what we need, another way to kill laboratory mice. But there is hope. Epibatidine now has been synthesized in the lab in a pure form (no more reason to skin frogs to isolate the chemical) that is available for research. With time, it should be possible to determine just what part of the molecule blocks pain receptors and which causes dead mice. Using modern chemical methods, it then will be possible to replace the toxic portion of the molecule with a neutral component that won't prevent the painkiller effects but will let mice live a long, healthy life (until the next experiment).

So if five or six years from now you break your leg and the doctor tells you to take one epibatidine and call him in the morning, remember that little red and yellow poison frog from the Ecuadorean rainforest.

THE SOCIAL POISON FROG

If *Epipedobates tricolor* should prove to be pharmaceutically exciting, either the species will have to be bred in much larger numbers or it will be over-collected and exterminated in its small range. Photo by R. D. Bartlett.

AND NOW A POISON BIRD

What lives in the gardens and villages of New Guinea, is orange-brown and black, 23 cm long, and made all the headlines in 1992? It's the Hooded Pitohui, *Pitohui dichrous*, a "rubbish bird" that New Guinea natives won't bother killing for the pot and basically leave alone. Biologist Jack Dumbacher was mistnetting birds and discovered that after freeing Hooded Pitohuis from the net his hands started to burn. Eventually he made a connection between the birds, cuts on his hands, and the burning sensation. Acting on a hunch, he tried biting into a bit of Hooded Pitohui feather and found it tasted like biting into hot pepper, complete with numbness and tingling. Two other local species of pitohuis produced no reaction. Dr. John Daly is a biochemist who since the 1970's has been working on the toxins of poison frogs. Many of his papers coauthored with Dr. C. W. Myers are cited in the bibliography, and he has many more dealing strictly with the chemical side of poison frogs. Dumbacher sent a sample of Hooded Pitohui to Daly for analysis and found his hunch proved beyond his wildest dreams. For the Hooded Pitohui

Poison frogs even are on stamps, as at least three countries (Surinam, shown here, Brazil, and Costa Rica) have used these colorful little frogs to grace their country's postage.

THE SOCIAL POISON FROG

The toxin homobatrachotoxin found in the feathers and skin of the Hooded Pitohui of New Guinea (top) seemingly is identical to the toxin in the Golden Poison Frog, *Phyllobates terribilis*, of Colombia. The Variable Pitohui (center) lacks toxicity, but in areas where its range overlaps that of the toxic Hooded Pitohui it develops a pattern that accurately mimics the dangerous bird (the model). The Rusty Pitohui (bottom) lacks toxins and is not a mimic, so it seems to be eaten freely by the natives.

THE SOCIAL POISON FROG

Strawberry Poison Frogs, *Dendrobates pumilio*, still are exported from Costa Rica in large numbers, mostly to face a lingering death. There have been several proposals to place the entire family Dendrobatidae on the CITES list as Appendix I to give them complete protection, but none has passed so far. Probably it is just a matter of a few years before exports are outlawed and any poison frog that is not captive-bred will disappear from the terrarium hobby. Photo by A. Kerstitch.

This slender little (25 mm) Panamanian poison frog may be just a variety of *Dendrobates auratus* or it might be a new species. Unless frogs are preserved in their habitats there will be no way to settle even these minor points in the future. Rainforests must be preserved, and not just as little oases in a desert of ranches and condominiums. Photo by A. Kerstitch.

feathers and skin proved to be liberally laced with batrachotoxins, the same toxins found in *Phyllobates terribilis* and other dangerous Colombian poison frogs. How did a bird (no other bird species was known to be toxic) develop the same toxin found in a group of frogs thousands of kilometers away on a different continent? No one can answer that question, but it seems certain that the batrachotoxins have the same function in both bird and frogs, preventing predation. New Guinea natives do not eat the Hooded Pitohui, though they will kill and eat its close relatives, which, as it turns out, contain no or very little batrachotoxins. Just as some brightly colored poison frogs that produce few toxins may mimic the colors and patterns of the more potent *Phyllobates* in their area, one non-toxic pitohui, the Variable Pitohui, appears to mimic the color pattern of its dangerous cousin where their ranges overlap.

In the past it has been suggested that poison frogs manufacture at least some of their toxins from chemicals in the ants that form the basis of their diets, and it is possible that the Hooded Pitohui also derives its toxins from some portion of its diet. There is a possibility that Hooded Pitohuis in some parts of the range are quite edible and may lack the toxins. If this proves to be true, it would be indirect evidence that the diet in different areas might not contain the necessary precursors to production of the batrachotoxins. A parallel with poison frogs is obvious—remember that the Golden Poison Frog seems to lose toxicity with increasing time and generations spent in captivity, where it does not get ants as part of its diet. (For an interesting discussion of how butterflies obtain protective chemicals from plants, see the article by Boppre in the January, 1994, issue of *Natural History* magazine.)

Pitohuis are rainforest residents like poison frogs, and as the New Guinea forests are logged and converted to human usages (like the American rainforests) they likely will become rarer. Their biological novelty probably will mean that extra efforts will be made to protect them, but their future still is tied directly to the survival of their home forests. Now a few other birds have been suggested to be toxic as well, including the Pink Pigeon, the last surviving native pigeon on the Indian Ocean island of Mauritius. All the other pigeon species were killed for the pot over the last two centuries, but the Pink Pigeon may produce a toxin in its flesh from seeds that only it eats. Will biological wonders ever cease? (Actually, I can answer that rhetorical question—the answer is "No.")

THEY'RE EVERYWHERE!

Quick, how many poison frog images did you receive at Christmas or for your birthday? None? Then your relatives must not realize that you are interested in frogs (leave more hints next year). Poison frogs are on teeshirts, umbrellas, and neckties. If you want golden earrings in the shape of poison frogs, no problem. Today many nature-oriented organizations have found that colorful poison frog images sell products. Their fund-raising catalogs are filled with whales, seals, parrots... and

THE SOCIAL POISON FROG

Red-eyed Treefrogs, *Agalychnis callidryas*, seem to be second only to poison frogs in the toy-dish-necktie competition. Photo by R. D. Bartlett.

poison frogs. Mall nature stores and toy stores sell their own poison frog images, from colorful magnets to very well done plastic models of *Dendrobates auratus*, *D. tinctorius*, and a few other species—often the paint jobs are good enough to identify the species with no hesitation. More fanciful creations in the form of beanbags and children's pillows may prove a bit harder to identify to species, but there is no doubting the intentions of the designers. Last year I even found a catalog selling serving dishes and mugs covered with a melange of various poison frogs. To the true poison frog fanatic there is only one problem—designers seem to think that Red-eyed Treefrogs (*Agalychnis callidryas*) are poison frogs, too, and keep inserting them in the purer and taxonomically more satisfying dendrobatid designs. But then again, perhaps I've just been sitting at this computer too long to appreciate *anything* but pure poison frogs.

So next time you are in the drugstore buying aspirin, are looking through a bird guide thinking about that next birding adventure into the tropics, or want a quick, cheap, colorful gift for that herper friend, think of the social poison frog. The dendrobatids are now a part of our culture...and reminders that the rainforests and their many jewels must survive into the next century and beyond.

THE SOCIAL POISON FROG

"No comment." Photo by R. Bechter.

APPENDIX
A Different Poison Frog Classification

Throughout this book I have used the current classification of poison frog genera as accepted by Myers and his students and co-workers. I also have mentioned the variant generic arrangement proposed by the Zimmermanns and accepted by many European workers. There is, however, a third generic system—that of Luuc Bauer—that is available but largely ignored by herpetologists, probably because it was published in the "gray" literature of terrarium hobby publications. Though several subfamily names and some differences in species and subspecies of various species are involved, I'll briefly mention here just two generic names and one specific name that seem to be validly published and may affect the rules of priority.

On March 25, 1985, Bauer published in *Het Paludarium* and soon after in a looseleaf, *RIPA*, both published in the Netherlands, the new generic name *Ranitomeya*, with *Dendrobates reticulatus* specified as the type species. The genus is described in some detail (though largely from characters in the literature) and a variety of small species of poison frogs are referred to it. It seems, from the publications I have examined, that the description meets the requirements for valid publication under the Code and must be considered if in the future the *Quinquevittatus*-Group is split from the remainder of *Dendrobates*, which seems at least somewhat likely.

On November 11, 1986, Bauer published in *Het Paludarium* and then again in *RIPA* another new generic name, *Ameerega*, for the type species *Hyla trivittata* (today usually called *Epipedobates trivittatus* or *Phobobates trivittatus*). Again the new genus is described in some detail mostly from characters in the literature and appears to be validly published under the minimal rules of the Code. It should be noted that *Ameerega* Bauer, 1986, has priority over both *Epipedobates* Myers, 1987, and *Phobobates* Zimmermann & Zimmermann, 1988. Because it seems probable that *Epipedobates* sensu Myers is polyphyletic and will have to be split, there is little to gain at the moment in attempting to apply *Ameerega* to this genus. More important is the fact that *Ameerega* and *Phobobates* are largely the same concept and if *Epipedobates* is split *Ameerega* definitely will be in contention with *Phobobates* as the proper name for one of the splits. The name *Ameerega* (as well as *Ranitomeya*) has been used by Bauer in several publications since its proposal, both in Dutch and American hobby publications, but has never appeared in the major catalogs of anuran generic names, being ignored by herpetologists. Both *Ranitomeya* and *Ameerega* appear to be validly proposed and must be at least inspected for purposes of priority.

In his 1986 paper, Bauer also commented on his "*trivittata*-group," recognizing *A. trivittata* from the "Amazon drainage west to the Cordillera de los Andes"; *A. nigerrima* (Spix) from the "Guayana shield and Amazon Delta"; a new species, *Ameerega peruviridis* Bauer, from the "Ucayali drainage of East Andean Peru"; and *A.* cf. *bassleri* for the hobby form referred to *bassleri* but possibly not conspecific with the type of that species. Each species was defined on color and skin texture characters, with *A. peruviridis* applying to the form with a granular skin and bright green back with a bright green stripe on each side of the back. A mention is given to figure 2 of Silverstone, 1976, as picturing a "typical *peruviridis*." This composite figure illustrates several variations of *trivittatus* sensu Silverstone, including the holotype (Fig. 2 A), a Surinam specimen (Fig. 2 C), the type of *bassleri* (Fig. 2 F), two variants of *trivittatus* from Peru (Fig. 2 D & E), and a Peru specimen with a solid green dorsum (Fig. 2 B). Presumably the specimen in Fig. 2 B (Santa Isabel, Peru, USNM 166764) represents the typification of Bauer's *peruviridis*, but the exact nomenclatural and biological status of this specimen should be determined. There is little doubt that *trivittatus* is a very variable species in need of revision.

Bauer also has proposed other generic and subgeneric names in the hobby literature, but these apparently have been circulated in Xerox copies only and never validly published under present rules. Only the three names discussed here appear to be validly published, and they must be considered, even if eventually discarded, in any future divisions of dendrobatid genera and the species *trivittatus*.

A green-backed *Epipedobates trivittatus* from the Ucayali area of Peru. This is the form—species, subspecies, or just individual color variant—described by Bauer as *Ameerega peruviridis*, a validly proposed name ignored in herpetological literature. Such specimens appear to be uncommon and occur alongside more normally patterned *E. trivittatus*. Photo by P. Freed

Bibliography

The following bibliography is far from complete and is meant largely as a supplement to the more extensive bibliographies in Silverstone 1975 and 1976. Older literature is not listed here but will be found in the Silverstone references. Papers have been selected not only for direct usefulness in researching this book, but also for use in forming a secondary bibliography. Papers on the taxonomy of *Colostethus* generally are not included, but basic references on the subject may be found in Duellman (1993), Frost (1985), and Myers, Paolillo, and Daly (1991). No attempt has been made to list all the recent popular articles on the group (there are many in both English and German), though several of the better ones on breeding techniques have been included.

Aichinger, M. 1991. "A new species of poison-dart frog (Anura: Dendrobatidae) from the Serrania de Sira, Peru," *Herpetologica*, 47(1): 1-5, pl. [*D. sirensis*]

Aichinger, M. 1992. "Fecundity and breeding sites of an anuran community in a seasonal tropical environment," *Stud. Neotrop. Fauna Environ.*, 27(1): 9-18. [Panguana, Peru]

Bauer, L. 1989. "Updating dendrobatid nomenclature for terrarists," *I.S.S.D. Newsletter* (Tucson, AZ), 2(5): 13-19. [review of unusual classification]

Bertram, D. 1989. "Dart-poison frogs: Some general husbandry principles," *J. Northern Ohio Assoc. Herp.*, 15(1): 1-13.

Boppre, M. 1994. "Sex, drugs, and butterflies," *Nat. Hist. (N.Y.)*, 103(1): 26-33. [plant-derived butterfly chemicals]

Bradley, D. 1993. "Frog venom cocktail yields a one-handed painkiller," *Science*, 261: 1117.

Brust, D. G. 1993. "Maternal brood care by *Dendrobates pumilio*: A frog that feeds its young," *J. Herp.*, 27(1): 96-98.

Bunnell, P. 1973. "Vocalizations in the territorial behavior of the frog *Dendrobates pumilio*," *Copeia*, 1973(2): 277-284.

Caldwell, J. P. and C. W. Myers. 1990. "A new poison frog from Amazonian Brazil, with further revision of the *quinquevittatus* Group of *Dendrobates*," *Amer. Mus. Novitates*, No. 2988: 1-21. [*D. castaneoticus*, redescription *D. quinquevittatus*]

Crump, M. L. 1972. "Territoriality and mating behavior in *Dendrobates granuliferus* (Anura: Dendrobatidae)," *Herpetologica*, 28(3): 195-198.

Daly, J. W., G. B. Brown, M. Mensah-Dwumah, and C. W. Myers. 1978. "Classification of skin alkaloids from neotropical poison dart frogs (Dendrobatidae)," *Toxicon*, 16: 163-188.

Diamond, J. 1994. "Stinking birds and burning books," *Nat. Hist. (N.Y.)*, 103(2): 4/12. [pitohuis and other protected birds]

Dole, J. W. 1974. "Courtship behavior in *Colostethus collaris* (Dendrobatidae)," *Copeia*, 1974(4): 988-990.

Donnelly, M. A. 1989. "Reproductive phenology and age structure of *Dendrobates pumilio* in northeastern Costa Rica," *J. Herp.*, 23(4): 362-367.

Donnelly, M. A. 1991. "Feeding patterns of the strawberry poison frog, *Dendrobates pumilio* (Anura: Dendrobatidae)," *Copeia*, 1991(3): 723-730.

Donnelly, M. A., C. Guyer, and R. O. de Sa. 1990. "The tadpole of a dart-poison frog *Phyllobates lugubris* (Anura: Dendrobatidae)," *Proc. Biol. Soc. Washington*, 103(2): 427-431.

Duellman, W. E. 1966. "Aggressive behavior in dendrobatid frogs," *Herpetologica*, 22(3): 217-221 [*D. galindoi = pumilio*]

Duellman, W. E. 1993. *Amphibian Species of the World: Additions and Corrections*. Univ. Kansas Press; Lawrence, KS.

Dunn, E. R. 1941. "Notes on *Dendrobates auratus*," *Copeia*, 1941(2): 88-93.

Durant, P. and J. W. Dole. 1975. "Aggressive behavior in *Colostethus (=Prostherapis) collaris* (Anura: Dendrobatidae)," *Herpetologica*, 31(1): 23-26.

Eaton, T. H., Jr. 1941. "Notes on the life history of *Dendrobates auratus*," *Copeia*, 1941(2): 93-95.

Emmer, R. 1990. "Husbandry and breeding of dart-poison frogs (*Dendrobates auratus* and *D. tinctorius*)," *The Vivarium*, 2(6): 8-11, 18, 35.

Ford, L.S. 1993. "The phylogenetic position of the dart-poison frogs (Dendrobatidae) among anurans: an examination of the competing hypotheses and their characters," *Eth. Ecol. & Evol.*, 5:219-231.

Ford, L.S. and D.C. Cannatella. 1993. "The major clades of frogs," *Herp. Monogr.*, 7:94-117.

Forester, D. C. and A. Wisnieski. 1991. "The significance of airborne olfactory cues to the recognition of home area by the dart-poison frog *Dendrobates pumilio*," *J. Herp.*, 25(4): 502-504.

Frost, D. (Editor). 1985. *Amphibian Species of the World: A Taxonomic and Geographic Reference*. Assoc. Syst. Coll., Allen Press; Lawrence, KS.

Goodman, D. E. 1971. "Territorial behavior in a Neotropical frog, *Dendrobates granuliferus*," *Copeia*, 1971(2): 365-370.

Gorzula, S. 1988[=1990]. "Una nueva especie de *Dendrobates* (Amphibia, Dendrobatidae) del Macizo del Chimanta, Estado Bolivar, Venezuela," *Mem. Soc. Cienc. Nat. La Salle*, 48(130): 143-149. [*E. rufulus*]

Hallowell, C. 1992. "The Hooded Pitohui's poisonous secret," *American Birds*, 46(5): 1084-1088.

Henle, K. 1992. "Zur Amphibienfauna Perus nebst Beschreibung eines neuen *Eleutherodactylus* (Leptodactylidae)," *Bonn. zool. Beitr.*, 43(1): 79-129. [includes comparison *E. bassleri* & *E. trivittatus*, synonymy *E. tricolor*; checklist amphibians Peru with extensive bibliography]

Heselhaus, R. 1992. *Poison-arrow Frogs. Their Natural History and Care in Captivity*. Ralph Curtis - Books; Sanibel Island, FL. [translation of *Pfeilgiftfrosche*, 1988, Eugen, Ulmer GmbH & Co., Stuttgart, Germany]

Heselhaus, R. 1993. "Keeping and breeding rocket frogs," *Tropical Fish Hobbyist*, 41(6): 90, 92-94. [*Colostethus inguinalis*]

Hoogmoed, M. S. 1971. "*Dendrobates*, eine farbenreiche Gattung," *DATZ*, 24(1): 1-7.

Hoogmoed, M. S. 1972. "Frosche, die ihre Kaulquappen huckepack traden. *Dendrobates azureus* und andere Baumsteigerfrosche," *Aquarien Magazin [Stuttgart]*, 6(7): 288-293.

Jungfer, K-H. 1989. "Pfeilgiftfrosche der Gattung *Epipedobates* mit rot granuliertem Rucken aus dem Oriente van Ecuador und Peru," *Salamandra*, 25(2): 81-98. [*E. ardens*, *E. bilinguis*]

Kneller, M. and K. Henle. 1985. "Ein neuer Blattsteiger-Frosch (Salientia: Dendrobatidae: *Phyllobates*) aus Peru," *Salamandra*, 21(1): 62-69. [*E. azureiventris*]

Lescure, J. and R. Bechter. 1982. "Le comportement de reproduction en captivite et le polymorphisme de *Dendrobates quinquevittatus* Steindachner (Amphibia, Anura, Dendrobatidae)," *Rev. Francaise Aquariol. Herpetol.*, 8(4): 107-118. [*D. ventrimaculatus*]

Limerick, S. 1980. "Courtship behavior and oviposition of the poison-arrow frog *Dendrobates pumilio*," *Herpetologica*, 36(1): 69-71.

Lockwood, R. 1989. "A mass production method for rearing poison dart frog larvae," *The Vivarium*, 2(1): 24-27.

Lynch, J. D. 1982. "Two new species of poison-dart frogs (*Colostethus*) from Colombia," *Herpetologica*, 38(3): 366-374. [unusual species]

Lynch, J. D. and P. M. Ruiz-Carranza. 1982. "A new genus and species of poison-dart frog (Amphibia: Dendrobatidae) from the Andes of northern Colombia," *Proc. Biol. Soc. Washington*, 95(3): 557-562. [*Atopophrynus syntomopus*, now placed in Leptodactylidae]

Maxson, L. R. and C. W. Myers. 1985. "Albumin evolution in tropical poison frogs (Dendrobatidae): A preliminary report," *Biotropica*, 17(1): 50-56.

McVey, M. E., R. G. Zahary, D. Perry, and J. MacDougal. 1981. "Territoriality and homing behavior in the poison dart frog (*Dendrobates pumilio*)," *Copeia*, 1981(1): 1-8.

Meede, U. 1980. "Beobactungen an *Dendrobates quinquevittatus* und *Phyllobates femoralis* (Amphibia: Salientia: Dendrobatidae)," *Salamandra*, 16(1): 38-51.

Morales, V. R. 1992. "Dos especies nuevas de *Dendrobates* (Anura: Dendrobatidae) para Peru," *Caribbean J. Sci.*, 28(3/4): 191-199. [*D. lamasi*, biolat]

Myers, C. W. 1969. "The ecological geography of cloud forest in Panama," *Amer. Mus. Novitates*, No. 2396: 1-52. [excellent description of habitats in Panama]

Myers, C. W. 1982. "Spotted poison frogs: descriptions of three new *Dendrobates* from western Amazonia, and resurrection of a lost species from 'Chiriqui'," *Amer. Mus. Novitates*, No. 2721: 1-23. [*D. vanzolinii, captivus, mysteriosus,*

BIBLIOGRAPHY

E. maculatus]

Myers, C. W. 1987. "New generic names for some Neotropical poison frogs (Dendrobatidae)," *Papeis Avulsos Zool., Sao Paulo*, 36(25): 301-306.

Myers, C. W. 1991. "Distribution of the dendrobatid frog *Colostethus chocoensis* and description of a related species occurring macrosympatrically," *Amer. Mus. Novitates*, No. 3010: 1-15. [good example of the problems distinguishing species in genus]

Myers, C. W. and P. A. Burrowes. 1987. "A new poison frog (*Dendrobates*) from Andean Colombia, with notes on a lowland relative," *Amer. Mus. Novitates*, No. 2899: 1-17. [*D. andinus*]

Myers, C. W. and J. W. Daly. 1976a. "Preliminary evaluation of skin toxins and vocalizations in taxonomic and evolutionary studies of poison-dart frogs (Dendrobatidae)," *Bull. Amer. Mus. Nat. Hist.*, 157( ): 173-262. [*D. lehmanni, occultator, M. viridis*, variation in *D. histrionicus*]

Myers, C. W. and J. W. Daly. 1976b. "A new species of poison frog (*Dendrobates*) from Andean Ecuador, including an analysis of its skin toxins," *Occas. Papers Mus. Nat. Hist., Univ. Kansas*, No. 59: 1-12. [*M. abditus*]

Myers, C. W. and J. W. Daly. 1979. "A name for the poison frog of Cordillera Azul, eastern Peru, with notes on its biology and skin toxins (Dendrobatidae)," *Amer. Mus. Novitates*, No. 2674: 1-24. [*E. silverstonei*]

Myers, C. W. and J. W. Daly. 1980. "Taxonomy and ecology of *Dendrobates bombetes*, a new Andean poison frog with new skin toxins," *Amer. Mus. Novitates*, No. 2692: 1-23.

Myers, C. W. and J. W. Daly. 1983. "Dart-poison frogs," *Scientific American*, 248(2): 120-133. [Feb.]

Myers, C. W., J. W. Daly, and B. Malkin. 1978. "A dangerously toxic new frog (*Phyllobates*) used by Embera Indians of western Colombia, with discussion of blowgun fabrication and dart poisoning," *Bull. Amer. Mus. Nat. Hist.*, 161(2): 307-365. [*P. terribilis*]

Myers, C. W., J. W. Daly, and V. Martinez. 1984. "An arboreal poison frog (*Dendrobates*) from western Panama," *Amer. Mus. Novitates*, No. 2783: 1-20. [*D. arboreus*]

Myers, C. W. and L. S. Ford. 1986. "On *Atopophrynus*, a recently described frog wrongly assigned to the Dendrobatidae," *Amer. Mus. Novitates*, 2843: 1-15. [family characters]

Myers, C. W., A. Paolillo O., and J. W. Daly. 1991. "Discovery of a defensively malodorous and nocturnal frog in the family Dendrobatidae: Phylogenetic significance of a new genus and species from the Venezuelan Andes," *American Mus. Novitates*, No. 3002: 1-33. [*Aromobates nocturnus* and discussion *Colostethus*]

Noble, G. K. 1921. "Five new species of Salientia from South America," *Amer. Mus. Novitates*, No. 29: 1-7. [*E. anthonyi*]

Pefaur, J. E. 1984. "A new species of dendrobatid frog from the coast of Peru," *J. Herp.*, 18(4): 492-494. [*Colostethus littoralis* from beach ponds near Lima, unusual habitat]

Pinney, R. 1991. "Poison arrow frogs," *Reptile & Amphibian Mag.*, Mar./Apr.: 3-7.

Pyburn, W. F. 1981. "A new poison-dart frog (Anura: Dendrobatidae) from the forest of southeastern Colombia," *Proc. Biol. Soc. Washington*, 94(1): 67-75. [*D. myersi*]

Ramos, L. 1989. "The toxins of Dendrobatidae," *J. Northern Ohio Assoc. Herp.*, 15(1): 14-24.

Rasotto, M. B., P. Cardellini, and M. Sala. 1987. "Karyotypes of five species of Dendrobatidae (Anura: Amphibia)," *Herpetologica*, 43(2): 177-182.

Rivero, J. A. 1971. "Un nuevo e interesante *Dendrobates* (Amphibia, Salientia) del Cerro Yapacana de Venezuela," *Kasmera (Univ. Zulia)*, 3(4): 389-396. [*M. steyermarki*]

Rivero, J. A. 1991. "New *Colostethus* (Amphibia, Dendrobatidae) from South America," *Breviora (Harvard)*, No. 493: 1-28. [*C. paradoxus* = *E. tricolor*]

Rodriguez, L. and C. W. Myers. 1993. "A new poison frog from Manu National Park, southeastern Peru (Dendrobatidae, *Epipedobates*)," *Amer. Mus. Novitates*, No. 3068: 1-15. [*E. macero*]

Roithmair, M.E. 1994. "Male territoriality and female mate selection in the dart-poison frog, *Epipedobates trivittatus* (Dendrobatidae, Anura)," *Copeia*, 1994 (1): 107-115.

Ruiz-Carranza, P. M. & M. P. Ramirez-Pinilla. 1992. "Una nueva especie de *Minyobates* (Anura: Dendrobatidae) de Colombia," *Lozania (Acta Zool. Colombiana)*, No. 61: 1-16. [*M. virolinensis* and review of genus *Minyobates*]

Savage, J. M. 1968. "The dendrobatid frogs of Central America," *Copeia*, 1968(4): 745-776.

Schluter, A. 1980. "Bio-akustische Untersuchungen an Dendrobatiden in einem begrenzten Gebiet des tropischen Regenwaldes von Peru (Amphibia: Salientia: Dendrobatidae)," *Salamandra*, 16(3): 149-161.

Schmidt, W. 1993. "Funfstreifen-Baumsteigerfrosch," *DATZ*, 46(3): 164-167.

Schulte, R. 1981. "*Dendrobates bassleri*—Feilandbeobactungen Haltung und Zucht," *Herpetofauna (Ludwigsburg)*, 12: 23-28.

Schulte, R. 1986. "Eine neue *Dendrobates*-Art aus Ostperu (Amphibia: Salientia: Dendrobatidae)," *Sauria*, 8: 11-20. [*D. imitator*]

Schulte, R. 1987. "Der Erstnachweis von *Dendrobates zaparo* (Silverstone, 1976) fur Peru (Amphibia: Salientia: Dendrobatidae)," *Sauria*, 9(1): 17-18.

Schulte, R. 1989. "Nueva especie de rana venenosa del genero *Epipedobates* registrada en la Cordillera Oriental, Departmento de San Martin," *Bol. Lima*, No. 63: 41-46. [*Epipedobates cainarachi*]

Schulte, R. 1990. "Redescubrimiento y redefinicion de *Dendrobates mysteriosus* (Myers, 1982) de la Cordillera del Condor," *Bol. Lima*, No. 70: 57-68.

Sexton, O. J. 1960. "Some aspects of the behavior and of the territory of a dendrobatid frog, *Prostherapis trinitatis*," *Ecology*, 41(1): 107-115.

Silverstone, P. A. 1973. "Observations on the behavior and ecology of a Colombian poison-arrow frog, the kokoe-pa (*Dendrobates histrionicus* Berthold)," *Herpetologica*, 29(4): 295-301.

Silverstone, P. A. 1975. "A revision of the poison-arrow frogs of the genus *Dendrobates* Wagler," *Sci. Bull. Nat. Hist. Mus. Los Angeles Co.*, 21: 1-55. [*Minyobates altobueyensis, M. fulguritus*]

Silverstone, P. A. 1976. "A revision of the poison-arrow frogs of the genus *Phyllobates* Bibron In Sagra (family Dendrobatidae)," *Sci. Bull. Nat. Hist. Mus. Los Angeles Co.*, 27: 1-53. [*Epipedobates petersi, E. pulchripectus, E. smaragdinus, E. zaparo*]

Toft, C. A. 1981. "Feeding ecology of Panamanian litter anurans: Patterns in diet and foraging mode," *J. Herp.*, 15(2): 139-144. [*Dendrobates* vs. *Colostethus*]

Toft, C. A. and W. E. Duellman. 1979. "Anurans of the Lower Rio Llullapichis, Amazonian Peru: A preliminary analysis of community structure," *Herpetologica*, 35(1): 71-77.

Vigle, G. O. and K. Miyata. 1980. "A new species of *Dendrobates* (Anura: Dendrobatidae) from the lowland rain forests of western Ecuador," *Breviora (Harvard)*, No. 459: 1-7. [*E. erythromos*]

Walls, J.G. 1994. *Keeping Poison Frogs*. T.F.H. Publ.; Neptune, N.J.

Wells, K. D. 1978. "Courtship and parental behavior in a Panamanian poison-arrow frog (*Dendrobates auratus*)," *Herpetologica*, 34(2): 148-155.

Wells, K. D. 1980a. "Social behavior and communication of a dendrobatid frog (*Colostethus trinitatis*)," *Herpetologica*, 36(2): 189-199.

Wells, K. D. 1980b. "Behavioral ecology and social organization of a dendrobatid frog (*Colostethus inguinalis*)," *Behav. Ecol. Sociobiol.*, 6: 199-209.

Wells, K. D. 1980c. "Evidence for growth of tadpoles during parental transport in *Colostethus inguinalis*," *J. Herp.*, 14(4): 428-430.

Weygoldt, P. 1980. "Complex brood care and reproductive behavior in captive poison-arrow frogs, *Dendrobates pumilio* O. Schmidt," *Behav. Ecol. Sociobiol.*, 7: 329-332.

Wijngaarden, R. van and F. Bolanos. 1992. "Parental care in *Dendrobates granuliferus* (Anura: Dendrobatidae), with a description of the tadpole," *J. Herp.*, 26(1): 102-105.

Zimmermann, E. 1986. *Breeding Terrarium Animals*. T.F.H. Publ.; Neptune, NJ. [reprinted under new title *Reptiles and Amphibians: Care, Behavior, Reproduction* in 1992; translation of *Das Zuchten von Terrarientieren*, 1983, Franckh'sche Verlag., Stuttgart, Germany].

Zimmermann, H. and E. Zimmermann. 1988. "Etho-Taxonomie und zoogeographische Artengruppenbildung bei Pfeilgiftfroschen," *Salamandra*, 24(2): 125-160. [*D. variabilis, Phobobates, Allobates*]

INDEX

Page numbers in **boldface** refer to illustrations.

Agalychnis callidryas, **281**
Allobates, 16
Alto del Buey Poison Frog, 247–248, **248**
Alto del Buey Poison Frog = *M. altobueyensis*
Amazonian Poison Frog, 157–159, **157–165**
Amazonian Poison Frog = *D. ventrimaculatus*
Ameerega, 17, 283
Amplexus, 6, 9
Amplexus = grasping and positioning behavior of mating frogs
Andean Poison Frog, 250, **250**
Andean Poison Frog = *M. opisthomelas*
Ants, 29, **48**, 49
Aposematic = brilliant coloration suddenly exposed to confuse a predator
Aposematic coloration, 29
Aromobates nocturnus, 272–273, **272**
Atelopus, 9
Atelopus flavescens, **12**
Atelopus varius, **7**, **8**, **10**, **12**
Atelopus zeteki, **7**
Axil = where a leaf or branch meets the stem
Bauer classification, 16–17, 283
Behavior and classification, 17
Biolat Poison Frog, 166–167, **167**
Biolat Poison Frog = *D. biolat*
Birds, toxic, 278, 280
Black-legged Poison Frog, 267, **267–268**, 270
Black-legged Poison Frog = *P. bicolor*
Bloodworms, **51**, **52**
Blowflies, **53**
Blue Poison Frog, 74–75, **74–83**, **140**
Blue Poison Frog = *D. azureus*
Blue-bellied Poison Frog, **27**, 249–250, **249**
Blue-bellied Poison Frog = *M. minutus*
Blue-breasted Poison Frog, 241, **241**
Blue-breasted Poison Frog = *E. pulchripectus*
Bolivian Poison Frog, 227, **227**
Bolivian Poison Frog = *E. bolivianus*
Bower = egg deposition site
Bowers, 31
Bowers, artificial, 46
Brazil-nut Poison Frog, 168, **169**
Brazil-nut Poison Frog = *D. castaneoticus*
Brazilian Poison Frog, 202–203, **203**
Brazilian Poison Frog = *D. vanzolinii*
Breeding behavior, natural, 31
Breeding cycles, 47
Breeding stations, artificial, 46
Brilliant-thighed Poison Frog, **25**, 229–230, **230–232**
Brilliant-thighed Poison Frog = *E. femoralis*
Bromeliad = an airplant related to the pineapple
Bromeliads, **56**, **58**, **59**
Cainarachi Poison Frog, 228, **228**
Cainarachi Poison Frog = *E. cainarachi*
Calls, 31
Cauca Poison Frog, 248, **248**
Cauca Poison Frog = *M. bombetes*
Cephalic amplexus, 31
Choco = region of northwestern Colombia and adjacent Panama
Chromosomes, 17
Collins's Poison Frog, 247, **247**
Collins's Poison Frog = *M. abditus*
Colostethus, 6, 11, 13, 273–275
Colostethus collaris, 273–274
Colostethus inguinalis, 273–274, **273–274**
Colostethus marchesianus, **274**
Colostethus nubicola, 273
Colostethus olfersoides, **18**
Colostethus paradoxus = *Epipedobates tricolor*
Colostethus trinitatus, 273–274, **275–276**
Common names, 5–6
Confusing Poison Frog, 234–235, **234**
Confusing Poison Frog = *E. maculatus*
Crickets, 46, **50**, **53**
Demonic Poison Frog, 250–251, **250**
Demonic Poison Frog = *M. steyermarki*
Dendrobates arboreus, 166, **166**
Dendrobates arboreus = Polka-dot Poison Frog
Dendrobates auratus, 61–63, **61–73**, **280**
Dendrobates auratus = Green and Black Poison Frog
Dendrobates auratus X *azureus*, **71**, **72**
Dendrobates azureus, 74–75, **74–83**, **140**
Dendrobates azureus = Blue Poison Frog
Dendrobates biolat, 166–167, **167**
Dendrobates biolat = Biolat Poison Frog
Dendrobates captivus, 167–168, **168**
Dendrobates captivus = Rio Santiago Poison Frog
Dendrobates castaneoticus, 168, **169**
Dendrobates castaneoticus = Brazil-nut Poison Frog
Dendrobates fantasticus, 169, **169–173**
Dendrobates fantasticus = Red-headed Poison Frog
Dendrobates galactonotus, 174, **174**
Dendrobates galactonotus = Splash-backed Poison Frog
Dendrobates "galindoi" = *Dendrobates pumilio*, 117
Dendrobates granuliferus, **5**, **6**, 84, **84–88**, 86
Dendrobates granuliferus = Granular Poison Frog
Dendrobates histrionicus, **21**, **44**, **48**, 89–110, **89–91**, **182**, **183**, **184**, **185**
Dendrobates histrionicus = Harlequin Poison Frog
Dendrobates imitator, 174, **174–179**, 176
Dendrobates imitator = Mimic Poison Frog
Dendrobates labialis, 19
Dendrobates lamasi, 179–180, **179**
Dendrobates lamasi = Pasco Poison Frog
Dendrobates lehmanni, **30**, 180–181, **180–186**
Dendrobates lehmanni = Lehmann's Poison Frog
Dendrobates leucomelas, 111–112, **111–116**
Dendrobates leucomelas = Yellow-banded Poison Frog
Dendrobates leucomelas X *auratus*, **69**, 114
Dendrobates mysteriosus, 187–188, **187**
Dendrobates mysteriosus = Maranon Poison Frog
Dendrobates occultator, 188, **188**
Dendrobates occultator = La Brea Poison Frog
Dendrobates pumilio, **5**, **9**, **35**, **37**, 117–119, **117–138**, **280**
Dendrobates pumilio = Strawberry Poison Frog
Dendrobates quinquevittatus, 188–189, **189**
Dendrobates quinquevittatus = Rio Madeira Poison Frog
Dendrobates reticulatus, 189–190, **189–196**
Dendrobates reticulatus = Red-backed Poison Frog
Dendrobates sirensis, 197, **197**
Dendrobates sirensis = Sira Poison Frog
Dendrobates speciosus, **6**, 197–198, **198–201**
Dendrobates speciosus = Splendid Poison Frog
Dendrobates tinctorius, **23**, **32**, **33**, **34**, **35**, 139–140, **139–156**, 143, 202, **202**
Dendrobates tinctorius = Dyeing Poison Frog
Dendrobates tinctorius X *azureus*, **151**
Dendrobates truncatus = Yellow-striped Poison Frog
Dendrobates vanzolinii, 202–203, **203**
Dendrobates vanzolinii = Brazilian Poison Frog
Dendrobates variabilis, 203–204, **203–206**
Dendrobates variabilis = Zimmermann's Poison Frog
Dendrobates ventrimaculatus, 157–159, **157–165**
Dendrobates ventrimaculatus = Amazonian Poison Frog
Dendrobates, definition, 13, 15
Dendrobates, groups, 19
Dendrobatid vs. poison frog, 6
Dendrobatidae, relationships, 9, 11
Dendrobatids, names, 5–6
Dextral = arising from the right side
Dorsolateral = on the side of the back
Dyeing Poison Frog, **23**, **32**, **33**, **34**, **35**, 139–140, **139–156**, 143
Dyeing Poison Frog = *D. tinctorius*
Ecotourism, 5
Ecuadorean Poison Frog, 224, **224–226**

INDEX

Ecuadorean Poison Frog = *E. bilinguis*
Egg tending, 31
Eleutherodactylus limbatus, **15**
Emerald Poison Frog, 246, **246**
Emerald Poison Frog = *E. smaragdinus*
Epibatidine, 277
Epipedobates andinus, 219–220, **219**
Epipedobates andinus = La Planada Poison Frog
Epipedobates "anthonyi" = *Epipedobates tricolor*, **207**
Epipedobates ardens = *Epipedobates cainarachi*
Epipedobates azureiventris, 220, **220**
Epipedobates azureiventris = Sky-blue Poison Frog
Epipedobates bassleri, 220–221, **221–223**
Epipedobates bassleri = Pleasing Poison Frog
Epipedobates bilinguis, 224, **224–226**
Epipedobates bilinguis = Ecuadorean Poison Frog
Epipedobates bolivianus, 227, **227**
Epipedobates bolivianus = Bolivian Poison Frog
Epipedobates boulengeri, 227, **227**
Epipedobates boulengeri = Marbled Poison Frog
Epipedobates cainarachi, 228, **228**
Epipedobates cainarachi = Cainarachi Poison Frog
Epipedobates erythromos, 228–229, **228**
Epipedobates erythromos = Palenque Poison Frog
Epipedobates espinosai, 229, **229**
Epipedobates espinosai = Espinosa Poison Frog
Epipedobates femoralis, **25**, 229–230, **230–232**
Epipedobates femoralis = Brilliant-thighed Poison Frog
Epipedobates flavopictus, 233, **233**
Epipedobates flavopictus = Lutz's Poison Frog
Epipedobates ingeri, 233, **233**
Epipedobates ingeri = Niceforo's Poison Frog
Epipedobates macero, 234, **234**
Epipedobates macero = Manu Poison Frog
Epipedobates maculatus, 234–235, **234**
Epipedobates maculatus = Confusing Poison Frog
Epipedobates myersi, 235, **235**
Epipedobates myersi = Myers's Poison Frog
Epipedobates parvulus, 235–236, **235–236**
Epipedobates parvulus = Ruby Poison Frog
Epipedobates "peruviridis", 283, **283**
Epipedobates petersi, 236–237, **237–238**
Epipedobates petersi = Peruvian Poison Frog
Epipedobates pictus, 230, 239, **239–240**
Epipedobates pictus = Spot-legged Poison Frog
Epipedobates pulchripectus, 241, **241**
Epipedobates pulchripectus = Blue-breasted Poison Frog
Epipedobates rufulus, 241–242, **241**
Epipedobates rufulus = Tepui Poison Frog
Epipedobates silverstonei, **22**, 242–243–246, **242–245**
Epipedobates silverstonei = Silverstone's Poison Frog
Epipedobates smaragdinus, 246, **246**
Epipedobates smaragdinus = Emerald Poison Frog
Epipedobates tricolor, **19**, **20**, **43**, 107–209, **207–211**, 277, **277**, **278**
Epipedobates tricolor = Phantasmal Poison Frog
Epipedobates trivittatus, **36**, 212–213, **212–218**
Epipedobates trivittatus = Three-striped Poison Frog
Epipedobates trivittatus, classification, 283
Epipedobates zaparo, 246, **246**
Epipedobates zaparo = Sanguine Poison Frog
Epipedobates, definition, 15–16
Epiphyte = a plant living on another plant and drawing its food from the air and from solids accumulating around its base
Espinosa Poison Frog, 229, **229**
Espinosa Poison Frog = *E. espinosai*
Fighting, 31
"Flash marks", 29
"Flash marks" = colorful spots at the bases of the limbs
Food egg feeders, 35–36
Food eggs = unfertilized eggs laid by a frog to feed her tadpoles
Foods, natural, 29
Foods, terrarium, 46
Froglet, 36
—*Dendrobates fantasticus*, **42**
—*Dendrobates tinctorius*, **41**
Froglets, raising, 47–48

Fruitflies, 46, **49**
Genera of poison frogs, 13, 15–16
Golden Mantella, **11**, **13**, **14**
Golden Poison Frog, **252**, 253–254, **254–258**
Golden Poison Frog = *P. terribilis*
Golfodulcean Poison Frog, **28**, 259, **259–265**
Golfodulcean Poison Frog = *P. vittatus*
Granular Poison Frog, **5**, **6**, 84, **84–88**, 86
Granular Poison Frog = *D. granuliferus*
Green and Black Poison Frog, 61–63, **61–73**, 280
Green and Black Poison Frog = *D. auratus*
Green Poison Frog, 251, **251**
Green Poison Frog = *M. viridis*
Groin = area where the thigh inserts into the trunk
Habitat, natural, 29
Harlequin Poison Frog, **21**, **44**, **48**, 89–110, **89–91**, **182**, **183**, **184**, **185**
Harlequin Poison Frog = *D. histrionicus*
Harlequin toads, **7**, **8**, 9, **10**, **12**
Heating, terrarium, 45–46
Hooded Pitohui, 278, **279**
Humidity, terrarium, 45–46
Identification procedure, 18
Kokoe Poison Frog, **266**, 276
Kokoe Poison Frog = *P. aurotaenia*
La Brea Poison Frog, 188, **188**
La Brea Poison Frog = *D. occultator*
La Planada Poison Frog, 219–220, **219**
La Planada Poison Frog = *E. andinus*
Leafhoppers, **49**
Lehmann's Poison Frog, **30**, 180–181, **180–186**
Lehmann's Poison Frog = *D. lehmanni*
Leptodactylidae, 9, 11
Lithodytes lineatus, **15**
Longevity, 48
Lovely Poison Frog, 270, **270–271**
Lovely Poison Frog = *P. lugubris*
Lutz's Poison Frog, 233, **233**
Lutz's Poison Frog = *E. flavopictus*
Mannophryne, 273
Mannophryne yustizi, 273
Mantella, 9
Mantella aurantiaca, **11**, **13**, **14**
Mantella crocea, **15**
Mantella expectata, 18
Mantella viridis, **14**, **17**
Mantellas, 9
Manu Poison Frog, 234, **234**
Manu Poison Frog = *E. macero*
Maranon Poison Frog, 187–188, **187**
Maranon Poison Frog = *D. mysteriosus*
Marbled Poison Frog, 227, **227**
Marbled Poison Frog = *E. boulengeri*
Maturity, 48
Metamorphosis, 36
Mimic Poison Frog, 174, **174–179**, 176
Mimic Poison Frog = *D. imitator*
Minyobates abditus, 247, **247**
Minyobates abditus = Collins's Poison Frog
Minyobates altobueyensis, 247–248, **248**
Minyobates altobueyensis = Alto del Buey Poison Frog
Minyobates bombetes, 248, **248**
Minyobates bombetes = Cauca Poison Frog
Minyobates fulguritus, 248–249, **249**
Minyobates fulguritus = Yellow-bellied Poison Frog
Minyobates minutus, **27**, 249–250, **249**
Minyobates minutus = Blue-bellied Poison Frog
Minyobates opisthomelas, 250, **250**
Minyobates opisthomelas = Andean Poison Frog
Minyobates steyermarki, 250–251, **250**
Minyobates steyermarki = Demonic Poison Frog
Minyobates viridis, 251, **251**
Minyobates viridis = Green Poison Frog
Minyobates virolinensis, 251–252, **251**
Minyobates virolinensis = Santander Poison Frog
Minyobates, definition, 15
Misting, 46

INDEX

Mites, 29
Monophyletic = derived from a common immediate ancestor
Mosquitoes, **50**, **52**
Moths, **53**
Myers classification, 13, 15–16
Myers's Poison Frog, 235, **235**
Myers's Poison Frog = *E. myersi*
Niceforo's Poison Frog, 233, **233**
Niceforo's Poison Frog = *E. ingeri*
Omosternum = anteriormost bone of the sternum, above the base of the pectoral girdle
Oral disc = area under the head containing the mouthparts of a tadpole
Painkillers, 277
Palenque Poison Frog, 228–229, **228**
Palenque Poison Frog = *E. erythromos*
Papillae = fleshy projections from the margins of the oral disc
Pasco Poison Frog, 179–180, **179**
Pasco Poison Frog = *D. lamasi*
Peruvian Poison Frog, 236–237, **237–238**
Peruvian Poison Frog = *E. petersi*
Phantasmal Poison Frog, **19**, **20**, **43**, 207–209, **207–211**, 277, **277**, **278**
Phantasmal Poison Frog = *E. tricolor*
Phantom midges, **51**, **53**
Phobobates, 16
Phyllobates aurotaenia, **266**, 267
Phyllobates aurotaenia = Kokoe Poison Frog
Phyllobates bicolor, 267, **267–268**, 270
Phyllobates bicolor = Black-legged Poison Frog
Phyllobates lugubris, 270, **270–271**
Phyllobates lugubris = Lovely Poison Frog
Phyllobates terribilis, **252**, 253–254, **254–258**
Phyllobates terribilis = Golden Poison Frog
Phyllobates vittatus, **28**, 259, **259–265**
Phyllobates vittatus = Golfodulcean Poison Frog
Phyllobates, definition, 16
Pitohui dichrous, 278, **279**
Pitohuis, toxic birds, 278, **279**, 280
Planted terraria, **54**, **55**, **56**, **58**, **59**
Pleasing Poison Frog, 220–221, **221–223**
Pleasing Poison Frog = *E. bassleri*
Poison frogs, checklist, 19–20, 22, 24–26, 28
Poison frogs, definition, 6, 9
Poison frogs, relationships, 9, 11
Poison frogs, taxonomy, 11, 13, 15–18
Poison-arrow frogs, 5–6
Poison-dart frogs, 5–6
Polka-dot Poison Frog, 166, **166**
Polka-dot Poison Frog = *D. arboreus*
Polyphyletic = unnatural group derived from two or more different ancestors
Predation, 29
Prostherapis, 273
Rainforest loss, 5
Rainfrogs, 9
Ranitomeya, 283
Rearing aquarium, **60**
Red-backed Poison Frog, 189–190, **189–196**
Red-backed Poison Frog = *D. reticulatus*
Red-eyed Treefrog, **281**
Red-headed Poison Frog, 169, **169–173**
Red-headed Poison Frog = *D. fantasticus*
Rio Madeira Poison Frog, 188–189, **189**
Rio Madeira Poison Frog = *D. quinquevittatus*
Rio Santiago Poison Frog, 167–168, **168**
Rio Santiago Poison Frog = *D. captivus*
Rocket frogs, 6, 273–275
Ruby Poison Frog, 235–236, **235–236**
Ruby Poison Frog = *E. parvulus*
Sanguine Poison Frog, 246, **246**
Sanguine Poison Frog = *E. zaparo*
Santander Poison Frog, 251–252, **251**
Santander Poison Frog = *M. virolinensis*
Sexing, 31
Shank = tarsus

Silverstone classification, 13
Silverstone's Poison Frog, **22**, 242–243, **242–245**, 246
Silverstone's Poison Frog = *E. silverstonei*
Sinistral = arising from the left side
Sira Poison Frog, 197, **197**
Sira Poison Frog = *D. sirensis*
Skunk frogs, 6
Skunk Frog, 272–273, **272**
Sky-blue Poison Frog, 220, **220**
Sky-blue Poison Frog = *E. azureiventris*
Spindly leg syndrome, 48, **260**, 262
Spiracle = small tube for water exiting gills of a tadpole
Splash-backed Poison Frog, 174, **174**
Splash-backed Poison Frog = *D. galactonotus*
Splendid Harlequin Toad, **7**, **8**, **10**, **12**
Splendid Poison Frog, 6, 197–198, **198–201**
Splendid Poison Frog = *D. speciosus*
Spot-legged Poison Frog, **230**, 239, **239–240**
Spot-legged Poison Frog = *E. pictus*
Springtails, 48
Stamps, 278
Strawberry Poison Frog, **5**, **9**, **35**, **37**, 117–119, **117–138**, **280**
Strawberry Poison Frog = *D. pumilio*
Stream, terrarium, 46
Substrate, terrarium, 45
Sympatric = occurring in the same locality
Tadpole, 35–36
—*Aromobates nocturnus*, **40**
—*Colostethus nubicola*, **38**
—*Dendrobates auratus*, **38**
—*Dendrobates histrionicus*, **187**
—*Dendrobates mysteriosus*, **187**
—*Dendrobates pumilio*, **38**
—*Dendrobates ventrimaculatus*, **40**
—*Epipedobates boulengeri*, **39**
—*Epipedobates espinosai*, **39**
—*Epipedobates femoralis*, **39**
—*Epipedobates petersi*, **39**
—*Epipedobates pictus*, **39**
—*Epipedobates smaragdinus*, **39**
—*Epipedobates trivittatus*, **39**
—*Minyobates bombetes*, **40**
—*Minyobates minutus*, **38**
—*Minyobates opisthomelas*, **38**
—*Minyobates virolinensis*, **40**
—*Phyllobates lugubris*, **40**
—*Phyllobates vittatus*, **39**
Tadpole transport, 31
Tadpoles, raising, 47
Tapirage, 143
Tarsus = the region of a frog's leg between the thigh and the ankle
Tepui Poison Frog, 241–242, **241**
Tepui Poison Frog = *E. rufulus*
Terraria, design, 45
Three-striped Poison Frog, **36**, 212–213, **212–218**
Three-striped Poison Frog = *E. trivittatus*
Toxicity, 29
Toxins and classification, 13
Tubifex worms, **53**
Type-locality = exact locality from which the holotype of a species was collected
Versant = mountain slope
Vocal sacs, 31
Vocalizations, 17
Wax moths, 46
Waxworms, 49
Yellow-banded Poison Frog, 111–112, **111–116**
Yellow-banded Poison Frog = *D. leucomelas*
Yellow-bellied Poison Frog, 248–249, **249**
Yellow-bellied Poison Frog = *M. fulguritus*
Yellow-striped Poison Frog, 202, **202**
Yellow-striped Poison Frog = *D. truncatus*
Zimmermann & Zimmermann classification, 16
Zimmermann's Poison Frog, 203–204, **203–206**
Zimmermann's Poison Frog = *D. variabilis*

Back endpaper:
Dendrobates azureus. Photo by R. D. Bartlett